AF324168

STEVE KAHN
THE HOLLYWOOD SUITES

STEVE KAHN
THE HOLLYWOOD SUITES

JAMES A. GANZ

WITH
**CONSTANCE M. LEWALLEN,
MATTHEW SIMMS, AND
JODI THROCKMORTON**

de Young \ Legion of Honor
fine arts museums of san francisco

DELMONICO BOOKS · PRESTEL
Munich, London, New York

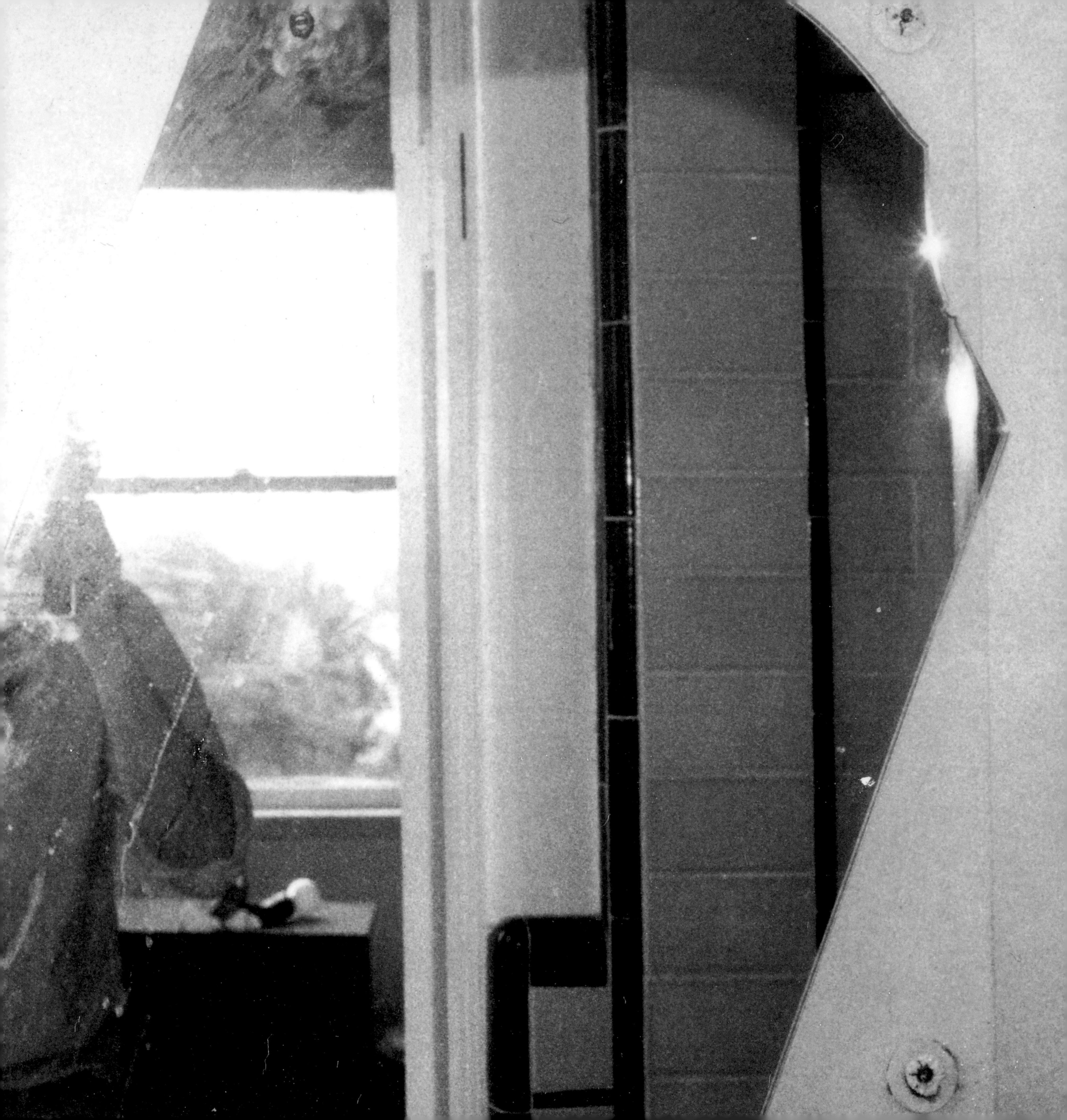

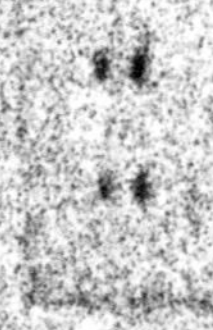

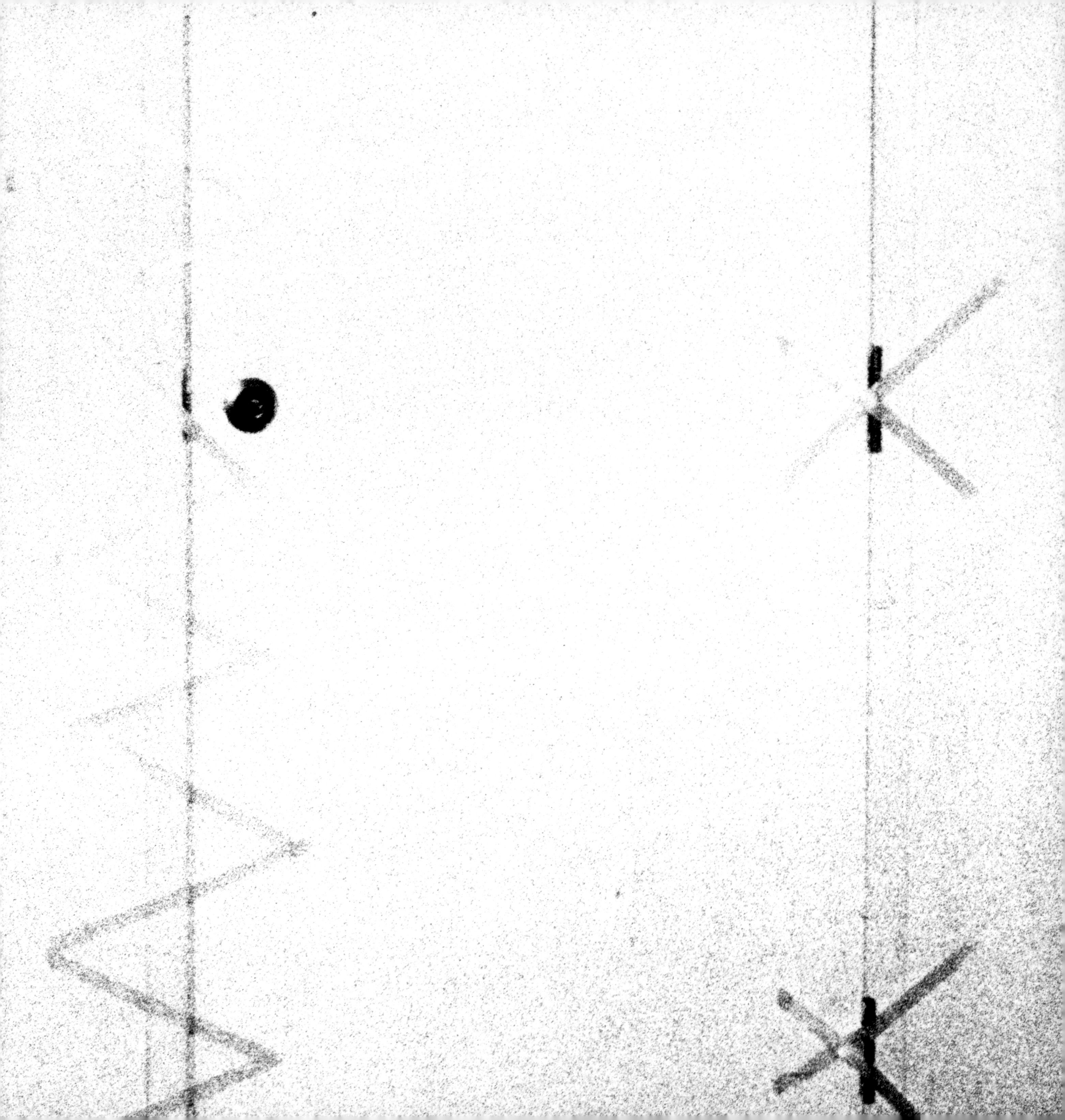

FOREWORD

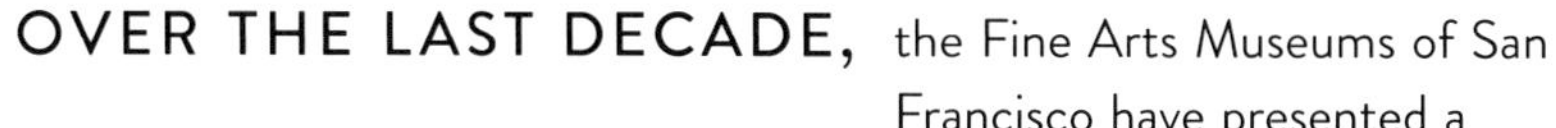

OVER THE LAST DECADE, the Fine Arts Museums of San Francisco have presented a series of exhibitions showcasing important photographers with ties to the Bay Area. Steve Kahn, who spent his final years in Berkeley, is the latest to join this roster, which includes such seminal artists of both regional and national significance as Judy Dater, Janet Delaney, Anthony Friedkin, Danny Lyon, Rose Mandel, Peter Stackpole, and Arthur Tress.

Kahn's early career was centered on Los Angeles, where he came of age artistically during the 1970s. It was a challenging era for the metropolis, which was undergoing profound and destructive economic and social crises. Such seismic cultural shifts inevitably penetrated the contemporary art world of Southern California, whose own instability was crystallized in such events as the closing of the avant-garde Ferus Gallery in 1966, the relocation of *Artforum* to New York in 1967, and wealthy collector Norton Simon's financial bailout of the cutting-edge Pasadena Art Museum, which became the Norton Simon Museum in 1974.

Amid this air of uncertainty and new opportunity, many LA-based artists felt liberated to explore nontraditional venues and novel approaches to conceptual, installation, and performance art. Artists such as Eleanor Antin, Robert Heinecken, Robert Overby, De Wain Valentine, and Beatrice Wood created rigorously experimental work that reflected the expanding and flexible social mores of the period. Kahn took part as well. Departing from the traditional street photography he had practiced a decade earlier, in 1974 the artist began to work on the project that would grow into the series *The Hollywood Suites*. Inspired by a brief foray into S&M photography, Kahn rented out rooms in a seedy motel on Melrose Avenue and began photographing professional bondage models posed in various stages of undress within. However, his attention did not remain with the women. As James A. Ganz, former curator of the Achenbach Foundation for

Graphic Arts, now senior curator of photographs at the J. Paul Getty Museum in Los Angeles, writes in his introduction to this catalogue, "The project evolved into a multifaceted conceptual series in which [Kahn] turned his lens from nude models and their body parts to study the mundane and monotonous rooms in which they worked. Kahn's intention with this work was to transcend pornography so as to seriously explore issues of dehumanization and alienation. Ultimately, he found he could best treat these themes through photographs that had no tangible human presence."

In 1986, Kahn moved to New York to pursue a career in commercial photography. Upon doing so, he put into storage his large body of *Hollywood Suites* Polaroids and gelatin silver prints, which were well known in LA's avant-garde circles during the 1970s but had, by then, fallen off the greater radar of art history. The work of his contemporaries had similarly been overlooked by historians and critics, who were more attuned to the New York art scene.

It was not until the revival of interest in this period generated by such exhibitions as the Centre Pompidou's groundbreaking survey *Los Angeles 1955–1985: the birth of an art capital* (2006) and the Getty Foundation's Pacific Standard Time initiatives of 2011 and 2017 that Kahn was encouraged to revisit his early work. His renewed efforts proved quickly and overwhelmingly fruitful, leading to several gallery exhibitions, new editions, and artist's books. This resurgence of interest in Kahn's *Hollywood Suites* photographs was particularly stoked by the encouragement from art dealers Joseph Bellows, Julie Casemore, Howard Greenberg, and Stefan Kirkeby, and from the publisher Chris Pichler.

This project at the Fine Arts Museums of San Francisco grew out of a series of conversations beginning in 2016 between the artist, collector Dan Solomon, and curators Julian Cox (formerly chief curator and founding curator of photography at the Museums, now chief curator and deputy director of the Art Gallery of Ontario in Toronto) and Ganz. Unfortunately, Kahn's fragile health deteriorated rapidly as the work neared completion. In February 2018, at a point when the production of this catalogue was well underway, Kahn passed away. The artist took comfort in knowing that his first museum exhibition would take place at the de Young and would be accompanied by this first scholarly publication documenting his artistic legacy.

We are grateful to the Stephen H. Kahn Trust, including Jo Ann Montoya, which has greatly supported this project after Kahn's death. We also extend our appreciation to Mary and Dan Solomon, Howard Greenberg and the Howard Greenberg Gallery, Nancy Ganz and Mitchell Steir, and Dr. Nancy Ascher and Dr. John Roberts for sharing Kahn's work with our Museums. We hope that this presentation will shine new light on Kahn's incredible and groundbreaking photographic oeuvre.

MAX HOLLEIN
Director and CEO
Fine Arts Museums of San Francisco

THE HOLLYWOOD SUITES
ORIGINS, CREATIONS, INTERVENTIONS, AND GENERATIONS

JAMES A. GANZ

ORIGINS. When it opened in March 1930, the Villa Constance Apartments at 5244 Melrose Avenue, in Los Angeles, offered numerous modern amenities, including electric refrigerators, private garages, an elevator, and daily maid service. The building was designed by noted architect Carl Jules Weyl, who was also responsible for the Brown Derby Restaurant on Vine Street, in Hollywood, and who later served as the art director on *The Adventures of Robin Hood* (1938) and *Casablanca* (1942).[1] Located around the corner from Paramount Pictures' Main Lot, the Constance was originally home to a number of blue-collar studio workers and B-actors. A slightly damaged photograph from 1935 (fig. 1) shows the Mission Revival structure with its original terracotta roof tiles and ornamental ironwork and a pair of medallions containing relief busts of conquistadors. Behind a broader facade, the four-story building stretched 130 feet, with thirty-one small apartments distributed on opposite sides of long corridors.

Never fashionable, the working-class neighborhood around Paramount slowly deteriorated after World War II. The Constance eventually shed its romantic name, and by the 1970s, it functioned essentially as a "no-tell hotel," offering studio apartments for twenty dollars per week, with unadvertised rates by the hour. The most noteworthy residents during this period were Lynette "Squeaky" Fromme and fellow members of the Manson Family.[2] Continuing its decline, by 1995 the building was in violation of so many health and safety codes that it was uninhabitable, and its slumlord owner was arrested and ordered to tear it down.[3]

Steve Kahn was attracted to LA's vernacular architecture, but his interest was less in the midcentury modern facades favored by such artists as Ed Ruscha than in the rundown interiors of older apartment buildings, like the former Villa Constance, that still lined the seedy streets of Hollywood. The

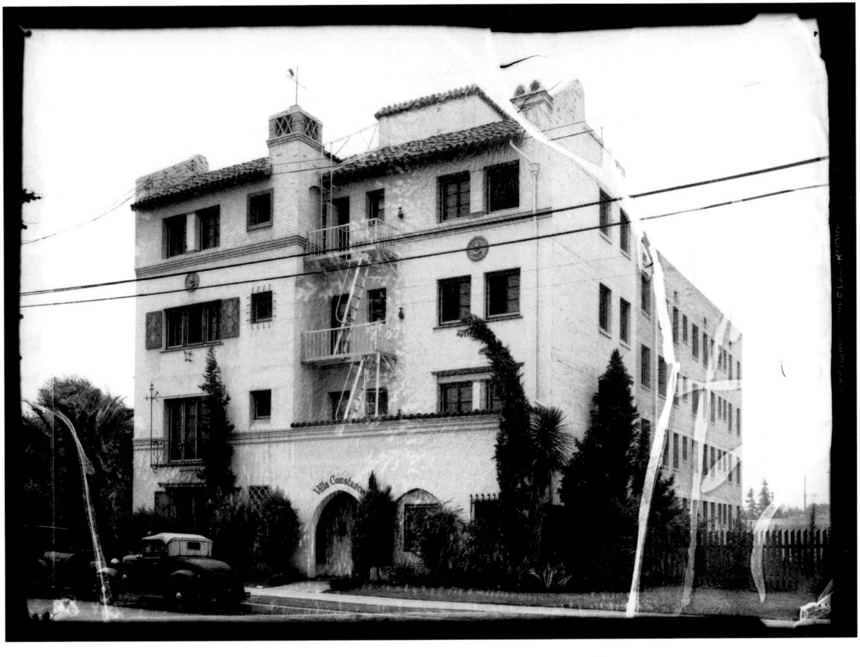

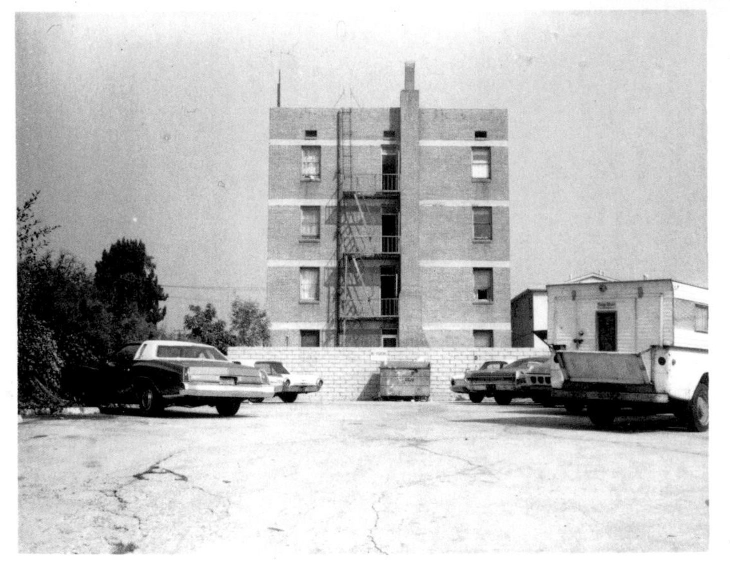

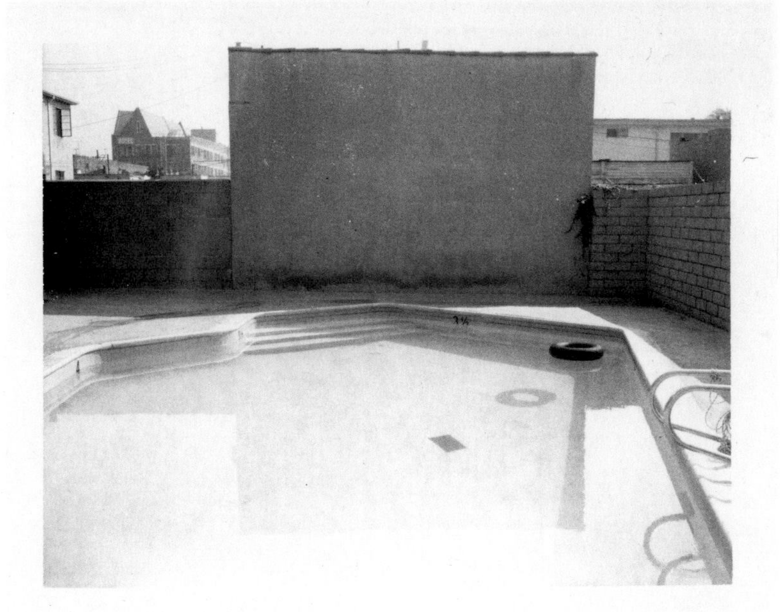

1
DICK WHITTINGTON STUDIO
Villa Constance Apartments, Los Angeles, 1935.
USC Libraries Special Collections

2
STEVE KAHN
Back of 5244 Melrose Avenue, Los Angeles,
1976. Polaroid. Stephen H. Kahn Trust

3
STEVE KAHN
Swimming pool, 5244 Melrose Avenue, Los
Angeles, 1976. Polaroid. Stephen H. Kahn Trust

Constance would be one of the primary settings for the extended photographic series that Kahn undertook from 1974 to 1977 called *The Hollywood Suites.* Having no interest in the building's history or the fine architectural details on its facade—indeed, the only exteriors he documented were the nondescript back of the building overlooking a cracked parking lot (fig. 2) and the uninviting swimming pool (fig. 3)—Kahn was drawn to the very dullness of the sparsely furnished rooms and gloomy corridors, which were utterly and ironically at odds with the splendor his overarching title evoked.

Kahn's artistic journey to 5244 Melrose Avenue can be traced to 1962, his freshman year at Reed College, in Portland, Oregon. There he made a crucial connection through his roommate, Paul Overby, to Paul's older brother, Robert, then working as a professional graphic designer. Jumping forward to 1968—after Kahn had graduated from Reed, started a PhD in physics, and dropped out to spend two years studying and performing flamenco guitar in Andalusia—he returned to his native Los Angeles, where Robert Overby would become his best friend and mentor. Shortly after this time, in 1969, Overby decided to move away from his commercial design work to reinvent himself as a Post-Minimalist artist, introducing unconventional materials like polyurethane, latex, and concrete into his work. As well as being interested in the human body, Overby was particularly drawn to architectural subjects, creating a series of sculptural works on the theme of the door that foreshadowed Kahn's later preoccupation with the form. "I see the door definitely as a body," Overby later said. "There's no doubt about that. But the door's also something that you set your scale by. . . . It's also a barrier—I have that kind of peeping Tom mentality you know, wanting to know what's behind it."[4] In 1971, Overby produced his seminal *Barclay House* series, twenty-eight latex casts of walls, doors, windows, and other elements from the charred ruins of an apartment building at 675 North Kenmore Avenue, near the intersection of Melrose Avenue and the Hollywood Freeway (see fig. 4).

In Los Angeles, Kahn also met Lita Albuquerque, a student at the Otis College of Art and Design, and the two were married the day after New Year's, 1972.[5] Albuquerque would emerge, over the course of the decade, as an acclaimed member of the Light and Space Movement. From 1971 to 1978, the couple lived in a ramshackle communal home in Malibu (fig. 5) perched above the Topanga Canyon and the Pacific Coast Highway among 130 acres of wild brush and chaparral. The site was originally part of the Rancho Budwood, owned by comedian Bud Abbott and film director Sam Wood during the 1940s. In 1957, it was transformed into the avant-garde Coffee House Positano, a hangout of celebrities, artists, and writers, from Rock Hudson to Ray Bradbury to Allen Ginsberg.[6] After the café closed in 1962, the building served as the central residence of an informal artists' and writers' colony that became known as "the Property" until it burned to the ground in the Malibu wildfire of 1993.[7] Tenants at various times included sculptor Elyn Zimmerman, landscape architect Pamela Burton, actress Mia Farrow, and playwright David Seidler. Kahn and Albuquerque occupied apartment no. 2, a former dining room. Kahn set up a fully equipped professional darkroom and took many photographs of the dramatic view of the Pacific Ocean from the front porch.

By the time he turned thirty, in December 1973, Kahn had achieved success as a photojournalist, working as a stringer for magazines like *Newsweek*, *Time*, and *Life*, and had self-published *Stasis* (1973), an artist's book of experimental photographs of "blurred reality" shot on the grounds of the Property and sold by mail order from its Malibu address. (Kahn's first solo exhibition of the *Stasis* photographs would take place at the Photographers' Gallery, London, in 1974, and would travel to venues in Milan, Rome, Naples, Paris, and Los Angeles.) These

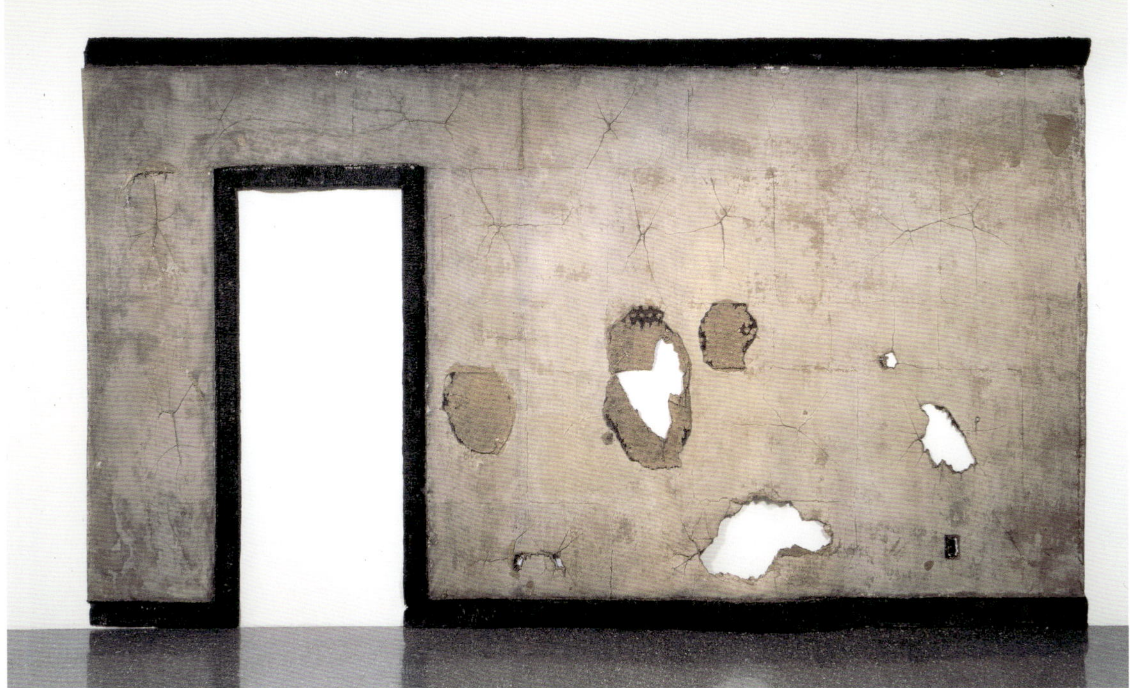

4
ROBERT OVERBY
*East Hall Wall, Third Floor
(Grey Wall),* August 4, 1971. Latex rubber.
104¼ x 182 x ⅛ in. (264.8 x 462.3 x
0.3 cm). The Museum of Contemporary
Art, Los Angeles, purchased with funds
provided by The Acquisition and Collection
Committee

5
STEVE KAHN
Northern end of the main house, Malibu,
ca. 1970. Stephen H. Kahn Trust

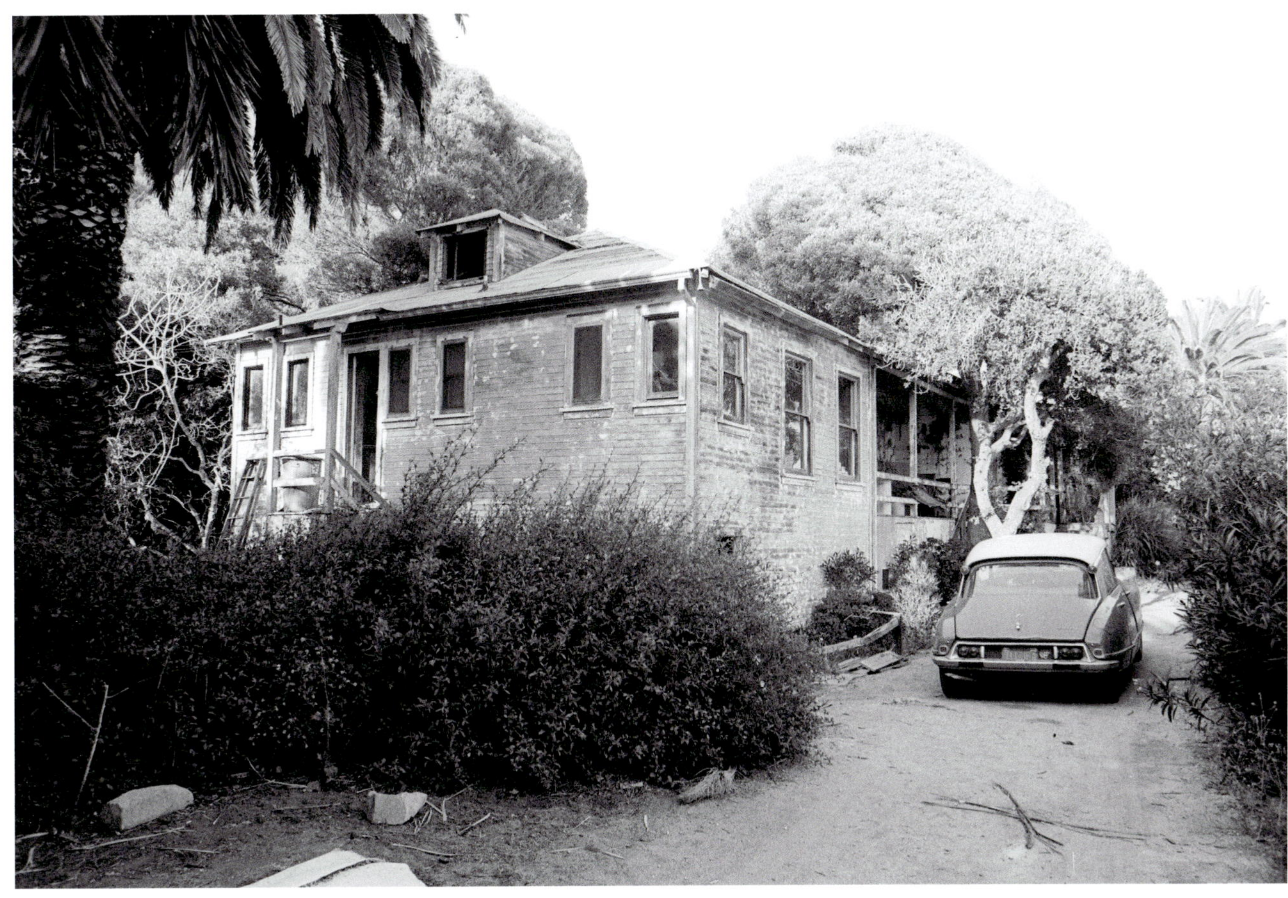

Possible Titles for nudes:

Hollywood Suites

w/ pun on Sweets / Suite-ees

- Shoot some overexposed polis ɟ
  just the shadow of objects against
  wall reveal shapes

- more scratched out images

Frame portrait of Chris
& one small getting around

accomplishments coincided, however, with the start of the historic recession of 1973–1975, which took a toll on every aspect of the US economy. Struggling to make ends meet, Kahn joined in a scheme proposed by Overby and painter Robert Blue to produce a series of three commercial fetish magazines. They employed an offset printer of S&M porn whose office was located in an alley behind Overby's studio, with the plan to each individually create one complete issue. The product of this venture was a single issue of *Photo-Bondage*, with photographs and text by Kahn. Published by Lyndon Distributors of Van Nuys, it sold for four dollars and was issued in a plain envelope out of a post-office box in Hollywood, with enlargements of individual illustrations suitable for framing available.

Kahn later characterized his brief venture into the porn industry as an unnatural experience, as he himself was not a consumer of sexually explicit material and could not tie suitable knots. Because potential customers were as aroused by the complexity of the binding and related paraphernalia as they were by explicit nudity, he had to employ Blue's brother, Tom, a former high school acquaintance and magician who could tie elaborate knots that could be instantly unraveled. After the publication of the inaugural issue of *Photo-Bondage*, the printer absconded to Mexico with the proceeds. Despite the project's financial disappointment, the endeavor is notable for setting Kahn on a path to his major body of photography, *The Hollywood Suites*.[8]

CREATIONS. *The Hollywood Suites* began in 1974 as a directorial essay in staged photography and portraiture, featuring some of the same professional models who posed for *Photo-Bondage*, such as Serena Czarnecki. Although Kahn produced the *Hollywood Suites* nudes in an artistic context, only a fine line separates them from the magazine's pornographic content; this resemblance is particularly pronounced in the uncomfortable images of women performing bondage scenarios that make up the first part of *The Hollywood Suites* (see Jodi Throckmorton, "Memoirs of a Bound Photographer," and Matthew Simms, "Steve Kahn: Displacements," both in this catalogue). But Kahn's intention with this work was to transcend pornography so as to seriously explore issues of dehumanization and alienation. Ultimately, he found he could best treat these themes through photographs that had no tangible human presence. Consequently, over the next three years, the project evolved into a multifaceted conceptual series in which he turned his lens from nude models and their body parts to study the mundane and monotonous rooms in which they worked. He came to focus on the scuffed doors and walls adorned with pieces of banal hotel room art, the mismatched curtains framing windows overlooking the bland cityscape, and the haunting outlines of mirrors long since broken or removed. Writing in his journal, he contemplated a project documenting motel decor, "the logic of it, the insensitivity of it."[9]

Our understanding of the project's evolution, as well as Kahn's working methods and thought process, is informed by five primary sources: Kahn's personal journals, starting in 1975, with his notes, sketches, diagrams, and a few inserted photographs; the transcript of a lengthy interview conducted in late 1977 or 1978 in which he discusses his work up to that point, found among the artist's papers;[10] an artist's statement entitled "Notes for The Hollywood Suites," dated November 7, 2012, published on his website; the original set of Polaroids, taken from 1974 to 1977, now in the collection of the Fine Arts Museums of San Francisco; and finally, a cache of more than one thousand original Polaroid outtakes and 35 mm contact sheets of the re-photographed Polaroids that the artist kept in his archive.[11]

The series, in its prototypical form, consists of 110 Polaroid studies of nudes and interiors that Kahn re-photographed and editioned as gelatin silver prints. Kahn exhibited enlargements of the nudes as early as the fall of 1975, as part of the group show *Eight Artists from Los Angeles*, held in the Emmanuel Walter Gallery of the San Francisco Art Institute, but it was not until August 1976 that he devised the title "Hollywood Suites," specifically for the figure studies. Eventually this title would encompass the interiors, and in later years Kahn characterized related projects such as his *Triptychs* (pls. 53–56, and figs. 32 and 40), *Quadrants* (pl. 57 and fig. 33), and *Corridors* (figs. 14 and 34), which all began as Polaroids, as extended chapters of a more expansive conception of *The Hollywood Suites*.

  Although Kahn never published a comprehensive list of *The Hollywood Suites*, in his studio inventory he assigned individual numbers to the images within seven categories: *Portraits, Nudes, Windows, Doors, Bound Doors, Mirrors,* and *Rooms*. Kahn's enumeration is not chronological, but data encapsulated in the original prints allows us to partly reconstruct the sequence in which they were taken.[12] Kahn's Polaroid 195 camera used Type 107 (black and white) and 108 (color) format film sold in packs of eight, and the verso of each 3¼-by-4¼-inch print bears a seven- to nine-character production code that can be deciphered to determine the date its film pack was produced in Polaroid's Waltham, Massachusetts, plant.[13] With this information it is possible to establish an earliest possible date for each print. Though we don't know precisely how long it took manufactured film packs to reach Los Angeles consumers, we can date several of Kahn's Polaroid outtakes based on their content, which reveals that two to three months typically elapsed between a film pack's manufacture and his use of it.[14] Because Kahn purchased his film in small quantities on an ongoing basis, rather than in bulk for use over an extended period, we can organize the *Hollywood Suites* Polaroids roughly sequentially by manufacturing code and can even reconstruct individual sessions (see Appendix).[15]

  Arranging the *Hollywood Suites* Polaroids from its earliest film pack, made on March 28, 1974, to its last one, made on May 27, 1977, we can both discern an outline of the project's progression and detect minor inaccuracies in Kahn's retelling of its evolution. In a 1978 interview and in his 2012 artist's statement, he maintained that he did not turn his attention to the interior studies until a model failed to show up for a session and that he stopped photographing the women altogether after that point. We can date this shift to sometime after June 10, 1975, as film packs manufactured on this date include photographs of both models and interiors (three *Rooms* and one *Window*, one *Door*, and one *Bound Door*). However, a single *Window* picture also unexpectedly appears on a film pack produced almost a full year earlier (pl. 31). Further complicating Kahn's chronology is a mixture of *Nudes* and *Portraits* and one *Room* image that appears on film packs produced on August 9, 1975 (apps. 55–58 and pls. 6 and 12), as well as journal notes from fall and early winter documenting his continued work with nude models.[16] Such discrepancies speak to the artist's desire to simplify rather than complicate his own narrative.

INTERVENTIONS. Although Kahn shot *The Hollywood Suites* in multiple locations, including at a friend's studio in Santa Monica, by mid-1976, the former Villa Constance apartment building on Melrose Avenue had become his preferred venue. In a few instances, scenes glimpsed through the windows establish a precise viewpoint, as in *Window* 10 and *Window* 12 (two photographs of the same window; pls. 17 and 18), *Window* 21 (pl. 19), and *Window* 9 (fig. 12), which all look out on an office building at 662 North Van Ness Avenue that is now part of the Raleigh Studios complex; *Window* 21 also includes a partial view of the Hollywood Encore Theatre, beyond the studio on the next block west of Van Ness.[17] In addition to photographing the

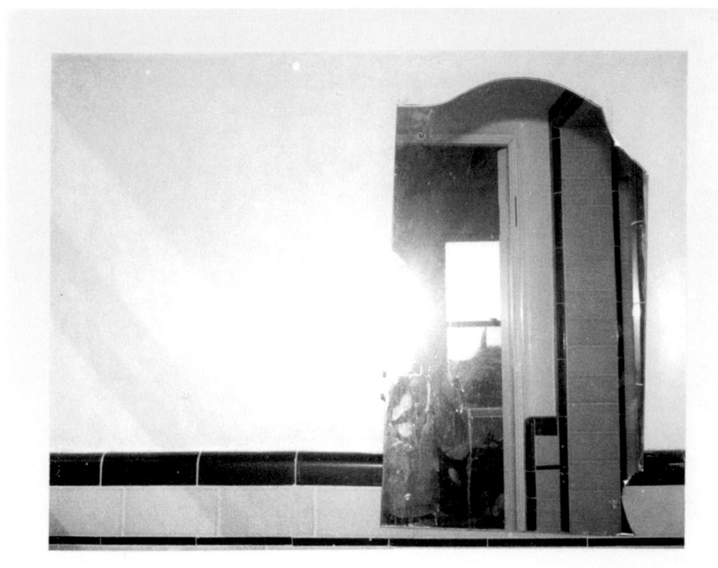 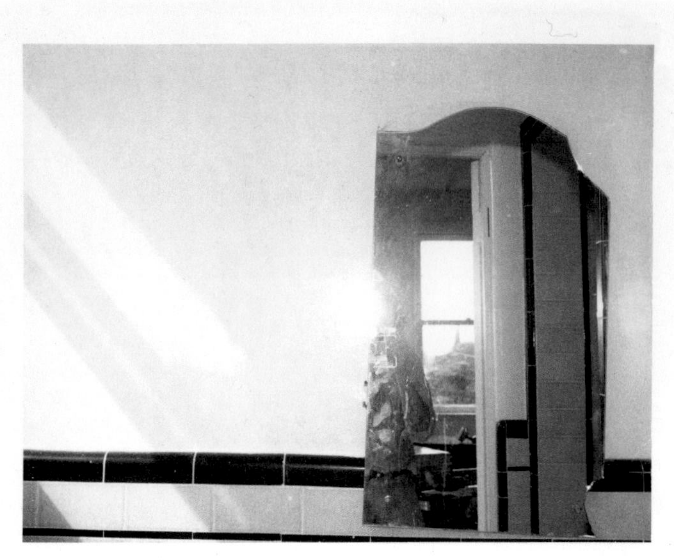

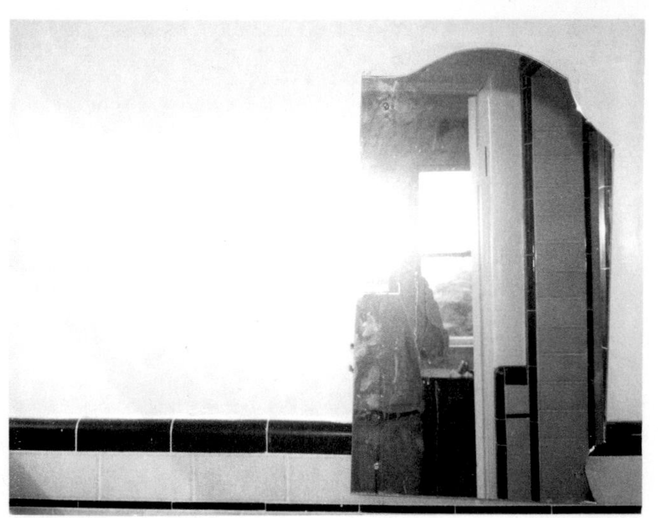 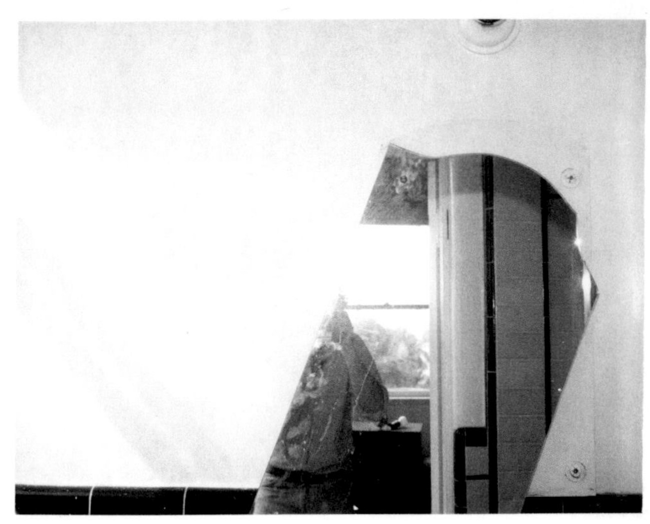

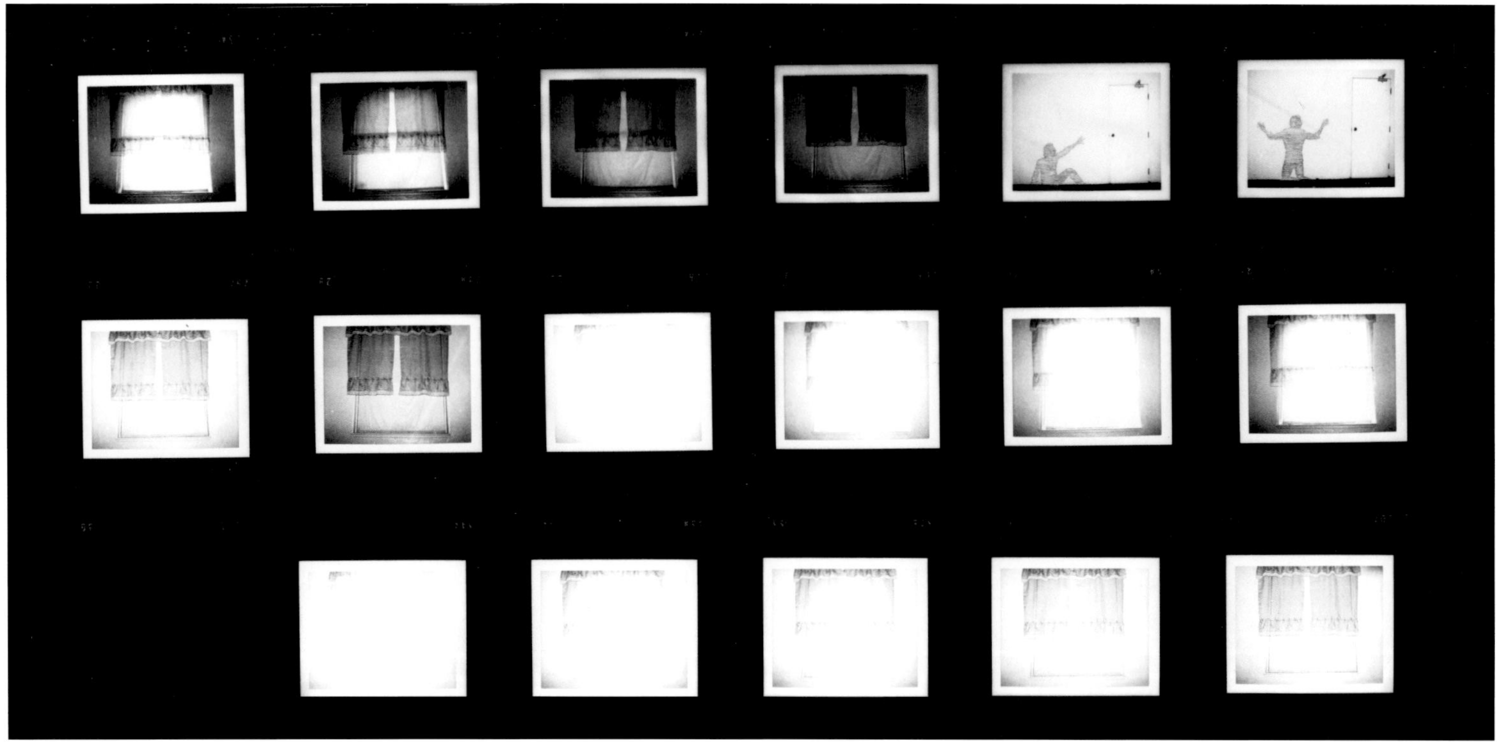

windows of the 5244 Melrose apartments, Kahn also developed an affinity for its interior doors, a subject that had strong associations with his mentor Robert Overby. With their subtle variations of knobs, hinges, security hardware, and scuffmarks, the inherently mysterious doors have their own identities and become stand-ins for the models, even to the point of being submitted to bondage.

In his 2012 artist statement, Kahn emphasized his objectivity in documenting the apartment interiors, writing that, with the exception of the *Bound Doors*, he "rarely altered the walls or curtains . . . or posters or framed lithos. They were photographed as I found them. Flat white plaster walls in need of repair and paint. These were (the) lowest common denominators of such living spaces." Here, again, Kahn's account oversimplifies his process, which actually did include modifications of the interior furnishings, experimentation with lighting effects, and occasional retouching of the Polaroids.

Outfitted with a Speedlight flash, Kahn's Polaroid 195 was a top-of-the-line professional-grade camera that gave him full control over exposure and shutter speed (the camera is partially visible in four photographs of mirrors; fig. 7). The instant processing of prints meant that he could critique his work in progress and make immediate corrections. This capability is reflected in his archive's numerous outtakes and contact sheets, which reveal his adjustments of illumination and other environmental factors. In many cases Kahn bracketed his exposures to explore variations in lighting, which could be especially difficult to control when shooting through windows.

In setting up his window shots, he sometimes incorporated opaque fabrics to mask the daylight and frequently varied the arrangement of shades and curtains from one Polaroid to the next (compare, for instance, *Window* 18 and *Window* 18a [apps. 69 and 70], *Window* 10 and *Window* 12 [apps. 87 and 88], and *Window* 25 and *Window* 14 [apps. 105 and 106]). In one extreme instance, he produced seventeen variants of a single window (the subject of *Window* 3 and *Window* 2 [apps. 60 and 61]) with a range of subtle gradations of exposure (fig. 8).[18]

Kahn believed that the Polaroids would eventually vanish from the record, taking with them all documentation of the experimentation that preceded each gelatin silver print. He wrote in his journal, "the Polaroids will fade away & the 'Final Choice' [i.e., gelatin silver print] will prevail with, in time, no memory or visual chart as to the decision-making process!!"[19] Fortunately, the hundreds of Polaroid variants kept by Kahn survive in generally pristine condition. Along with the contact sheets he made when re-photographing the Polaroids, they provide fascinating insight into his working methods. For example, the archive contains twenty-three variants and studies of *Bound Door* 6 (fig. 9), which reveal his rigorous trial and error. To make this image, he began by covering the interior of the room's narrow door opening with dark fabric and photographing the empty space. He then scratched patterns in the emulsion of several resulting Polaroids to visualize potential configurations of white rope he envisioned securing by pushpins or nails to the actual doorframe. One of these scratched studies shows the actual rope on the floor. Eventually, he settled on a minimalist pattern, using black yarn zigzagging between the pins as the source for his edition (pl. 41). In effect, Kahn's site of intervention was manifold and intersecting, consisting of the literal mise-en-scène of the rope and the door in concert with the two-dimensional surface of the Polaroid, which functioned as a kind of sketch pad, leading to his re-photography of the Polaroid and production of a gelatin silver print.

Further reviewing the archive, we find multiple variants of specific motifs, as well as unique subjects that he ultimately rejected. Among the *Nudes*, the outtakes include examples of more elaborately staged bondage and explicit poses that might have been intended for a second issue of *Photo-Bondage*. Among the non-figurative castoffs are images of a Philco refrigerator, a radiator, a medicine cabinet interior (fig. 10), and exterior views of 5244 Melrose Avenue (see figs. 2 and 3). The archive also contains Polaroids and related contact sheets that served as the basis for the *Triptychs*, *Quadrants*, and *Door/Window* constructions, as well as Malibu seascapes that would become part of the *Storm/Wall* pairs (see *Storm/Wall Diptych* no. 6, pl. 58), and sequential works like *Acting Out* (pl. 59), *Getting Around*, and *Running*.

Kahn subtly manipulated several of the images during the process of translating them from Polaroid to gelatin silver. For instance, after carefully masking the main motifs, he methodically retouched discrete areas on the Polaroids of *Window* 1 (app. 7), *Window* 14 (app. 106), *Window* 20 (app. 68), and *Window* 23 (app. 77), applying opaque white paint with a miniature airbrush to eliminate unwanted shadows or blemishes. In addition, on *Window* 23 (app. 77) he used graphite and black ink to manually redraw two details accidentally covered by the paint: the molding line in the lower-left corner and the curtain rod at the upper left. Kahn similarly airbrushed the wall on *Door* 9 (app. 99) to hide graffiti. In a number of other instances, he simply cropped

the edges of the Polaroids when enlarging the compositions to eliminate unwanted details, most noticeably in *Window* 10 (app. 87 and pl. 17) and *Window* 21 (app. 89 and pl. 19). Such precise adjustments reveal Kahn's close attention to the formal qualities of the enlargements.

In September 1976, as Kahn's work on the project was reaching a feverish pace, he created a temporary art installation inside one of the apartments of 5244 Melrose Avenue. He recorded his inspiration in a journal entry dated September 18–19, noting that after working in apartment 203 all day he arrived at a "breakthrough idea":

The Polis [i.e., Polaroids] I've done in this room (including adjustments to 3 walls (& portals) + shooting windows in 4th wall) are of such strength & cohesiveness that the photos are really pale by comparison—too much that is relevantly going on that is outside the camera's realm—too many cues— . . . Maybe open this room up to visitors—a piece in #203 / With no lock on the door (i.e. no secrets) & perhaps photographs somewhere else like Broxton [Gallery]—i.e. the photographs of the pieces for comparison—It'd be heavy for my career as a photographer—maybe end it as such—open a dialogue / perhaps put the Polaroids in the room.[20]

Kahn described the *Apt. #203* installation as a series of four interventions or "adjustments" to the space, which he then photographed (figs. 11a–11f). His adjustments included leaning an unattached door alongside a door set into the wall and creating an illusionary corner within a closet by pinning a piece of black cloth in the form of a triangle within the shallow interior. He also installed four Polaroids of the interventions on the unit's walls to juxtapose what the camera sees and what it misses, thus creating an optical feedback loop for visitors to the space. "This is the first time I'm letting people 'in' to see the workings of my mind—to

STEVE KAHN
Variants of *Bound Door* 6, 1976. Twenty-three
Polaroids with scratching. Mary and Dan Solomon
Collection, Los Angeles

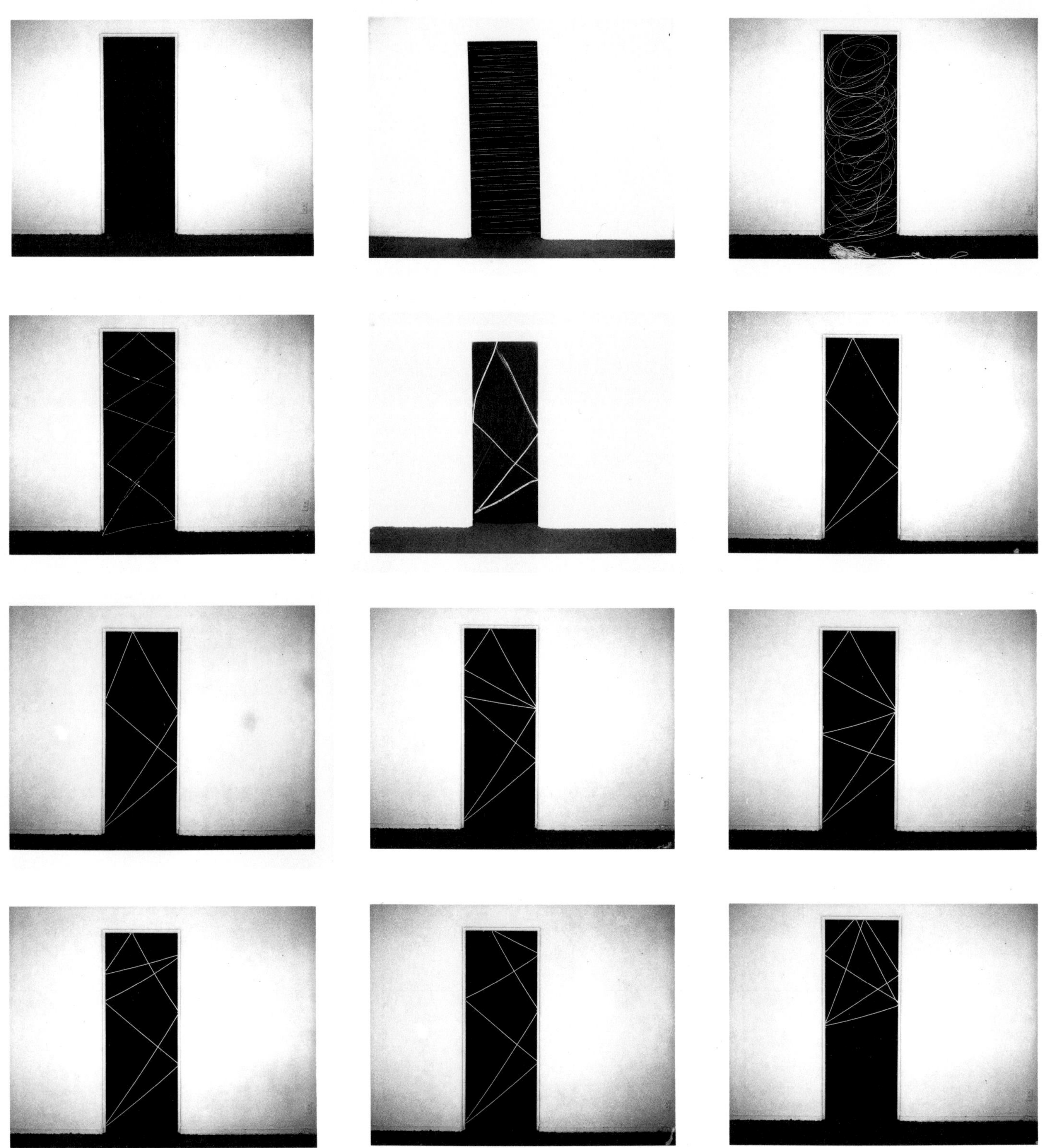

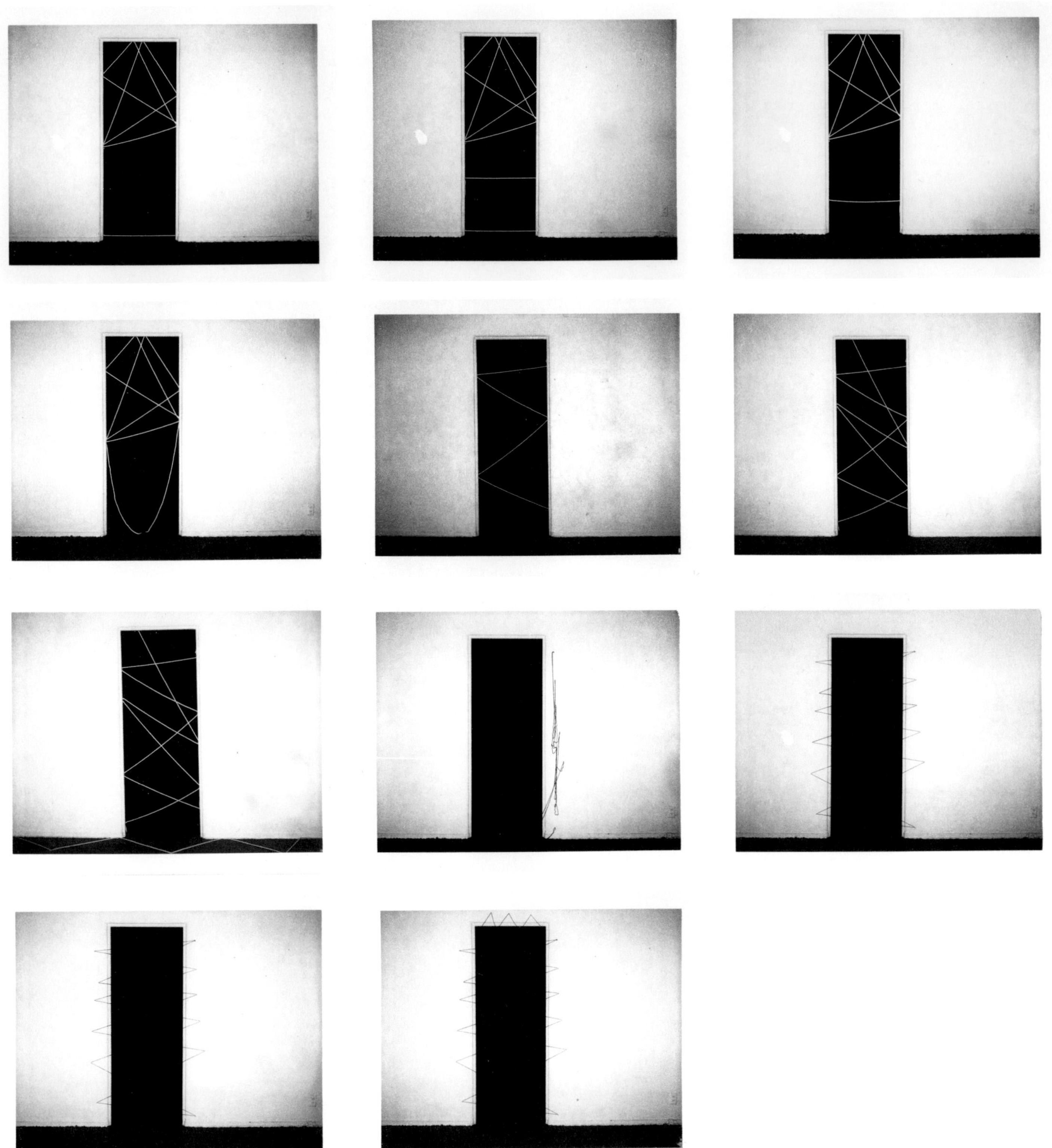

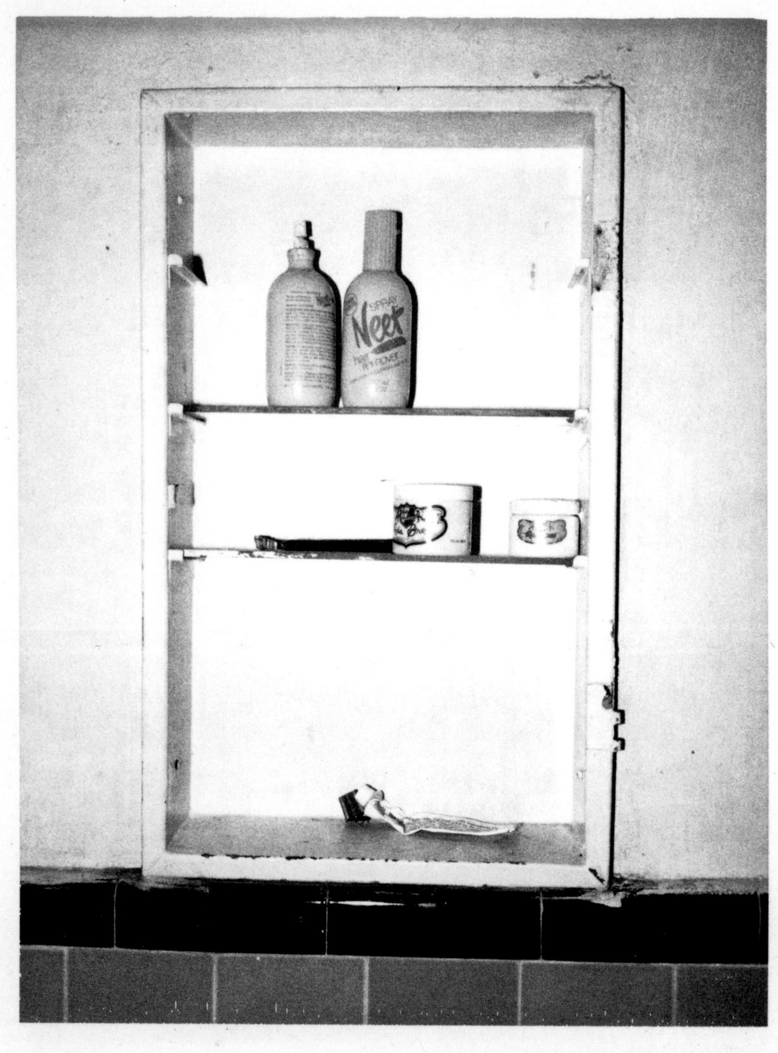

10
STEVE KAHN
Untitled (Medicine cabinet), 1976. Polaroid.
Mary and Dan Solomon Collection,
Los Angeles

11a–11f
STEVE KAHN
Untitled (Installation in Apt. 203), 1976.
Six Polaroids. Mary and Dan Solomon Collection,
Los Angeles

12 [overleaf]
[left] STEVE KAHN
Window 6, 1976. Polaroid. Fine Arts Museums
of San Francisco, Gift of Dr. Nancy Ascher and
Dr. John Roberts
[right] STEVE KAHN
Window 6, 1976. Gelatin silver print.
Fine Arts Museums of San Francisco,
Gift of Dr. Nancy Ascher and Dr. John Roberts

view for themselves the original material of which my Polaroids are only one interpretation,"[21] Kahn wrote, articulating his belief that 5244 Melrose—rather than the Polaroids or gelatin silver prints—constituted the "original material" of his work. "I wanted those people to come into that space and feel the paranoia of that space if they were so inclined," he said later, "and to experience unlocking the door and locking it behind them, being in the room for a certain period of time, seeing how they responded in there. Could they tolerate it? Could they tolerate that enclosure?"[22]

Kahn's adoption of this alternative exhibition space allies him with a number of experimental California artists of the late 1960s and early 1970s who independently created temporary installations outside the mainstream of museums and galleries. These include James Turrell (*Mendota Stoppages*, 1969–1974, in the Mendota Block on Main Street in Ocean Park, Santa Monica); Allen Ruppersberg (*Al's Café*, 1969, West 6th Street in the Westlake neighborhood of Los Angeles; and *Al's Grand Hotel*, 1971, Sunset Boulevard in Hollywood); Judy Chicago and Miriam Schapiro (*Womanhouse*, 1972, Mariposa Avenue in Hollywood); and Lynn Hershman and Eleanor Coppola (*The Dante Hotel*, 1973–1974, Columbus Avenue, San Francisco).

GENERATIONS. Despite his inclusion of Polaroids in the *Apt. #203* installation, Kahn wrote in his journal and his later artist's statement that he did not consider them to be finished works of art. Rather he saw the Polaroids as the raw "first generation" matrices for the gelatin silver prints that he would edition and exhibit, and as such he came to view them as if they were anonymous found objects. "The copying process," he explained, "allowed me to explore the effects of creating multiple generations of the images and the levels of abstraction that resulted." Offering a detailed account of this, he wrote:

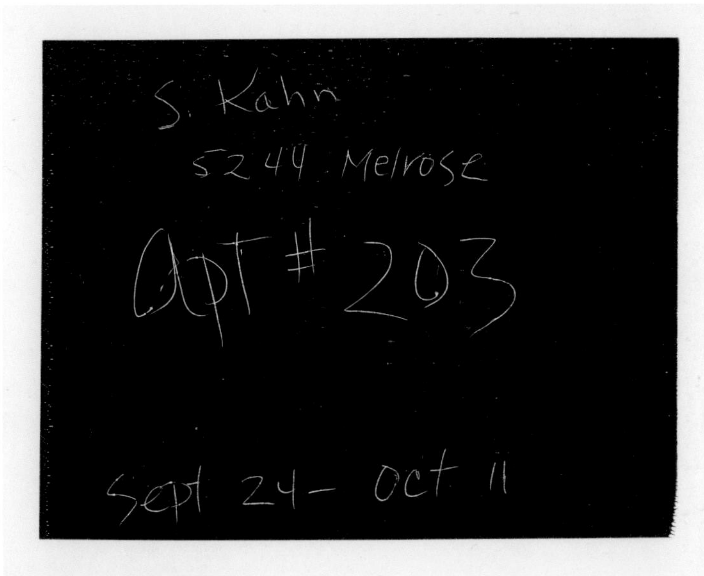
S. Kahn
5244 Melrose
apt # 203
Sept 24 - Oct 11
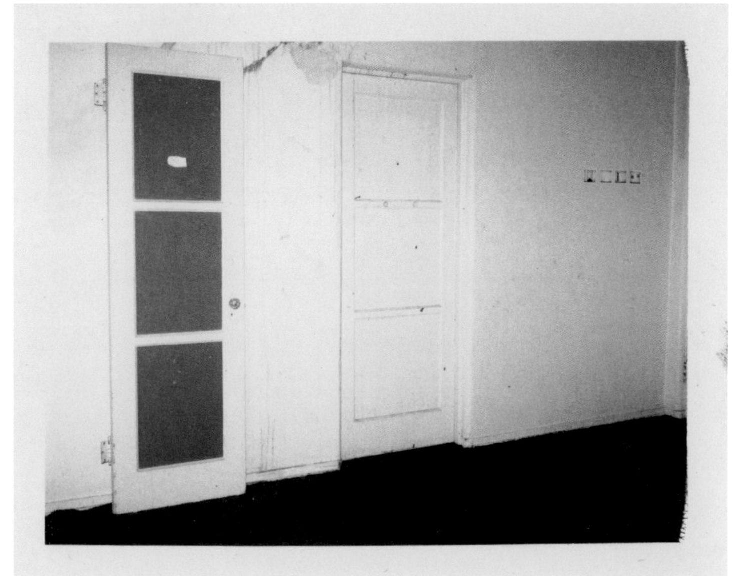
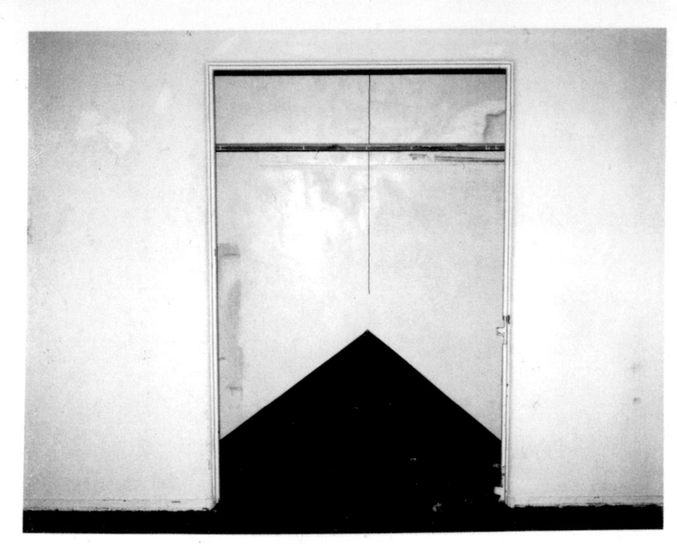
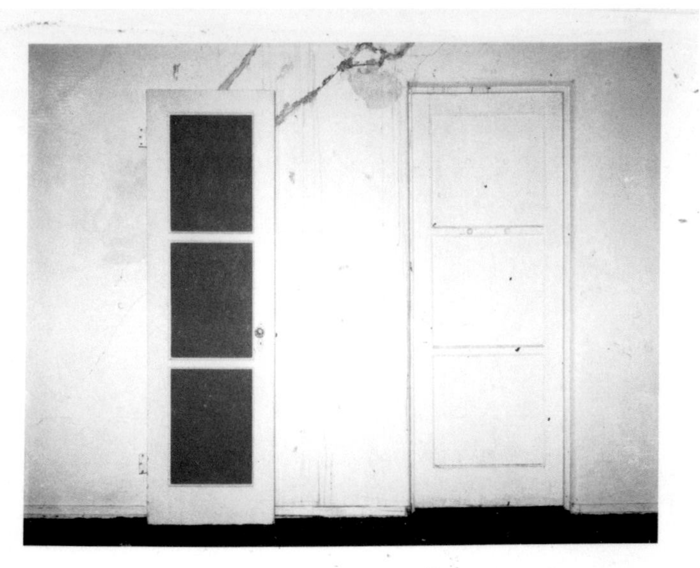
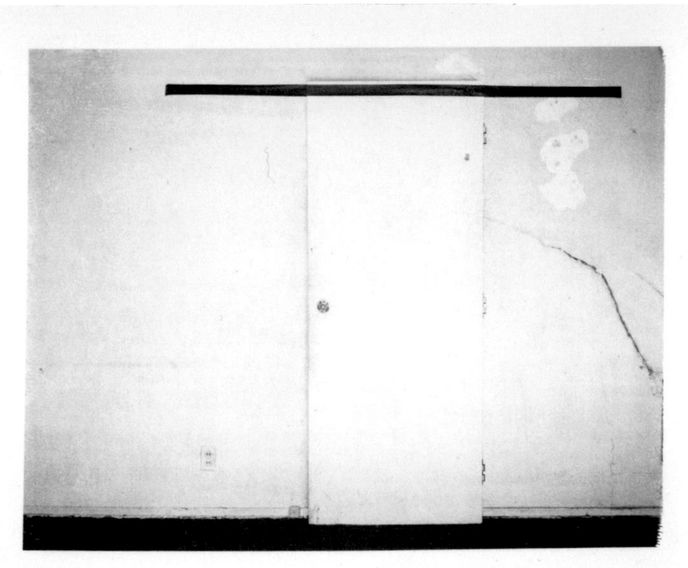
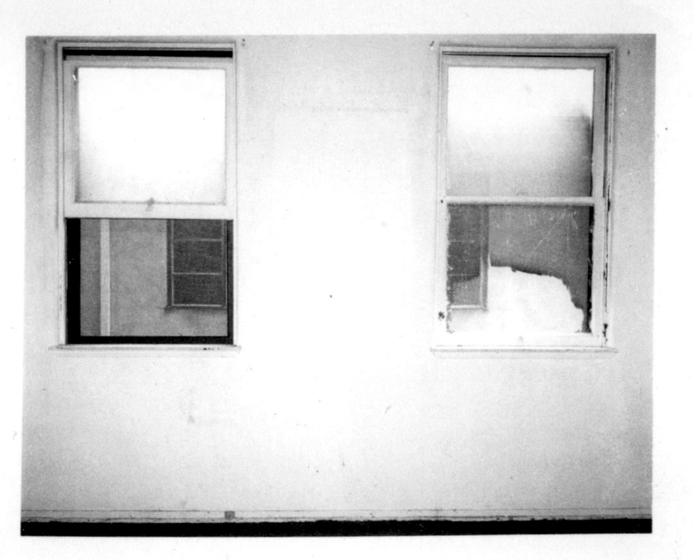

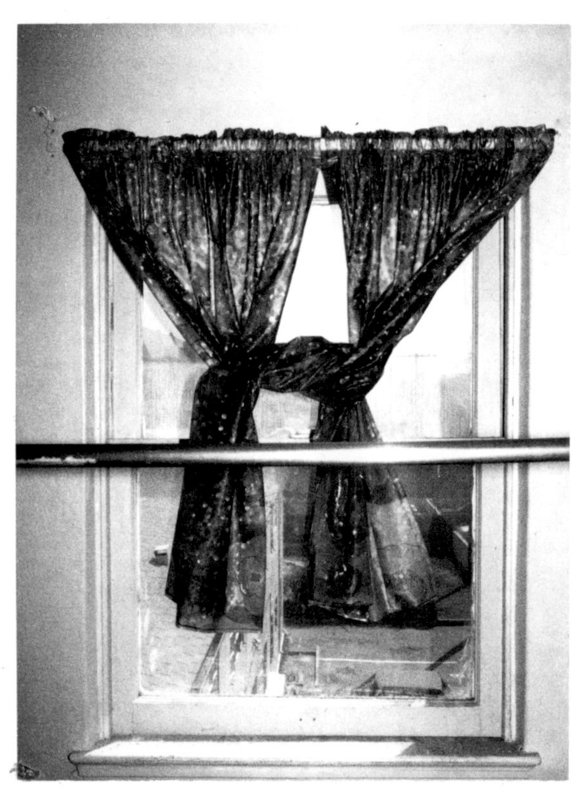

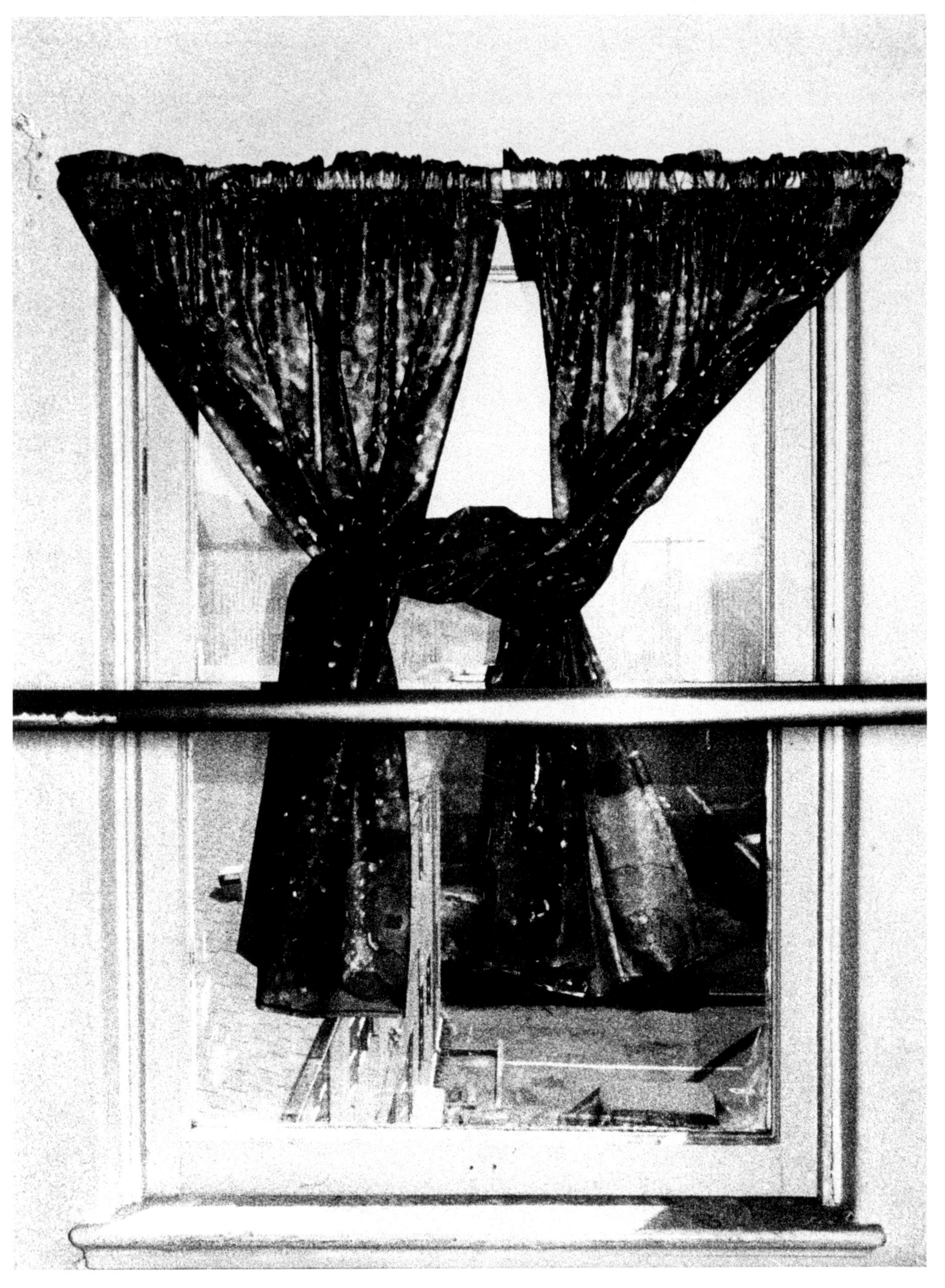

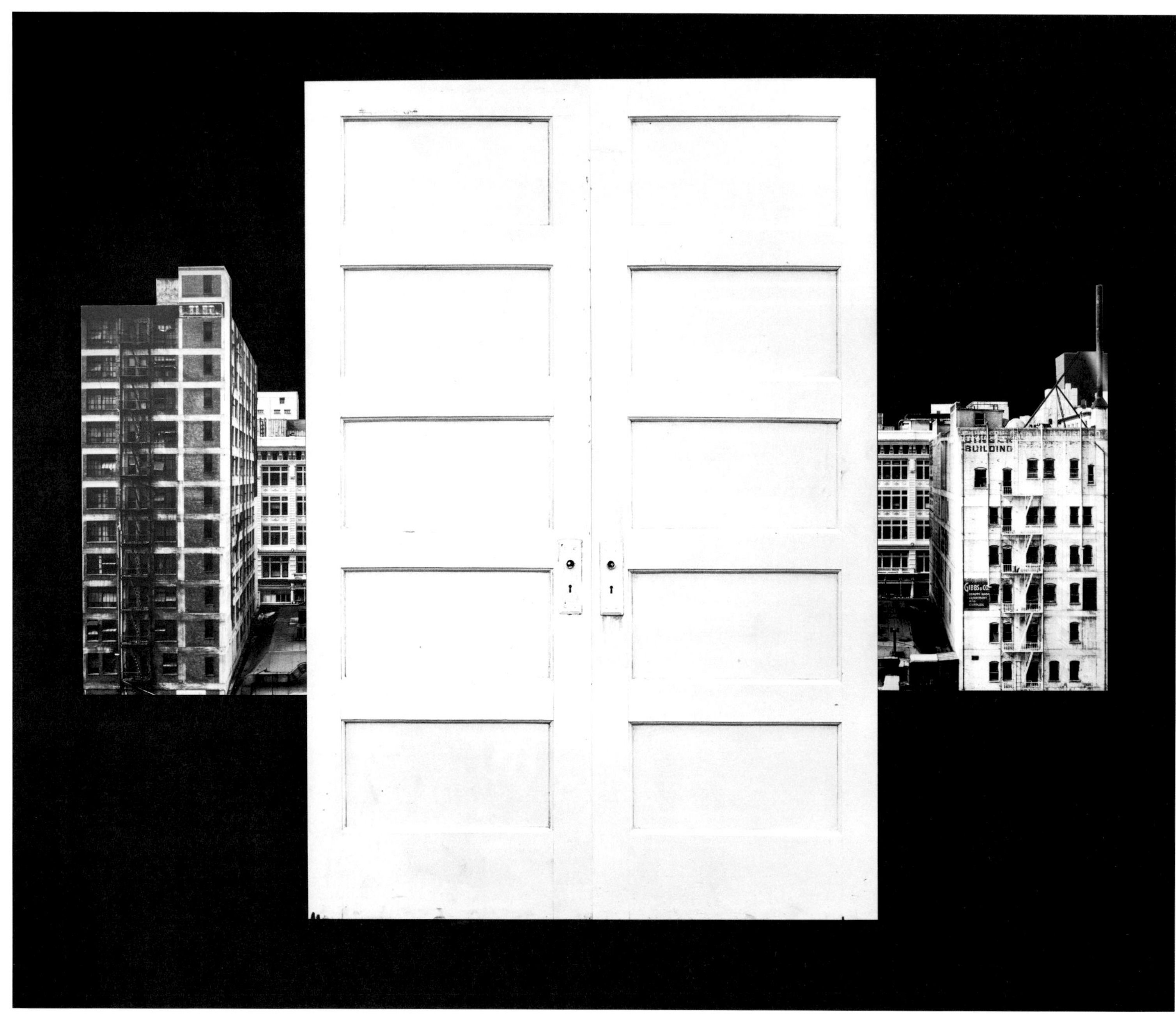

I copied the Polaroid prints onto high-speed, b/w 35mm film (Ilford HP-4) using a copy stand with my Leica, and processed the film in the German developer Rodinal for crisp grain that formed the underlying visual surface holding everything together and out of which details coalesced. . . . The vintage silver prints were made on Agfa Brovira grade #5 paper to spread the short value range of the Polaroids across the paper's response curve . . . and were finished in a light selenium toner bath for longevity, deep blacks and cool grays [see fig. 12].[23]

The editions were set at fifteen, but for most images he produced only six prints (exceptionally, he produced thirteen prints of *Window* 13 [pl. 16], perhaps one of the most superficially cheerful compositions in the series). Kahn inscribed the editioned gelatin silver prints of the *Nudes* and *Portraits* on the verso with the dates 1974–1975, while the *Windows, Doors, Bound Doors, Mirrors,* and *Rooms* he inscribed either 1976 or 1977.[24] When he reprinted the series in a small edition of pigment prints in 2012, he added eight previously unpublished images.

Although Kahn wrapped up shooting the *Doors, Windows,* and *Mirrors* for *The Hollywood Suites* in 1977, the Polaroids continued to serve as a source of inspiration and raw material for several of his future related projects, including his multipanel *Door/Window* constructions (1978), first shown at the Rosamund Felsen Gallery, Los Angeles, in late December 1978/ early January 1979. *Door/Window* 4 (fig. 13) was chosen by the curators and Modern and Contemporary Art Council of the Los Angeles County Museum of Art for the New Talent Purchase award in 1979, putting Kahn in the company of such past winners as Chris Burden, Mary Corse, and Llyn Foulkes. The *Storm/Wall*

diptychs (1978), first shown at the Cronin Gallery, Houston, in 1979, juxtapose *Hollywood Suites Doors* (minus the artwork on the walls) with views of storm clouds over the Pacific Ocean in Malibu (see *Storm/Wall Diptych* 6, pl. 58).[25] Kahn stated that the diptychs were inspired by the juxtapositions of the framed fantasy landscapes decorating the apartments with the plain surfaces of the walls, but they also reflected the extreme contrast between his pastoral lifestyle in Malibu and the urban decadence thirty miles to the east, where he commuted for several years while shooting *The Hollywood Suites.* "I would drive from this beautiful, funky setting to skuzzy Hollywood and make my explorations," he recalled a month before his death, in February 2018. "It was an adventure."[26]

Moving beyond the diptychs, Kahn became increasingly interested in serial imagery, participating in the exhibition *Sequences: Sequential Imagery in Photography,* which also included the work of John Baldessari, Hilla and Bernd Becher, Duane Michals, and Bruce Nauman, at Larry Gagosian's Broxton Gallery in the spring of 1976. Kahn's *Triptychs* and *Quadrants* (1976–1977), the first generations of which were shot concurrently with the *Doors, Bound Doors, Windows,* and *Mirrors* on 107 format Polaroid film, focus on austere structural elements in the rooms. Photographing and reassembling images of corners and junctures between floors, walls, ceilings, and doors, Kahn explained, "I created something new, consisting of the original information, yet quite skewed. This challenged me to re-think how I perceived the space initially and to consider what assumptions I brought to the problem."[27] Kahn printed the *Triptychs* and *Quadrants* both in 11-by-14-inch formats and as murals mounted on 36-by-48-inch aluminum panels. A breakthrough solo exhibition of *Triptychs* and *Quadrants* called

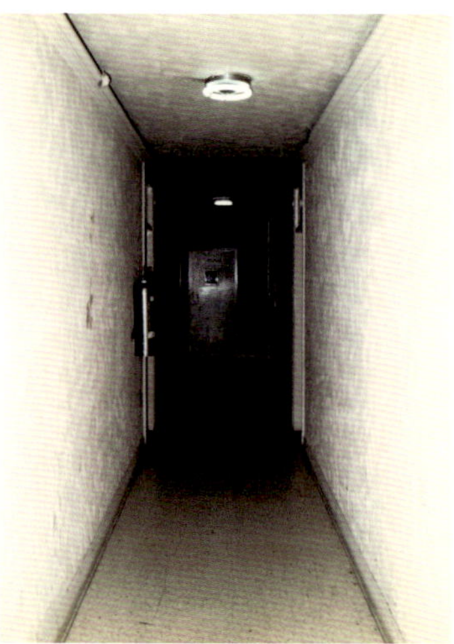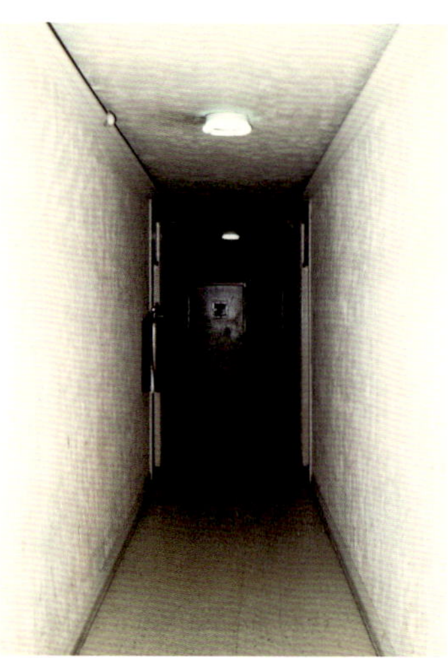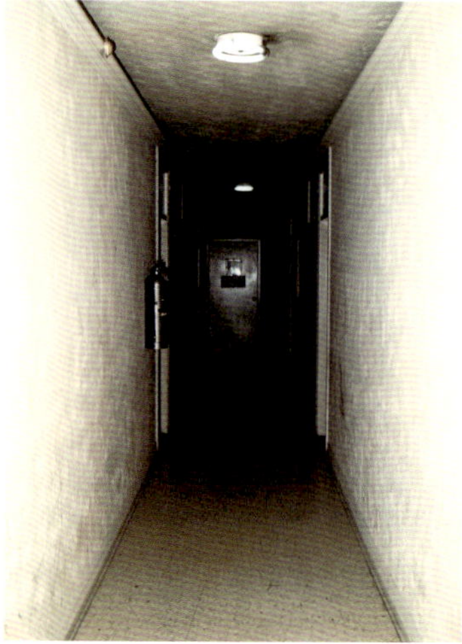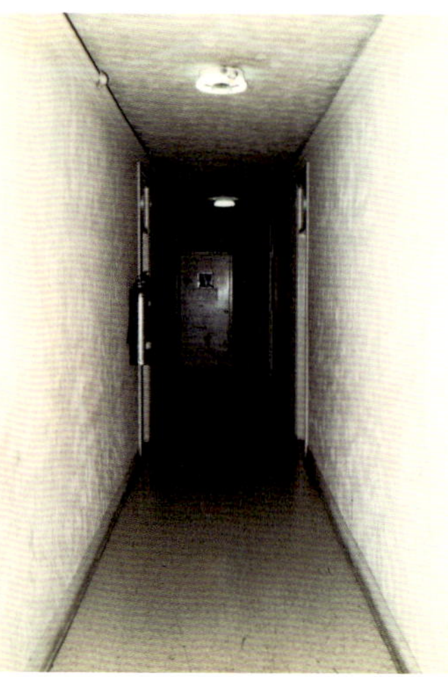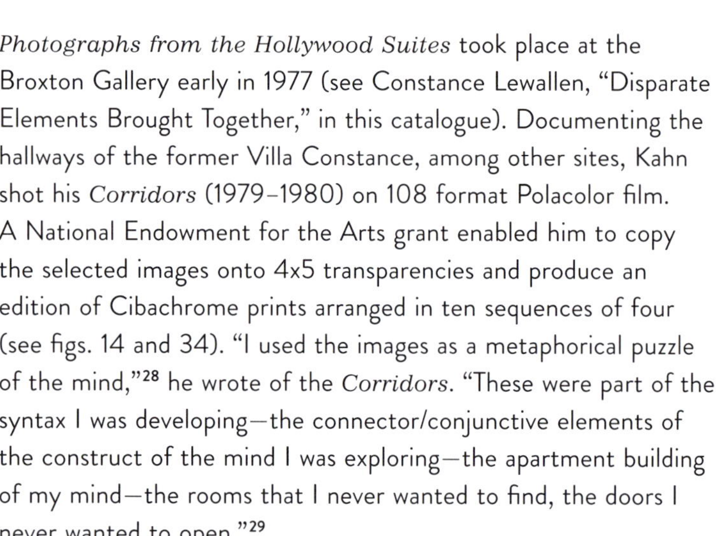

Photographs from the Hollywood Suites took place at the Broxton Gallery early in 1977 (see Constance Lewallen, "Disparate Elements Brought Together," in this catalogue). Documenting the hallways of the former Villa Constance, among other sites, Kahn shot his *Corridors* (1979–1980) on 108 format Polacolor film. A National Endowment for the Arts grant enabled him to copy the selected images onto 4x5 transparencies and produce an edition of Cibachrome prints arranged in ten sequences of four (see figs. 14 and 34). "I used the images as a metaphorical puzzle of the mind,"[28] he wrote of the *Corridors*. "These were part of the syntax I was developing—the connector/conjunctive elements of the construct of the mind I was exploring—the apartment building of my mind—the rooms that I never wanted to find, the doors I never wanted to open."[29]

Kahn continued to work and exhibit in Los Angeles until 1986, when he relocated to New York and shifted his full attention to commercial photography. It would be nearly twenty years, after he returned to the West Coast and settled in Berkeley, before he would revisit his 1970s work. A 2012 gallery show of *The Hollywood Suites* at the Joseph Bellows Gallery, in La Jolla, was followed two years later by a *Hollywood Suites* artist's book, published by Chris Pichler's Nazraeli Press, which reproduced fifty-one of the images in duotone and included several previously unpublished Polaroids. Kahn's first such publication since *Stasis,* in 1973, the book was dedicated by the photographer "to the memory of my dear friend, artist and mentor Robert Overby," who had died of cancer in 1993. Nazraeli followed up with a small book of Kahn's *Corridors* in 2015.

"There seems to be a performance aspect of my work which is gaining more importance in my mind than the photographs," Kahn ruminated in an October 1975 journal entry. "It's the experience of being confronted w/oneself—alone in a room (in this case)—confronted with the feelings of need, emptiness—fears of failure—fear of the light where 'things' are visible."[30] In his *Notes for The Hollywood Suites*, he stressed the element of containment as a fundamental theme of this body of work. "These were 'no-exit' situations," he wrote of the sessions, "entered into without plan, full of anxiety, in the hope of producing some document of the experience that was explicit, visually powerful, yet went beyond what it was."[31] In *Apt. #203*, Kahn attempted to share his experience by inviting the viewer into his makeshift studio. He considered another approach in a planned exhibition for the Newspace Gallery, in Los Angeles, consisting of photographs of nudes in the main space, shown with a video recording of Kahn participating in a bondage shooting session filmed in the back during the opening.[32] Although this project failed to materialize, he produced several multipart works during this period in which he appeared before the camera. In *Acting Out* (1976; pl. 59), Kahn's frantic body language expresses the peculiar angst of an artist who finds himself locked inside the room where the creative process is supposed to happen. In the twelfth and final frame of the sequence, the door at last opens, allowing the photographer to escape the work of art.

14
STEVE KAHN
Corridors 3, 1979–1980 (printed 2014).
Four archival pigment prints. 22½ x 55½ in.
Stephen H. Kahn Trust

1   Carl Jules Weyl is identified as the architect of 5244 Melrose on the original building permit, approved by the Department of Building and Safety of the city of Los Angeles on November 12, 1929.

2   Jess Bravin, *Squeaky: The Life and Times of Lynette Alice Fromme* (New York: St. Martin's Press, 1997).

3   The city of Los Angeles granted a permit to demolish the building in December 1994, and the work was carried out sometime in 1995 ("Landlord Told to Clean Up Building or Tear It Down," *Los Angeles Times*, January 5, 1995).

4   From a 1986 interview with Peter Clothier quoted in Terry R. Myers, *Robert Overby, Parallel: 1978–1969* (Los Angeles: UCLA Hammer Museum, 2000), 76.

5   The marriage ended after ten years. Albuquerque discussed their relationship in a 1990 interview conducted as part of the Archives of American Art oral history program: https://www.aaa.si.edu/collections/interviews/oral-history-interview-lita-albuquerque-11932#transcript.

6   Jay Ruby, *Coffee House Positano: A Bohemian Oasis in Malibu, 1957–1962* (Louisville, CO: University Press of Colorado, 2014).

7   Ruby, *The Property: Malibu's Other Colony* (self-pub., 2016).

8   Conversation with the author, Berkeley, California, December 12, 2017.

9   Steve Kahn, *Journal entry, November 1, 1976*, Journal 1, p. 86, Stephen H. Kahn Trust.

10   The forty-page transcript, discovered after Kahn's death, documents a conversation between the artist and two interviewers identified only by their initials—AS and CF. In it, Kahn recounts the evolution of his work in both pragmatic and philosophical terms. It is not known for what purpose the interview was conducted or if it was ever published. See: Steve Kahn, in discussion with unknown, [1977?]. In her essay in this catalogue, Jodi Throckmorton cites statements Kahn makes in the interview as she discusses potential feminist responses to *The Hollywood Suites*.

11   As of publication, Kahn's papers and archive are in the process of being transferred to the Archives of American Art, Washington, DC, per his wishes.

12   For instance, *Nude* 9 (app. 12) and *Nude* 30 (pl. 9) are clearly of the same model and were taken during the same session.

13   *Polaroid Film Codes* (America's Business Center [Bedford, MA: 1998]) explains how to interpret the codes that appear on Polaroid prints. See: http://tityrus.free.fr/polaroid/integral/Polaroid-FilmCode.pdf.

14   We arrived at this estimate by deciphering clues from multiple *Hollywood Suites* Polaroids, some of which are not published in this catalogue. Several Polaroids with manufacturing codes of April 8, 1975, feature a model with the travel section of the June 8, 1975, *Los Angeles Times* covering her body, indicating a period of two months between the film pack's manufacture and the photograph. Another group of Polaroids, taken on film packs manufactured on December 23, 1975, include the front page of the *Los Angeles Times* from March 31, 1976. Finally, the Polaroid reproduced in fig. 11a, which gives the date of Kahn's Room 203 installation opening on September 24, 1976, has a code dating from July 9 of that year.

15   Complicating efforts to determine the precise chronology is the fact that in many instances Kahn used multiple film packs with the same manufacturing codes.

16   Although *Nudes* do not appear on any of the 107 format film packs of *Hollywood Suites* manufactured after August 9, 1975, Kahn did continue to photograph nude models in color with a Polaroid consumer model SX-70; some of these prints became part of his *Torsos* and *Painted Ladies* series. A journal entry dated December 8, 1975, starts with the heading "Back to Bondage" and is followed by descriptions of bound women (Journal 1, p. 35). In another entry, dated November 26, 1977, he wrote "complete Polaroid SX70 nudes" (Journal 1, p. 123).

17   Extrapolating from other details in *Window* 10 (pl. 17), *Window* 12 (pl. 18), and *Window* 21 (pl. 19), we can determine that the distinctive light-and-dark-colored bathroom tile work recurs in *Window* 5 (app. 65), *Window* 9 (app. 81), *Window* 11 (pl. 20), *Window* 13 (pl. 16), *Window* 18 (app. 69), *Window* 18a (app. 70), and an untitled photograph of a medicine cabinet (fig. 10), establishing their location as also being 5244 Melrose. On the east side, *Window* 15 (pl. 21) looks out onto the Crown Apartments, next door at 5234 Melrose, whereas *Window* 16 (pl. 22) and *Window* 23 (pl. 23), two photographs of window triptychs partially obscured by curtains, correspond with a distinctive window configuration on the third-floor southern facade of 5244 Melrose visible in the 1935 view (fig. 1).

18   In only a few instances did Kahn select close variants of the same motif to enlarge as silver prints. These include *Windows* 2 and 3 (apps. 61 and 60); *Windows* 10 and 12 (pls. 17 and 18); *Windows* 14 and 25 (pl. 24 and app. 105); *Windows* 18 and 18a (apps. 69 and 70); and *Windows* 17 (pl. 25) and 27.

19   Kahn, *Journal entry, September 18–19, 1976*, Journal 1, p. 75.

20   Kahn, p. 75.

21   Kahn, *Journal entry, September 18–19, 1976*, Journal 1, p. 78.

22   Kahn, in discussion with unknown, [1977?], p. 36.

23   Kahn, "Notes for The Hollywood Suites" (artist statement, 2012), Stephen H. Kahn Trust.

24   We now know that some of the photographs Kahn marked as being from 1976 or 1977 were photographed as early as 1974. The manufacturing codes reveal discrepancies in Kahn's dating of the following interiors: *Window* 1 (pl. 31) and *Window* 4 (pl. 30), both inscribed 1976, were photographed in 1974 and 1975, respectively; *Door* 5 (pl. 35), inscribed 1976, was photographed in 1977; *Bound Door* 1 (pl. 39) and *Bound Door* 2 (pl. 43), both inscribed 1976, were photographed in 1975; and *Mirror* 6 (pl. 51), inscribed 1977, was photographed in 1976.

25   *Door* 1 (pl. 33) appears in *Storm/Wall Diptych* 7 with artwork removed; *Door* 2 (pl. 36) appears in *Storm/Wall Diptych* 1 with artwork removed; a variant of *Door* 6 (pl. 38) appears in *Storm/Wall Diptych* 4.

26   Kahn, email message to the author, December 21, 2017.

27   "Triptychs and Quadrants," Steve Kahn, accessed April 16, 2018, https://www.stevekahn.com/triptychs-and-quadrants.

28   "Corridors," Steve Kahn, accessed April 16, 2018, https://www.stevekahn.com/corridors.

29   Kahn, "Notes."

30   Kahn, *Journal entry, October 16, 1975*, Journal 1, p. 29.

31   Kahn, "Notes."

32   Kahn, *Journal entry, January 1, 1975*, Journal 1, p. 12; Kahn, in discussion with unknown, [1977?].

MEMOIRS OF A BOUND PHOTOGRAPHER
STEVE KAHN'S HOLLYWOOD SUITES

JODI THROCKMORTON

STEVE KAHN'S journals from the 1970s are filled with line drawings and written descriptions that detail bondage-inspired scenes for his *Hollywood Suites* photographs. These schematics were not necessarily instructions; in fact, the scenarios that Kahn enacted with professional bondage models in shabby Hollywood apartments and photographed with a Polaroid camera were improvisational, open to risk and chance. Nonetheless, Kahn's sketches and notes—such as "tied down like a rack" and "treat body contours like landscape"[1]—give insight into his primarily formal interest in the bound female form (see fig. 15).[2] When a scheduled model failed to show up for a session one day, Kahn, again inspired by chance circumstances, began to photograph the dismal interiors with the same formal rigor that he applied to the models, occasionally using bondage-like binds on doorframes and windows. Such oppositions—between "dead forms" and "live flesh,"[3] restraint and freedom, presence and absence—charge the series with a tension that is just barely contained, befitting the photographs that Kahn described as "anxiety projections,"[4] metaphors for his own state of mind.

The other authors in this catalogue thoroughly describe and examine Kahn's approach, formal interests, and context; this essay, therefore, considers his use of erotic subject matter to convey experiences of isolation, power, and vulnerability through the formally striking photographs of *The Hollywood Suites*. In addition, although I do not characterize his work as feminist, this essay also addresses Kahn's conflicted exploration of the sexualized gaze and the relationship between domestic spaces and the female body—burgeoning discussions in 1960s and 1970s feminism.

The Hollywood Suites grew out of Kahn's foray into the commercial pornography industry in the 1970s, specifically his work as a photographer for the one and only issue of *Photo-Bondage* magazine.[5] Kahn's main contribution was

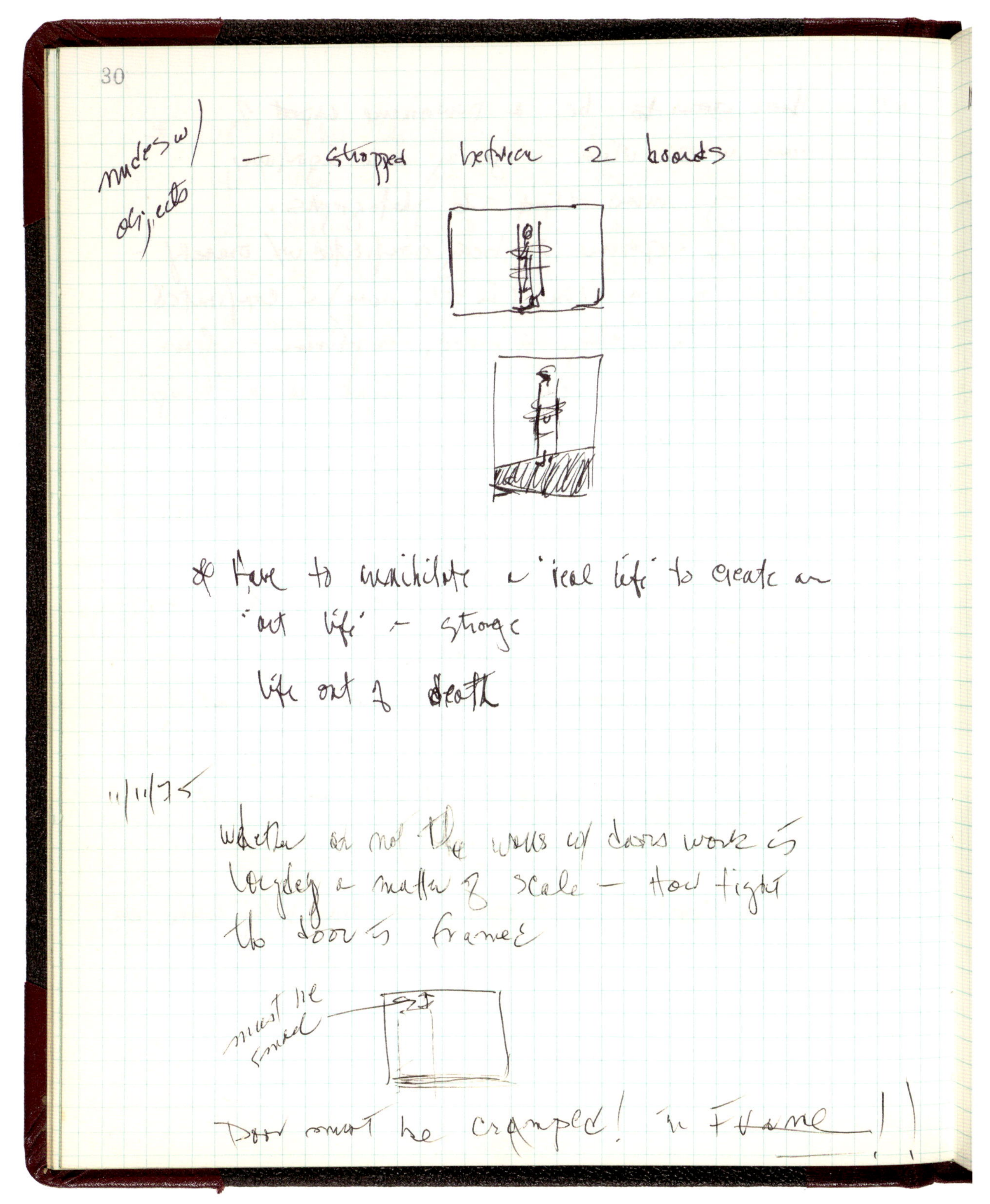

15
STEVE KAHN
Journal entry, October 16, 1975
(detail), Journal 1, p. 30, Stephen H.
Kahn Trust

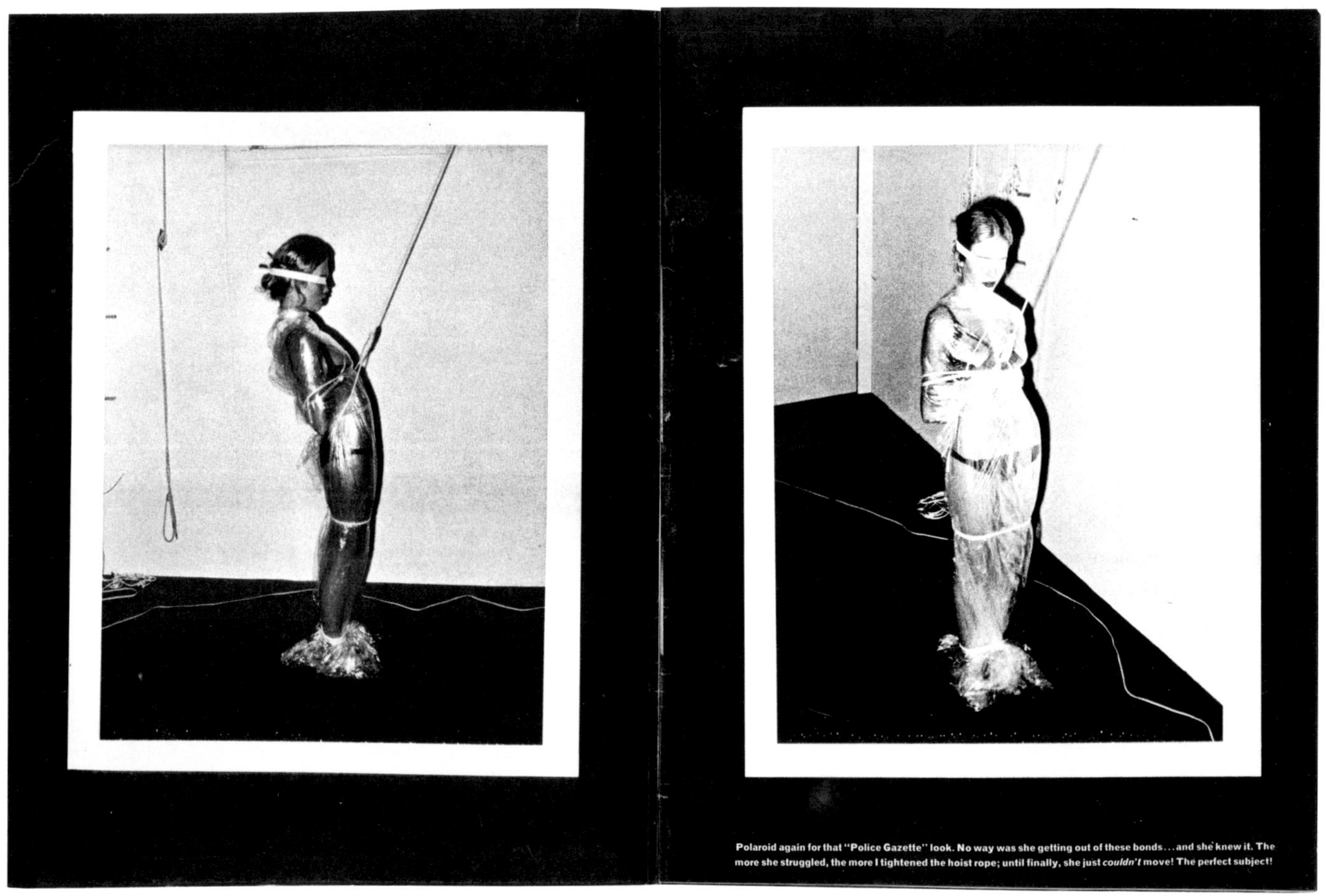

"Memoirs of a Bondage Photographer," a fictional photo-essay he composed and wrote that details a sexual scenario between a photographer and his female model. He begins this fantasy in the photographer's mind:

> It all started one night, late last summer, after a long day's shooting. I was alone in the studio, just lying there in the dim light, digging on some sounds and getting pleasantly stoned. My head was full of fantasies about this gorgeous, moody chick I'd been doing a fashion spread on a few hours before.[6]

He goes on to describe the model's submissiveness: "Weird chick . . . different from the others . . . hardly said a word all day, kept her eyes cast down, never looking at me . . ." Kahn keenly recognized the psychosexual tension that can result from the imbalance of power in an artist-model relationship, and he sought to translate this intensity from commercial bondage fantasy into *The Hollywood Suites*.

Kahn's *Hollywood Suites* photographs, which he made after he had shifted to working with professional bondage models in cheap apartments, are more minimal and distanced than those in "Memoirs of a Bondage Photographer." Compare, for example, an image from *Photo-Bondage* in which a model appears to be suffocating in a sheet of plastic (a material often found in artists' studios; fig. 16) with a photo from *The Hollywood Suites* (pl. 8) in which a woman is similarly sheathed in plastic wrapping. The photograph in the magazine places an emphasis on the woman's bound breasts, torn lingerie, and inability to move. Such intense visual information bluntly translates the sexual experience for the viewer, leaving little to the imagination.

Kahn's deftness with visual composition is apparent in this earlier photo—the tension he establishes between the rope's straight, taut line and the curves of the model's body, for example—but it is even clearer in the *Suites* photograph, in which the composition is reduced to the model, her arm, a plastic sheet, and the floor and wall. Kahn photographs the model from the side, denying the viewer the direct gaze of the sexualized female body that he allows in the commercial photographs, drawing focus to the radiating lines in the pulled plastic instead. A fascinating contradiction emerges between the photographs' inherent sexual tension and Kahn's denial of the viewer's erotic projections. The fantasy of the photographer introduced in "Memoirs of a Bondage Photographer" is obstructed for the viewer of *The Hollywood Suites*.

Despite the bravado Kahn projects in the text of his photo-essay, his actual experience of the bondage sessions was far from titillating. In an unpublished interview from the late 1970s, he remarked:

> *I was dealing with an issue of alienation and annihilation which meant that there had to be a real live situation in which that took place. And that was perhaps the most painful part of the whole thing: in other words, I had in fact to act that out as director, as creator, as orchestrator of it, as author of the situation.*[7]

It is the apprehension that Kahn experienced while making the *Photo-Bondage* work—his discomfort with the process of creating the photographs and using the models to enact violent scenarios— that he wanted to express in *The Hollywood Suites*. As such, the models come to reflect Kahn's uneasiness as an author. He diverts the viewer's gaze as an expression of the sexual frustration these scenarios generate in him and his anxiety over the dangerous sexuality they suggest. He also may have been conflicted about the models' relative acceptance of these manipulations. Serena Czarnecki, one of the models in *The Hollywood Suites*, who wrote a memoir about her time working in the pornography industry, described her experience: "I was able to do a kind of meditation that kept me comfortable while tied up. I would be hung upside down with a ball gag in my mouth and fall asleep!"[8] While one

cannot assume that all of the *Hollywood Suites* models felt this way, it's notable how these two statements—that of a distressed photographer and that of a calm and meditative model—flip Kahn's photo-essay script, complicating the assumed power dynamics between artist and model and between dominant and submissive.

Kahn did not intend for his photographs to give a sense of agency to his female models or to make a moral statement about violence against women; that is clear. Yet it is still worthwhile to compare his methods for diverting and controlling the viewer's sexualized gaze with the practices of contemporaneous feminist artists who sought to define and subvert the male gaze. Kahn's previously described photographs of women bound with plastic sheeting call to mind images from Carolee Schneemann's iconic *Eye Body: 36 Transformative Actions for the Camera*, done in 1963 (fig. 17). Schneemann foregrounds her body in these photographs, acting out the questions she was asking at the time: "Could I include myself as a formal aspect of my own materials? Could a nude woman artist be both image and image maker?"[9]

The Hollywood Suites and Schneemann's series both start with performative scenarios—Kahn responding to the "'no-exit' situations, entered into without plan,"[10] that he had created with the models, Schneemann "actively collaging [her] body with studio materials such as paint, fur, plastic, and garden snakes."[11] In Schneemann's photographs, she confronts the viewer with her nude body, staring directly into the camera. In contrast, the women in Kahn's photographs are muted, suspended, contained, and purposefully anonymous. Both artists use the female "body as visual territory,"[12] but their direction of the viewer's gaze differs. Kahn misdirects the gaze, de-personalizing his models as a means of sublimating sexual denial into a psychological state. Schneemann, contrastingly, encourages and embraces the viewer's sexualized gaze, reclaiming it as a mirror of female, rather than male, desire.

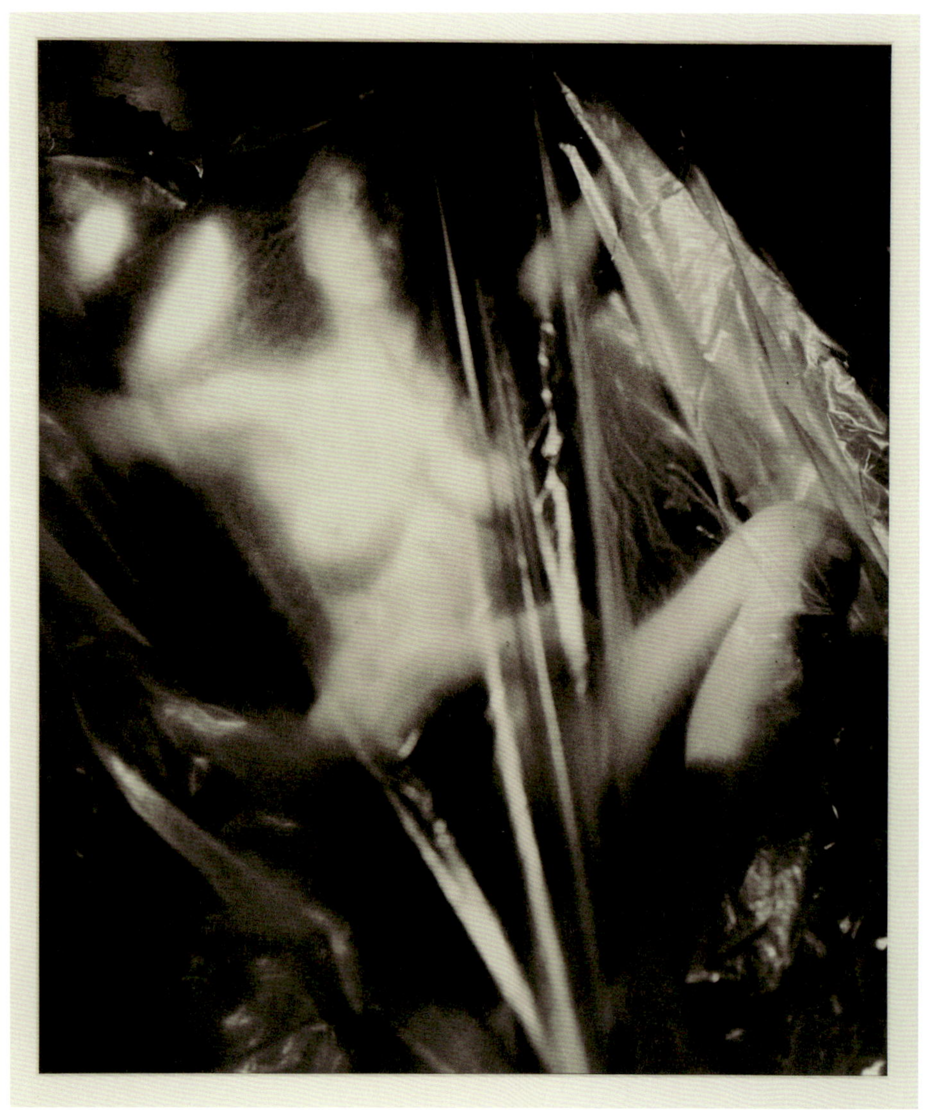

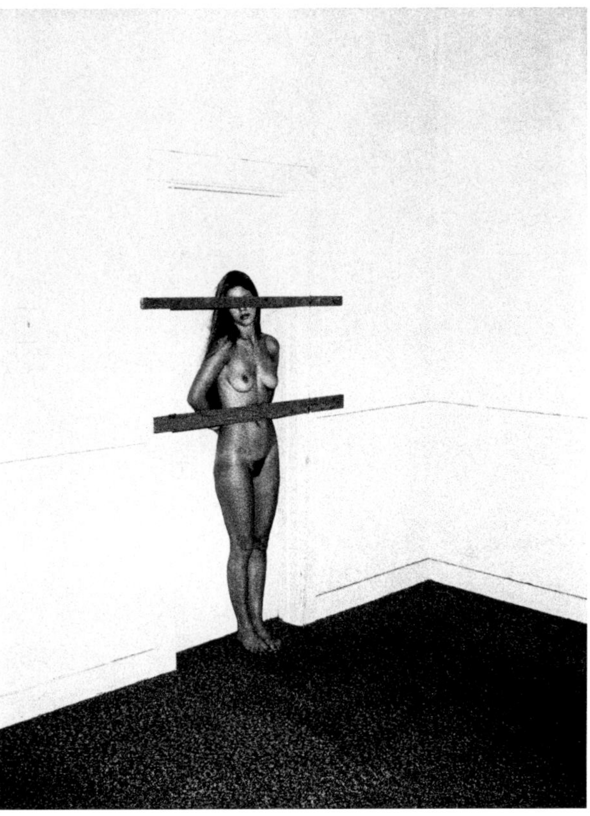

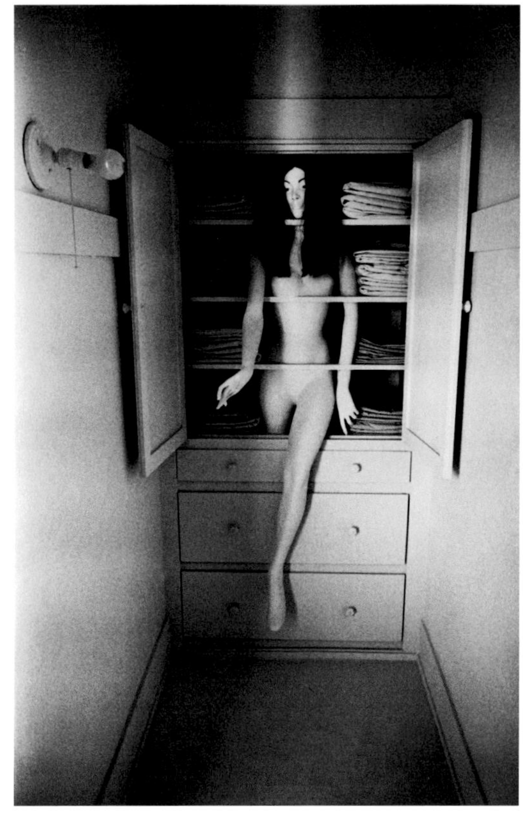

The disappearance of the "sweets" from the "suites" (a meaningful homophonic pun that Kahn mentions in his journal),[13] though provoked through unplanned circumstance, seems inevitable considering the artist's practice of positioning the models as though they were being absorbed into the corners, walls, and furniture of the apartments. Given the time period in which Kahn made these photographs, one cannot help but think about the metaphorical disappearance of women from domestic spaces, an absence that many feminist artists were then addressing. In fact, it was during this period, in 1972, that *Womanhouse*, one of the foundational artworks of the feminist art movement and part of the Feminist Art Program at California Institute of the Arts (CalArts), was staged in Hollywood, where Kahn took his photographs. Though no evidence exists that Kahn visited *Womanhouse*, his image of a nude woman standing inside a doorframe with wooden planks covering her waist and eyes (fig.

18) strikes a vivid comparison with Sandy Orgel's *Linen Closet* (fig. 19), from *Womanhouse*. Orgel's work presents the body of a female mannequin intersected and fragmented by a closet's shelves, so trapped and bound by domestic duties that she has become indistinguishable from her home. The women in Kahn's photographs are similarly isolated, transformed into objects and architectural elements or reduced to abstract forms.

Kahn did show projected slides of *The Hollywood Suites* to a group at CalArts, and he was aware of the feminist response that his work provoked. He recalled that:

> *Afterwards there was a strong feminist reaction to them—Cal Arts [sic] had a very strong feminist movement there. It was very interesting to me because almost none of them recognized that the issues I was dealing with in those images were the same issues that they were dealing with as feminists, which are issues of bondage.*[14]

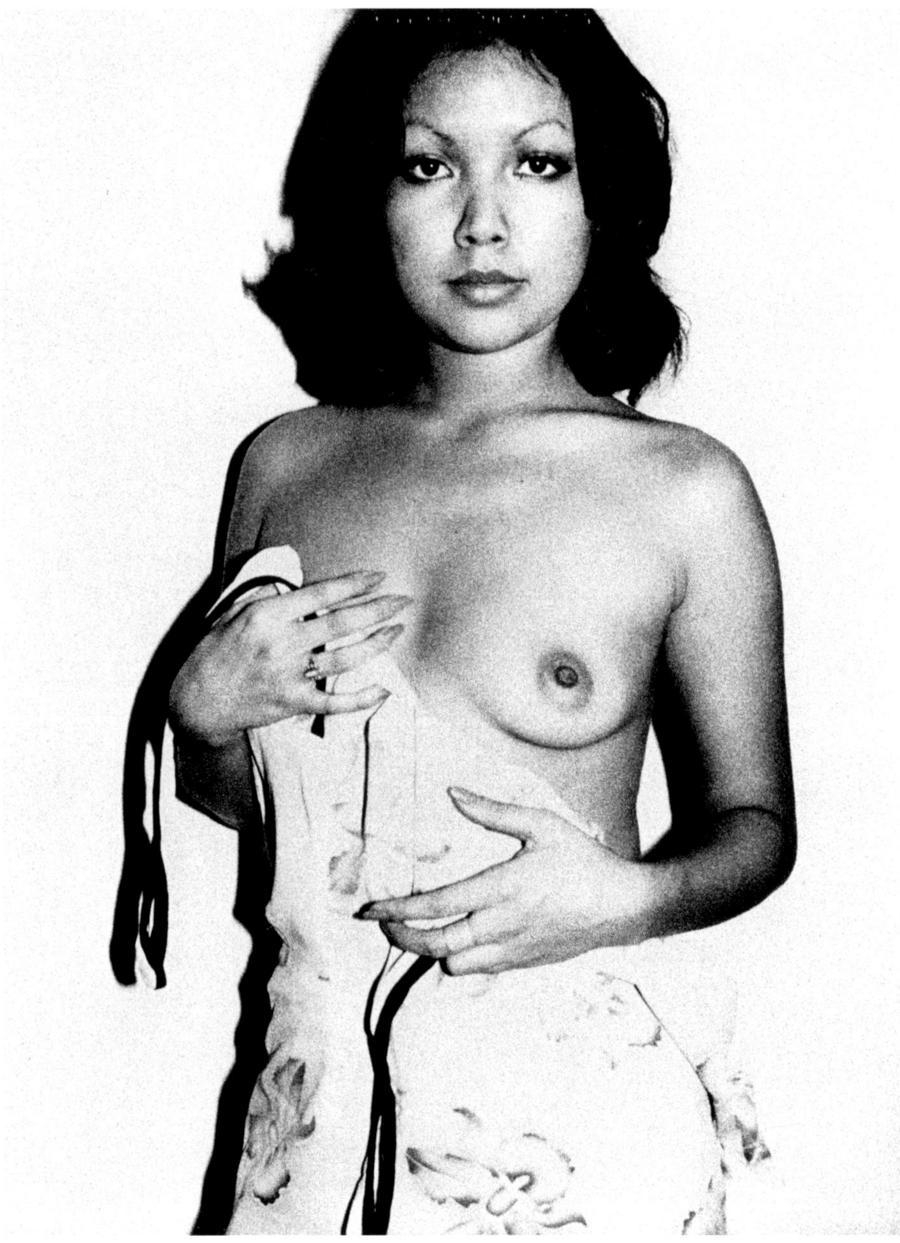

Kahn asserted that the series was "not exploitative, it was merely exploring the issue,"[15] but many of the students found the photographs to be denigrating to women and African Americans (as they related to issues stemming from bondage, entrapment, and slavery).[16]

Yet it is in his photographs' erasure of the female body that Kahn reached his goal of capturing an experience that was "visually powerful, yet went beyond what it was."[17] A testament to Kahn's skill, his photographs are most potent when formal tension replaces sexual transgression, creating a space for the viewer to contribute his or her mental associations. Interestingly, in his journal Kahn cited philosopher and early media theorist Marshall McLuhan's idea of "low resolution" media—the notion that images with less detail allow for more mental processing and even "fantasy projection"[18]—and he applied it to *The Hollywood Suites*. Looking at the series in its entirety, comparing the images with models to those without, one reads the eroticism of a dress falling from a woman's shoulders (fig. 20) in a "de-frocked window"[19] (pl. 32) and vice versa.

Kahn's photographs unsettle and disturb through their deep exploration of form and the aesthetics of transgression. He hoped that his photographs would "offer little escape or relief. They are contained/claustrophobic."[20] The force of these images—especially those without models—derives from the viewer's own feelings of immurement. They become a screen for the viewer's "anxiety projections"—provoked by Kahn but all the more powerful because of the space he left for the viewer's own terrible fantasies.

1   Steve Kahn, *Journal entry, Note inserted in journal, no date,* Journal 1, between pp. 4 and 5, Stephen H. Kahn Trust.

2   In an entry dated May 4, 1975, Kahn wrote: "woman's body as object—stone—tied, blindfolded[;] inert—not threatening—harmless" (Journal 1, p. 3).

3   Kahn, *Journal entry, May 4, 1975,* Journal 1, p. 3.

4   Kahn, *Journal entry, May 1, 1976,* Journal 1, p. 55.

5   For a more thorough account of Kahn's involvement in the project, see James A. Ganz, *"The Hollywood Suites:* Origins, Creations, Interventions, and Generations," and Matthew Simms, "Steve Kahn: Displacements," both in this catalogue.

6   Kahn, "Memoirs of a Bondage Photographer," *Photo-Bondage,* [1973?], p. 7, Stephen H. Kahn Trust.

7   Kahn, in discussion with unknown, [1977?], p. 33, Stephen H. Kahn Trust.

8   Serena Czarnecki, *Bright Lights, Lonely Nights—The Memories of Serena, Porn Star Pioneer of the 1970s* (Albany, GA: BearManor Bare, 2014).

9   Carolee Schneemann, *Imaging Her Erotics: Essays, Interviews, Projects* (Cambridge, MA: The MIT Press, 2001), 28.

10   Kahn, "Notes for The Hollywood Suites" (artist statement, 2012), Stephen H. Kahn Trust.

11   Gioni Massimiliano, "More Than Meat Joy: Carolee Schneemann," *Mousse Magazine* 48 (April–May 2015), http://moussemagazine.it/carolee-schneemann-massimilano-gioni-2015/.

12   Schneemann, *More Than Meat Joy* (New York: Documentext, 1979), 52.

13   Kahn, *Journal entry, August 3, 1976,* Journal 1, p. 69.

14   Kahn, in discussion with unknown, [1977?], p. 30.

15   Kahn, in discussion with unknown, [1977?], p. 31.

16   Kahn, p. 31.

17   Kahn, "Notes."

18   Kahn, *Journal entry, May 1, 1976,* Journal 1, p. 55.

19   Kahn, *Journal entry, November 26, 1976,* Journal 1, p. 90.

20   Kahn, *Note inserted in journal, no date,* Journal 1, after p. 185.

MATTHEW SIMMS

A YOUNG MODEL removes her clothes as she looks into the distance; a second, mostly undressed woman, also a professional model, sits impatiently, averting her gaze; and a single window, its floral-print curtains tied into knots, proffers a shiny metal towel bar: these are the subjects of the three earliest photographs that can be firmly associated with Steve Kahn's *Hollywood Suites* (fig. 21 and pls. 1 and 31).[1] The appearance of both nudes and an architectural detail in this selection is prophetic. As *The Hollywood Suites* unfolded, Kahn would eventually shift his attention completely away from the professional bondage models and toward the dingy rooms in which he photographed them. Art critic Melinda Wortz explained that the reorientation was "initiated by chance": "He had been renting these rooms of a former Hollywood hotel as [a] setting for a series of nudes. When a model failed to show up one day, it was a natural step for Kahn to transfer his attention from the female nudes to their environment."[2]

It is clear from the first photographs, however, that even before a model failed to arrive for a shoot, Kahn's attention was already moving easily between the women and their surroundings. The three photographs' common vertical orientation invites the discovery of associations and similarities. Fist-like knots, blouse-like and partially torn curtains: the window resonates with the women and vice versa. Kahn cultivated such analogies both between the models and architectural elements and between the interiors and his subjective experience. His associative imagination and photographic manipulations reflected his desire to reorder experience rather than simply document it, to bend appearances to match his subjective priorities. Kahn's taste for associations, as we will see, reached a crescendo in his photographs of vacant, or seemingly vacant, hotel rooms. "These were studies of the room," Kahn explained, "exploring the contained (content/me) through explorations of the container itself (the room). How one takes on the nature of the other."[3]

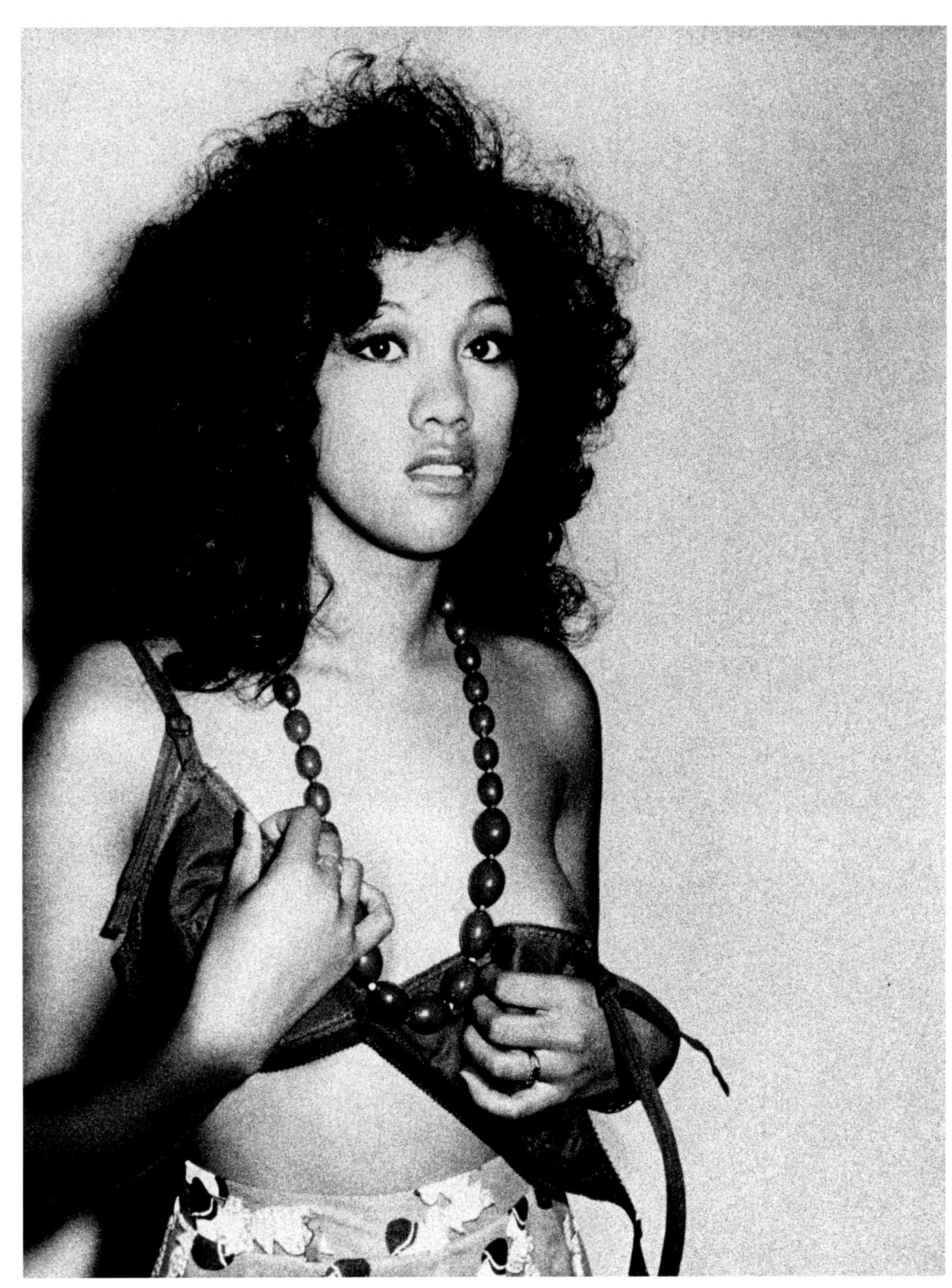

21
STEVE KAHN
Portrait 1, 1974–1975.
Gelatin silver print.
Fine Arts Museums of San
Francisco, Gift of Nancy Ganz
and Mitchell Steir

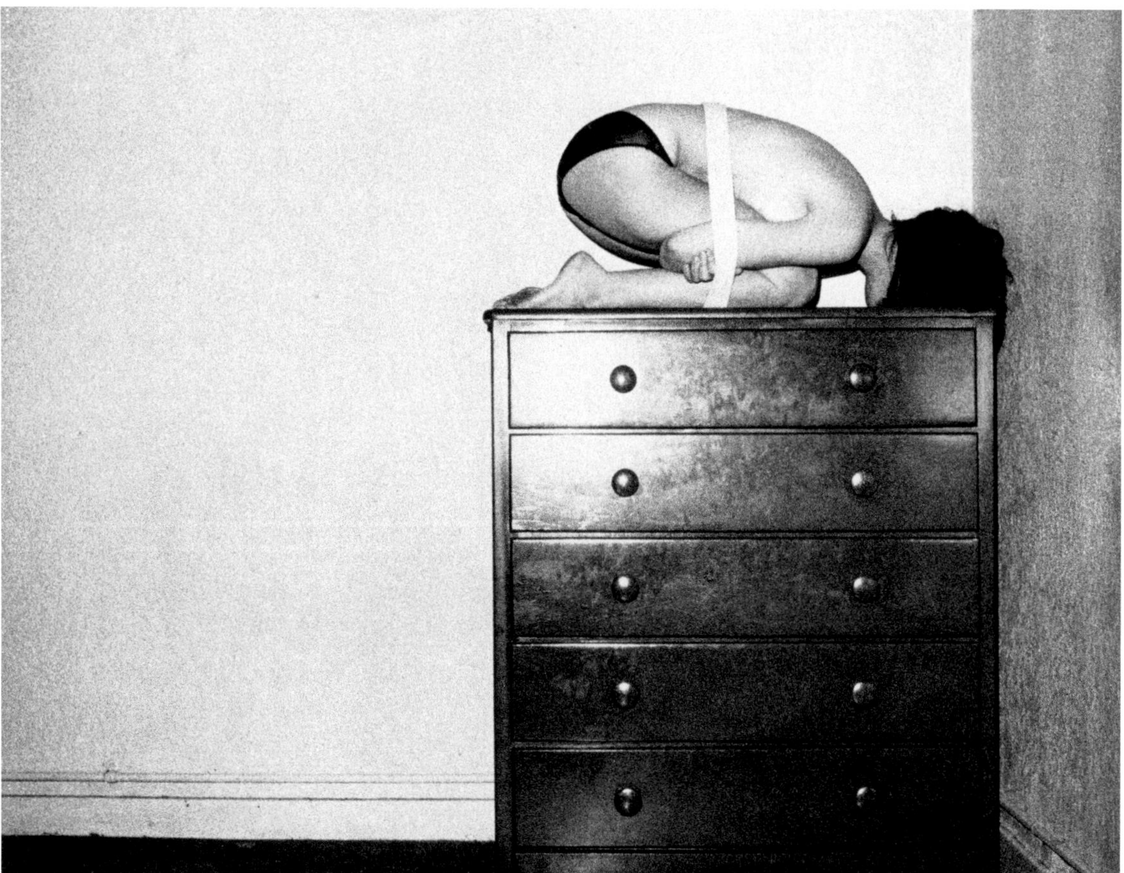

The Hollywood Suites began in what at first seems like inauspicious territory. Kahn recalled that his close friend and fellow artist Robert Overby maintained a studio in a seedy part of Los Angeles, next door to a printer who specialized in bondage pornography.[4] Kahn and Overby occasionally encountered discarded stacks of misprinted pages next to the garbage cans in the back alley. Both men were fascinated with the thrown-away images and the bondage scenarios they depicted. The staged fantasies were at once shocking and mesmerizing, pulp expressions of aggressive, repressed sexuality rendered in make-believe scenes of debasement. Kahn marveled at the rhetoric of the set-ups, which evoked both Surrealist transgression and peepshow scopophilia. Both he and Overby felt compelled to respond to the found images, first considering the idea of producing their own bondage magazine and eventually creating what, by Kahn's own admission, was an unsuccessful and somewhat misguided exploration of the genre.[5]

Kahn's most important and sweeping response to the found imagery, however, took place in his own photographs, in which he plumbed the erotic and subjective tensions between the models and himself as the photographer. "I would set up situations in funky, rent-by-the-day, one-room apartments in the old, run-down sections of Hollywood," Kahn explained. "[I] hired models [from an] industry agency and created images that somehow spoke to the broader issues of bondage, containment and isolation."[6] Yet, as we've seen, only two images of models, neither of whom are bound, appear in the first several photographs associated with *The Hollywood Suites*. Kahn admitted that he was not sure what to ask of the women: "These were 'no-exit' situations, entered into without plan, full of anxiety, in the hope of producing some document of the experience that was explicit, visually powerful, yet went beyond what it was."[7] As these first photographs and the numerous outtakes in Kahn's studio indicate, the photographer's intense editing process meant that a session might sometimes result in only one acceptable photograph.[8]

Kahn's photographs of the models fall into three general, equally weighted categories: portraits of women from the waist up, cropped images of women in striptease poses, and women engaged in bondage scenarios. The *Portraits* tend to engage the personalities of the different women, allowing their individual characters to emerge (pls. 1–5). Thanks to notes Kahn made in his personal journals and to more recent interviews, we know the names of four of the models: Serena Czarnecki, Mara Zhelutka, Candy Reynolds, and a woman referred to only as Joyce.[9] Though the photographs depict role-playing scenarios, in which professional models have voluntarily adopted a set of postures, a fantasy of coercion is clearly in play, particularly in the striptease and bondage photographs. In the former, Kahn crops the women's bodies into parts—legs, breasts, buttocks—shifting toward a fetishistic orientation that objectifies, abstracts, and eroticizes isolated figural elements (see apps. 28, 35, and 45). The process of abstraction deepens with the bondage scenarios, in which fetishism verges into dehumanization. One session resulted in at least three photographs in which Joyce is in situations of extreme subjugation (fig. 22, pl. 10, and app. 10). In the most striking of these images, she appears kneeling on a dresser, bound with rope coiled around her arms, torso, and legs (fig. 22). Such bindings become increasingly hyperbolic and decorative as Kahn's photographs progress. Ropes very quickly disappear and are replaced with more fanciful fetters, such as aluminum foil, stretched plastic cellophane, bubble wrap, and semi-transparent gauzy fabric (apps. 4 and 12 and pls. 8 and 9). However, Kahn's playful introduction of these tongue-in-cheek bondage materials does little to soften the psychological tension the viewer inevitably experiences when looking at some of the images.

Kahn was partly influenced in this project by the work of Ralph Gibson, whom he had met through Overby in the late 1960s; he was well acquainted with Gibson's photobook *The Somnambulist* (1970), which is punctuated with artfully cropped and strikingly foreshortened images of women's unclothed bodies.[10] But Kahn's stark and intense photographs of women's bodies are ultimately a far cry from Gibson's dreamy and aestheticized nudes. In some of Kahn's photographs (pls. 2, 3, and 5 and apps. 43 and 56), the models look back assertively and self-confidently at the camera, recalling the riveting gaze of Victorine Meurent in Édouard Manet's *Olympia* (1863). Kahn replaced the conventional nude model with sex workers—porn-industry models whom he hired and directed to act out bondage and striptease scenarios.

To make these images, Kahn used a Polaroid model 195 camera with an on-camera flash and pull-and-peel film. This equipment allowed him to see the photographs almost immediately after taking them and, after making adjustments, reshoot the picture if need be. Kahn did not treat the Polaroids as art objects. Instead, he placed the Polaroids on a copy stand and rephotographed them with his Leica. He considered the gelatin silver prints that emerged from this second step to be the finished works of art. In an entry in his journal, dated May 31, 1976, Kahn noted that this process was oriented toward a "natural distancing through generation (reproduction)":

The essential information survives (in many cases is revealed by way of passing through a sort of rigorous washing machine). The overtones which add dimension of a human sort . . . don't make it through the process—Devoid of the overtones which usually help to "fill out" the image, the image stands naked, without the "support" of what may be called sentiment, and either succeeds and remains as a strong object-presence or fails for lack of completeness. . . . It's also of interest to note that the Polaroid becomes a rather anonymous object, from which the image gets lifted—not unlike a "found object" photograph.[11]

Kahn's aim was to create a buffer that would hold the images' content at a remove, neutralizing it while also imparting a sense of uniformity and group identity to the photographs. Kahn wanted to filter out "overtones which add dimension of a human sort" by passing the image through stages of

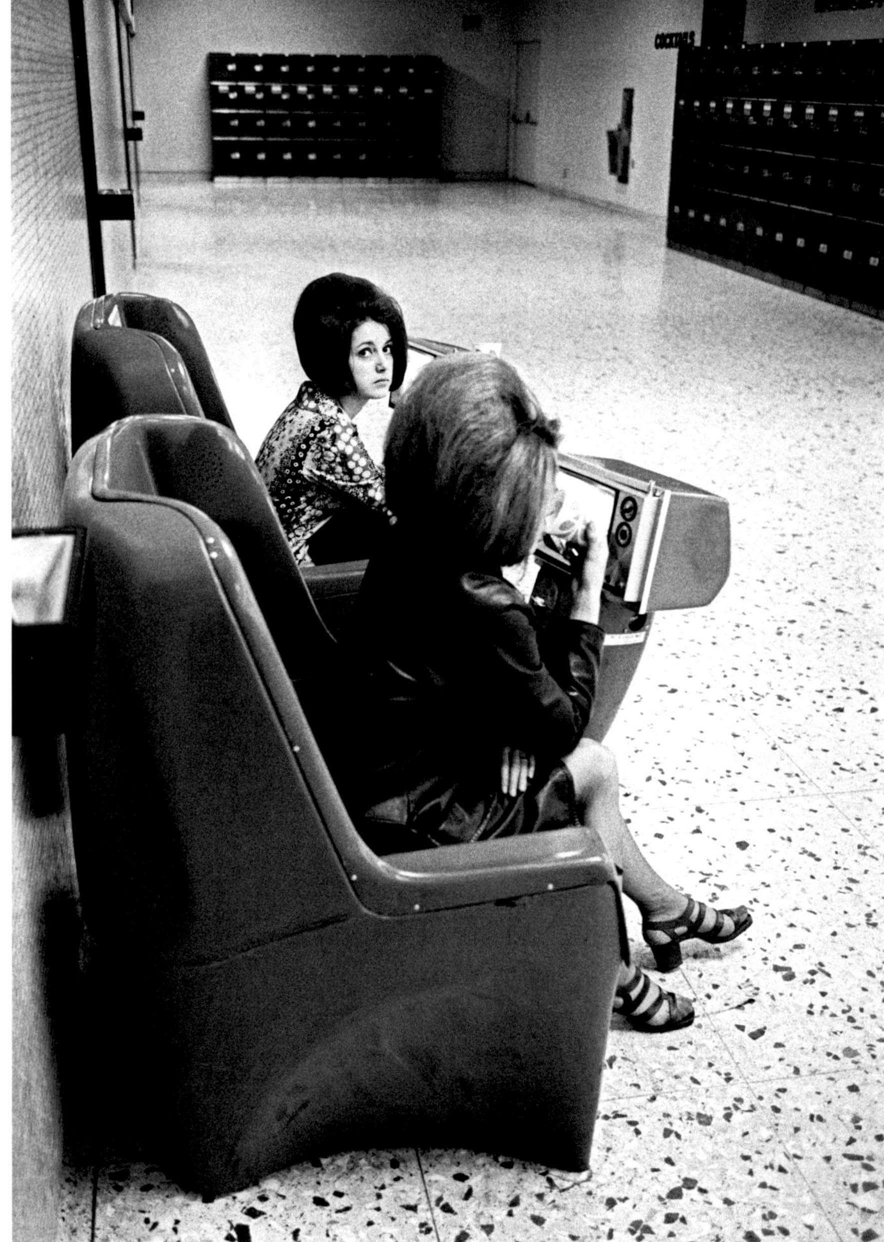

reproduction. One byproduct of this process was the images'
enlargement, from the Polaroids, which measure just 3¼ by 4¼
inches, to the gelatin silver prints, which measure 8 by 10 inches,
in the case of the nudes, and 11 by 14 inches, in the case of the
architectural interiors and details. Enlarging the images reduced
the photographs' visible details, which were already partially washed
out by Kahn's use of the on-camera flash at close quarters. As he
reported, he used a developer called Rodinal that allowed him to
achieve flatly delineated shapes and an abbreviation of tonal range,
all of which increased the striking visual impact of the final prints.
This flattening effect, by which three-dimensional form becomes
two-dimensional shape, seems to be in part what Kahn was
referring to when he wrote of washing away the *Nudes*' "human
dimension." Rodinal also enabled Kahn to achieve a grainy

appearance in the prints, a quality that he referred to as "the
underlying visual surface holding everything together and out of
which details coalesced."[12] Ironically, the hum and shimmer of this
"underlying visual surface" eroded, rather than reinforced, the
sharp edges and oppositions between figure and ground. In Kahn's
grainy photographs, details coalesce and then disintegrate into the
allover visual noise. "Like newspaper photos," reads a note in Kahn's
journal, calling to mind the dot-matrix effect of coarsely printed
images on brittle paper.[13] He also referred to the photographs'
graininess as "dirty," punning "dirty pictures."[14]

All of this distancing is a striking departure from
the objectivity and immediacy of Kahn's early reportage work,
which he practiced just a few years before embarking on *The
Hollywood Suites*. In Kahn's Robert Frank–inspired snapshots, he

40

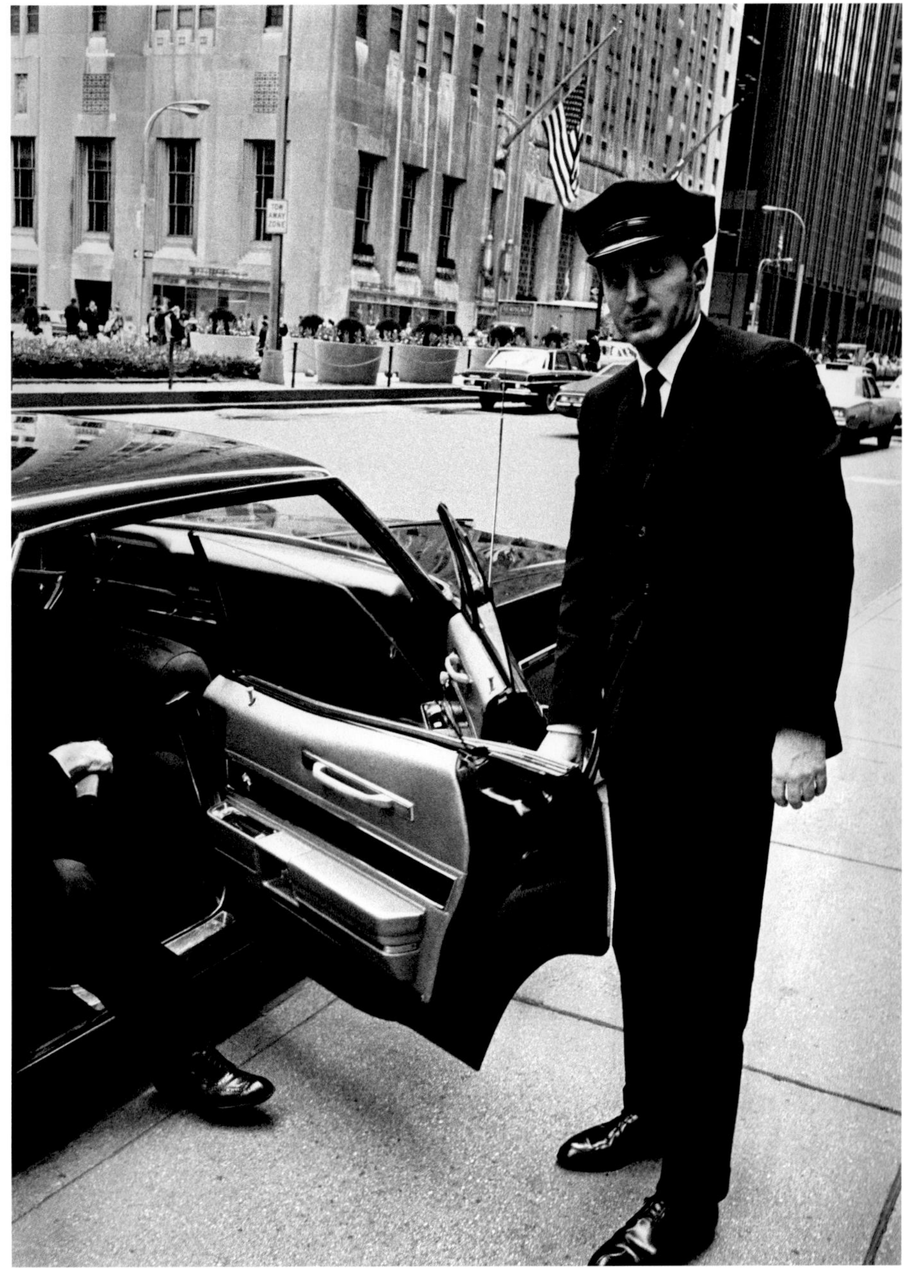

captured average people in candid moments that seemed to sum up a walk of life, a profession, or a broader cultural undercurrent: women watching televisions in Los Angeles's Union Station as they awaited a departure or an arrival, or a chauffeur holding open the door of a sedan for a VIP in front of New York's Rockefeller Center (figs. 23 and 24). Kahn's break with the eyewitness model of photography was influenced in part by his exposure to the work and ideas of Larry Bell, Peter Alexander, Craig Kauffman, and Robert Irwin, whom he was hired to photograph in their studios for the catalogue of a group show.[15] Approaching the project from a documentary perspective, Kahn originally intended to capture telling images of the artists at work. Instead, the artists turned their attention to Kahn and his work, critiquing his rather conventional understanding of photography's possibilities and

introducing him to sweeping questions about the aesthetics of light, space, reflection, and transparency (the theme of their group show). Kahn's resulting photographs swapped objective reporting for experimentation. In a photograph of Irwin in his pristine studio, Kahn captures the artist as he partially disappears behind one of his acrylic columns, responding with the camera to Irwin's concern with contextual conditions of light and space (fig. 25). This experimental thrust is even clearer in a photograph of Kauffman's reflection in which his silhouette appears to reach out and touch the point of a painted traffic arrow, patterns of concentric rings on the underlying wet pavement marking the impact of raindrops (fig. 26). The first substantial evidence that Kahn had fully internalized and adopted the speculative thrust of his encounter with these more established artists was *Stasis*, a photobook he published in

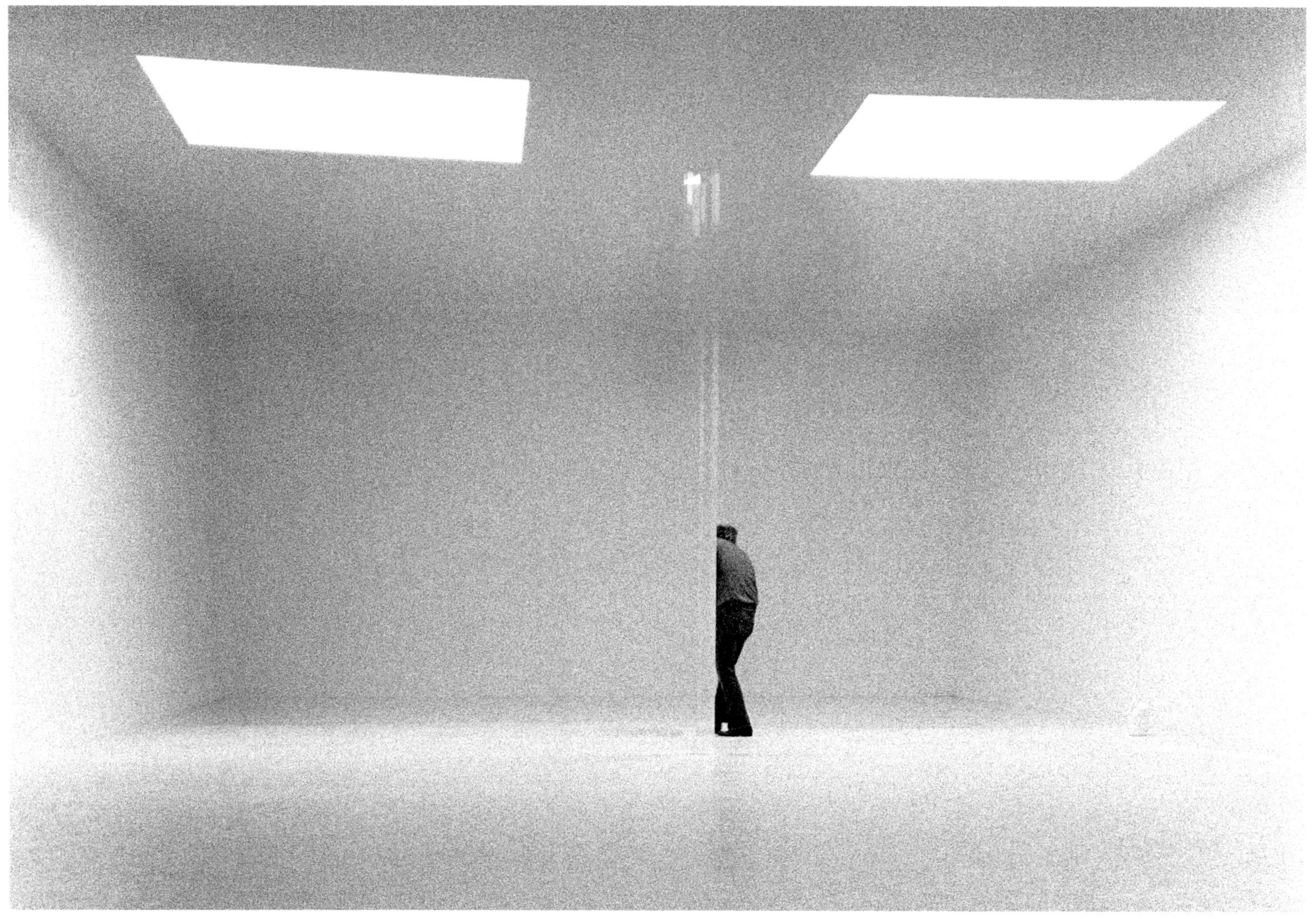

25
STEVE KAHN
Robert Irwin in His Studio, 1970.
Stephen H. Kahn Trust

26
STEVE KAHN
Craig Kauffman, ca. 1970.
Stephen H. Kahn Trust

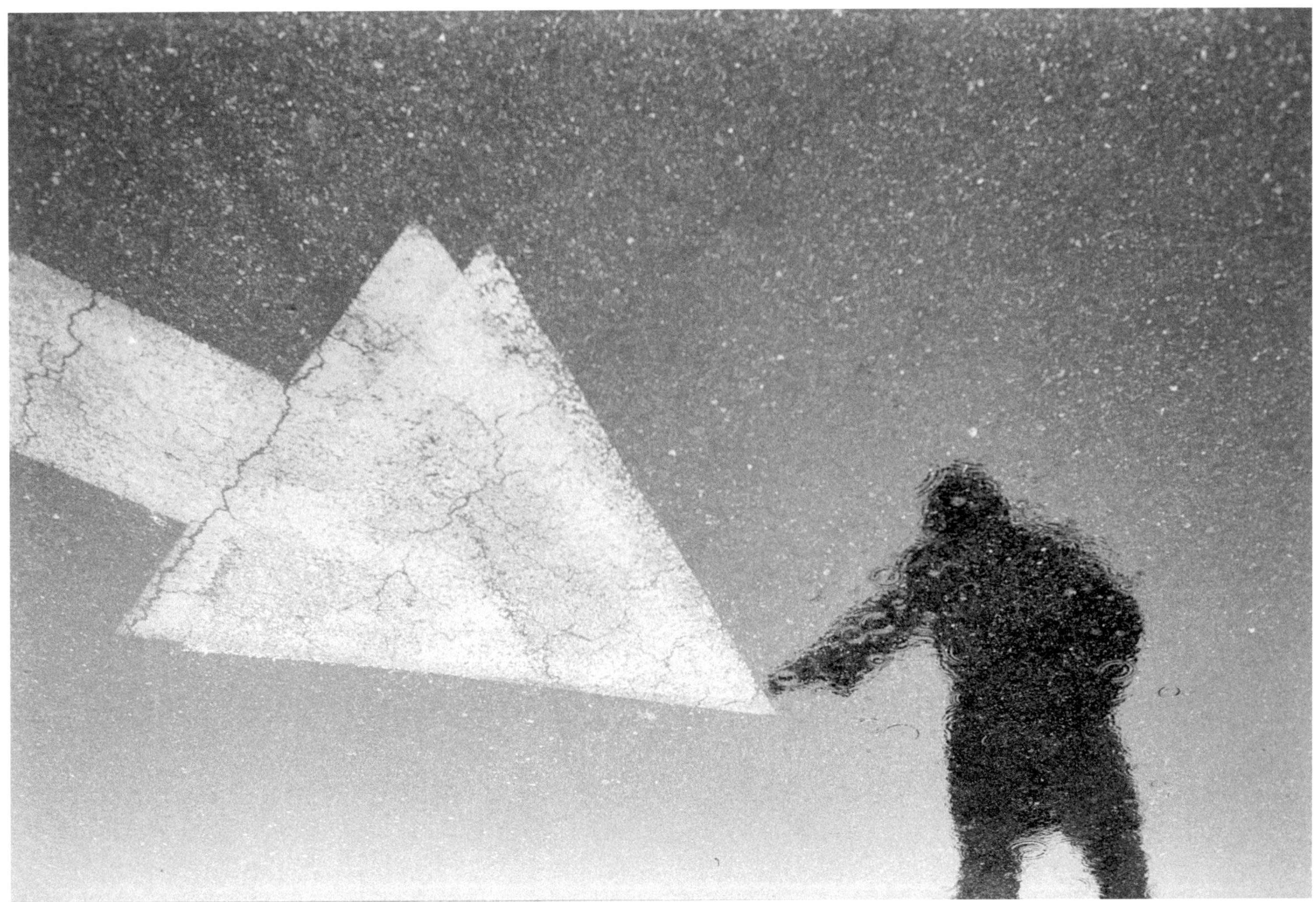

1973 consisting of twenty-two black-and-white images shot in the vicinity of his Malibu home.[16] The book's images unfold in a sequence of seven groups, separated by single or double blank pages. Some of the blurry photographs depict nudes; others include mirrors that reflect land or sky; still more capture the photographer's own body (see figs. 27a and 27b).[17] It is ironic, given the book's title, that the images represent anything but fixity, evincing duration and movement instead. In some cases, Kahn threw the camera into the air as the shutter snapped, creating photographs that could no longer be considered analogues for the artist's visual experience, be it reportage or anything else. The slow shutter speeds created visible displacements as the subjects before the camera or the camera itself moved. In his journal, Kahn privately referred to *Stasis* as an abstract expressionist experiment.[18] But we can also safely assert

that it represents the key step in his transition from being a reportage photographer to being an artist who used a camera to investigate larger conceptual and aesthetic issues.[19]

If *The Hollywood Suites* inverts some of the terms Kahn established in *Stasis*, exchanging the open horizons of the Pacific Ocean for the claustrophobic interiors of rent-by-day apartments, it nevertheless continues and expands upon *Stasis*'s serial orientation. Rather than treating a photograph as a testimony of observed reality, the serial photo project locates photographic meaning in the subjective sparks and associations that emerge between photographs. This is evident in Kahn's sequence of model portraits, which feel distinctly comparative in nature when viewed as a group. Even the bondage images appear as permutations and variations on a theme, assuming greater significance when one is compared to the next. Kahn likened the serial orientation of *The*

43

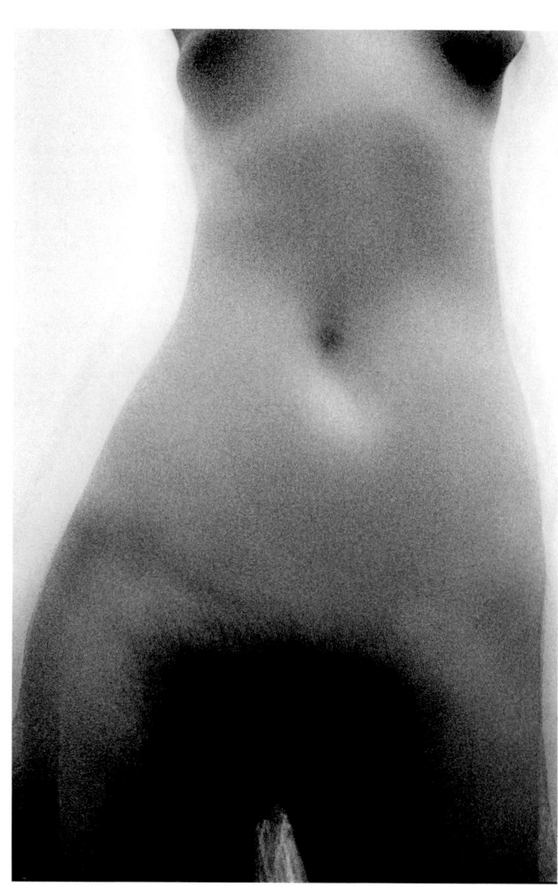

27a
STEVE KAHN
Stasis #4, 1973 (printed ca. 1973). Gelatin silver
print. 11¹/₈ x 16 in. Stephen H. Kahn Trust

27b
STEVE KAHN
Stasis #20, 1973 (printed ca. 1973). Gelatin silver
print. 16 x 11¹/₈ in. Stephen H. Kahn Trust

28
JUDY FISKIN
Peaked Roof #2, from the series *Dingbat*, 1982.
Gelatin silver print. 7¾ x 5½ in. (19.7 x 14 cm).
San Francisco Museum of Modern Art, Gift of
Jonathan M. Wiener

29
LEWIS BALTZ
*Northwest Wall, Unoccupied Industrial
Spaces, 17875 C and D Skypark Circle, Irvine*,
from the portfolio *The New Industrial Parks
near Irvine, California*, 1974. Gelatin silver
print. 6¹/₁₆ x 9 in. (15.4 x 22.9 cm). San Francisco
Museum of Modern Art, Gift of Carol Campbell
Wenaas

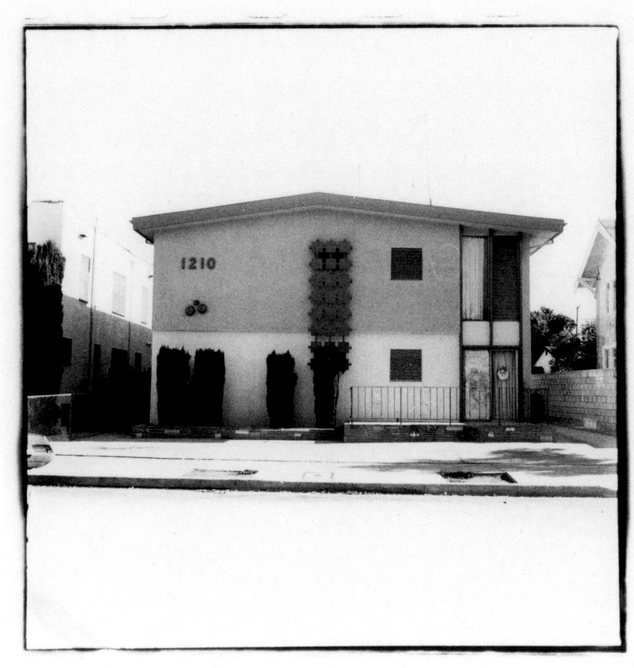

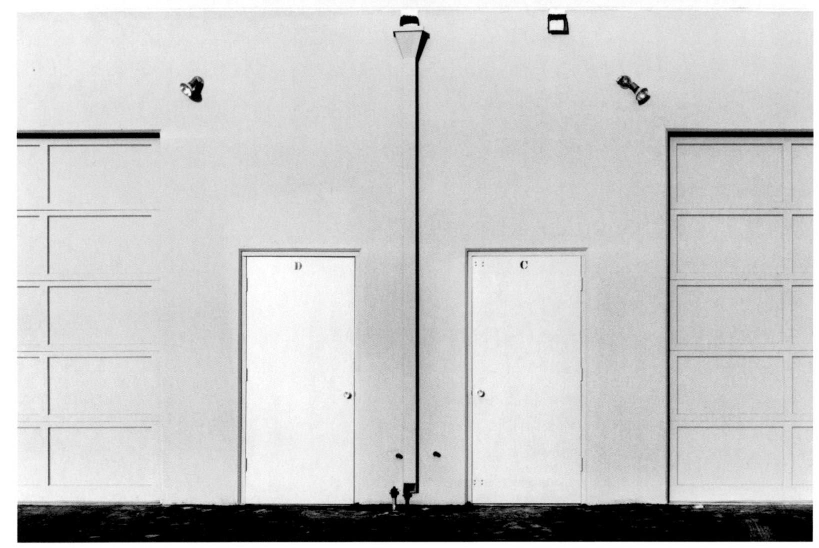

Hollywood Suites to a pattern of call-and-response, in which an initial action gives rise to a potentially endless range of interconnected effects: "A particular situation or a set of conditions will serve to generate a whole system of which the developing work becomes elements with relationships, cross references, etc."[20]

Kahn was not alone in his turn away from the single, stand-alone photographic masterpiece and toward a photographic system. Many of his Southern California peers, including Lewis Baltz and Judy Fiskin, also embraced seriality as a principle of photographic exploration.[21] Their respective bodies of work, which focus on vernacular Southern California architecture (figs. 28 and 29), have parallels with Kahn's images of tenement apartment interiors. But the deadpan mood of their work is far removed from the latent eroticism of *The Hollywood Suites*. In fact, we should not confuse Kahn's attempts to distance himself from his photographs' subject matter with an intent to eliminate affect. Distancing, for Kahn, referred to a suppression of sentiment, not of erotic charge. Affect is displaced from individual photographs to the relationships between them, just as it enters into the grain of the photographs themselves. Rather than the instantaneous glance, so central to the rhetorical force of reportage, *The Hollywood Suites* gains its significance from the displacement of subjective

affect across the system, freeing up feeling so that it might move unencumbered and, perhaps, unexpectedly in the gaps and interstices between images. "More erotic tension," he admonished himself in an early journal entry.[22] Erotic tension and emotional transitivity only increased as Kahn turned his camera away from the models and toward the worn architectural interiors. "It's like marbles, pushing them up against the wall," Kahn told a critic: "One day you look up and notice the context and the context becomes more interesting than the game."[23]

CONSIDER a pair of photographs Kahn made of two different windows (pl. 30 and fig. 30). Both are vertical, two-pane sliding sash, or double-hung, windows, with drawn half-length curtains, nearly identical trim, and similarly scalloped sills. Photographing them frontally and framed by surrounding areas of uninflected wall, Kahn treats the windows in roughly the same way. One has opaque, flower-print drapery; the other is dressed in a frilly, semi-transparent curtain with matching valance. One appears to be wide open, exposing unrelieved darkness outside, while the other is closed off by a drawn blind through which bright sunlight still manages to stream.[24] Other windows provide unobstructed views to the outside world, disclosing identifiable landmarks such as the Encore Theatre (pl. 19). Tile, towel racks, and shower curtain rods at times indicate that the window we are seeing is located in a bathroom or kitchen (see pls. 17 and 31 and apps. 69 and 76). Taken as a group, the *Windows* call forth differentiation and comparison. Each window's unique personality emerges in relationship to other, different windows, not unlike the way the personalities of the female models do.

The portraits of windows and models are also visually analogous to each other, due to shared aspects of format, like their isolation against walls and the photographs' frontal perspective. Like the models, the windows are sometimes slightly off-center in the picture frame, owing to Kahn's use of a handheld camera rather than a tripod. Other analogies also impress themselves upon us, such as the way some windows' half-length floral curtains start to resemble blouses or halter tops. Curtainless windows, conversely, appear strikingly naked, while windows with drapes torn, hanging off, or roughly pulled apart invite comparisons to Kahn's photographs of women in striptease scenarios. Kahn claimed not to have interfered with the way in which the curtains were drawn or the blinds were pulled, although the outtake variants indicate otherwise. The interiors were photographed, he attested, "as I found them."[25] Nevertheless, the *Windows* suggest that even after Kahn had stopped hiring models, he continued to think about the women.

Kahn was not trying to anthropomorphize windows, however. The associations between the *Windows* and the *Nudes* are more ambiguous than that. Indeed, Kahn noted in his journal that, with the *Nudes*, he had sought to create what he termed a mysterious blurring of distinctions between the women and the objects in their midst:

> In the bound figures, I'm treating the figure as an <u>object</u>,
> like Joyce on the dresser. She is without life, in a sense,
> just as the dresser which she is a part of (rather than

apart from). I wanted the wall elements (parts?) to be as functional as the human form—or the human presence to be as nonfunctional as the wall elements. A good example is Candy on her head. The two elements don't really relate according to any rational logic that I'm aware of, yet the two together make a definite gestalt—a mystery, an enigma, and definitely a presence.[26]

The image of Joyce posing on a dresser is among the photographs of bondage scenarios mentioned earlier. "Candy on her head," however, refers to one of three images in which Candy Reynolds assumes assorted postures of inversion or confinement (pls. 7 and 8 and app. 15). Kahn refers specifically to the image of Candy doing a headstand next to what appears to be a nightstand (pl. 7). The "two elements" he mentions, then, must be the animate women and the inanimate object, between which the eye moves instinctively, drawing comparisons and associations. In another journal passage, Kahn was even clearer about the form of associative abstraction he was pursuing. "What I attempt to do," he explained, "is single out (distill) the element(s) of the experience that is transcendent or relevant in a more general context of all experiences—that way a landscape can be perceived in such a way as to relate in [sic] common elements with a window curtain, bondage photo, or portrait."[27] Kahn's project was not a search for essential truth, we see here, but rather an effort to blur boundaries by emphasizing the ways associations form in the mobility of what he called "experience," a transience we might also locate within the pulsions of desire.

At one point in his journal, Kahn confesses to "reading heavily on [Marcel] Duchamp,"[28] adding, as if encouraged by Duchamp's example: "The windows I've been calling 'de-frocked windows' and [the doors] 'bound doors.' *Bride Stripped Bare by Her Bachelors, Even.*"[29] Kahn's readings may have included Duchamp's interviews, which first appeared in English translation in

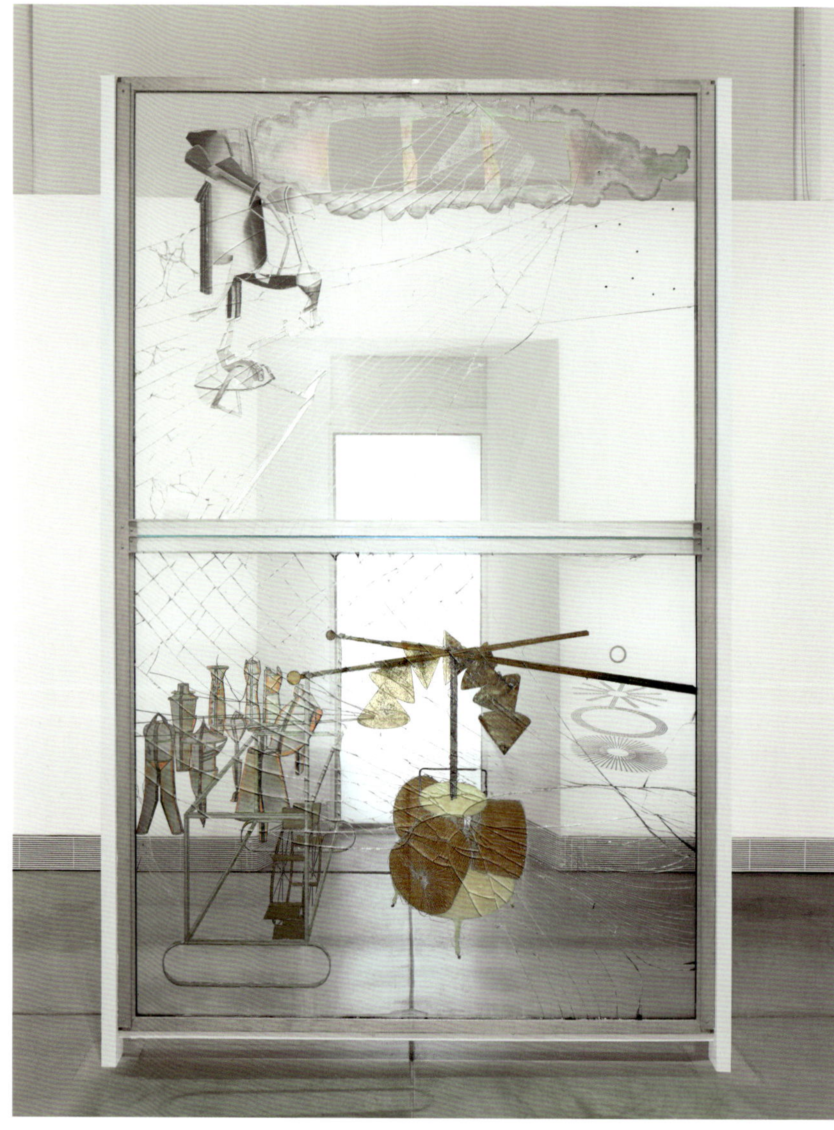

1971. In response to a question about the role of eroticism in *The Bride Stripped Bare by Her Bachelors, Even* (1915–1923; fig. 31), Duchamp responded: "It was a closed-in eroticism, if you like, an eroticism that wasn't overt. It wasn't implied, either. It's a sort of erotic climate."[30] Kahn's phrase "defrocked windows" also implies a covert and closed-in eroticism, suggesting a tacit reversibility between the nude women and the exposed windows. Likewise, "bound doors" calls forth analogies with the photographs of the bound women. In *Bound Door* 1 (pl. 39), a closed white door, rendered frontally and wrapped in white rope, recalls Joyce's pose on the dresser (fig. 22), as the rope loops and accumulates around the door just as it did around her kneeling body. Another photograph shows a pair of closed double doors, rendered frontally, with white rope tied in zigzag patterns across them (pl. 43). As in the *Nudes,* in the *Bound Doors* one discovers a range of restraints, from black yarn and white rope to translucent and opaque reflective tape (pl. 40 and app. 84). In two instances, the single and double doors are agape, revealing yawning darkness

beyond. In one, Kahn has pulled dark yarn tight across the opening in a double zigzag pattern (pl. 41); in another, light-colored string has been drawn into a star-like configuration (pl. 42). In a striking, blush-worthy passage in Kahn's journal, he referred to such bound openings as being like "laced up" vaginas.[31] Kahn seems to have been exploring how condensation and displacement can animate the world with fears and fantasies of a highly personal nature. "I am just realizing the very strong sexual symbolism—imagery in my work," Kahn confided, adding in a Duchampian vein: "The windows and doors that work the best are the most sexual."[32]

"MYSTERY," "ENIGMA": seriality provided Kahn with a form of abstraction that lifted everyday life onto a secondary plane, creating something like what Duchamp called an "erotic climate," in which nude women and windows, doors, and other inanimate objects exchange places. Patterns of analogy emerge between photographs, as does a sense of entropy that renders distinctions ambiguous. Such ambiguity was also a hallmark of Kahn's *Triptychs* and *Quadrants*, multi-image combinations that he began to make toward the end of 1975 (pls. 53–57 and figs. 32, 33, and 40). These works abandoned the strictly frontal formats of the "defrocked windows" and the "bound doors" in favor of oblique views that suggest spatial depth. Still working with his Polaroid camera, Kahn made multiple images at this time, either shifting the position of his camera to create images that would exclude distortions of perspective or cultivating such distortions by pivoting his camera from a single vantage point. Kahn's process of abstraction and distancing did not change with these larger works: he continued to copy and enlarge his original Polaroids, allowing the grain to become a fluid and energetic skin across the images. Nevertheless, in these multi-image pieces, Kahn seems to have wanted to push the original experience of the Polaroids even further away, employing manifestly artificial combinations to do so. *Triptych* 12 (fig. 32), for example, includes three photographs: a central image of a corner where adjacent walls meet a ceiling and two flanking images of the meeting of wall and ceiling away from the corner. Seen together, the images present a strong graphic design, but it is one that defies credibility. Kahn, in fact, used one photograph twice, reversing it for the triptych's two outer images. Something similar takes place in *Quadrant* 2, in which Kahn flipped and flopped two downward views of grimy walls concluding in dark carpet to create a clear spiral shape, a distinct form bought at the expense of a believable architectural environment (fig. 33). A note in Kahn's journal clarifies his aims: "I'm thinking about trying to group images that involve discontinuities—pools of indeterminate information—or barriers—or perplexing connections where connections may be made through reversal or mirror juxtapositions." [33] "The parts coming together," he added, "are <u>non-relational</u>, but they do succeed in forming a gestalt with an extraordinary <u>presence</u>." [34]

These "distorted triptychs" and "visual puzzles," as Kahn referred to them, shuffle and reorder architectural interiors to become sequential, serial objects in their own right. [35] They suggest parallels with both the additive empiricism of Minimalism and the logical games of Conceptualism. [36] "Triptychs deal with connections," Kahn noted in his journal, "connecting ideas—relationships." [37] Most importantly, they absorb and condense the larger, syntactical logic of *The Hollywood Suites* into single, multi-image configurations. This was already a factor in some of Kahn's interior photographs, as in his images of walls with doors and framed pictures and of walls with two windows. The comparative relationship between elements in a single image also informed some of his early bondage photographs. Kahn also experimented with a series of *Storm/Wall* combinations, which he aspired to publish as a book; in them, split attention becomes an invitation for imaginative expansion (see pl. 58). [38] Likewise, in the *Triptychs* and *Quadrants*, interstices of white space separating individual photographs coax vision into a pattern of continual displacement, as the eye skips from one photograph to the next. A tension emerges between this sequential seeing and the instantaneity of the gestalt. One either grasps Kahn's *Triptychs* and *Quadrants* as decisive shapes on the wall all at once, or one slips into a continuing, unfolding experience of looking from photograph to photograph. This tension became especially palpable when Kahn increased the size of his photo-ensembles to what he termed a mural format—three or four photographic prints, measuring 36 by 48 inches each, mounted on aluminum panels, margins of white wall visible between each. By increasing these images to near life-size, Kahn strove to create competition between the impossible spaces represented in the *Triptychs* and *Quadrants* and the actual spaces of the gallery. As one critic noted, "[W]e are uncertain about the actual structure of Kahn's segmented rooms, for he simultaneously makes references to

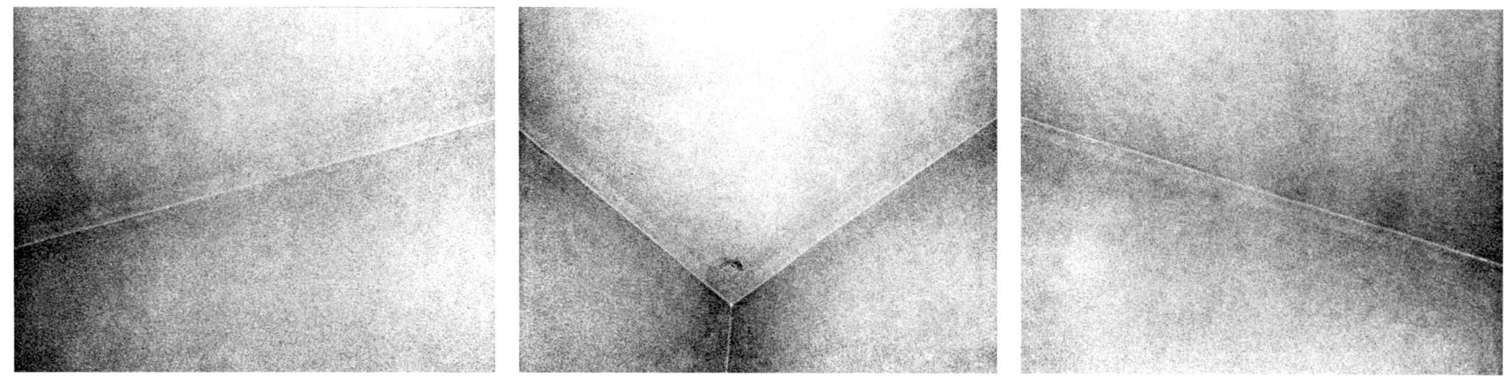

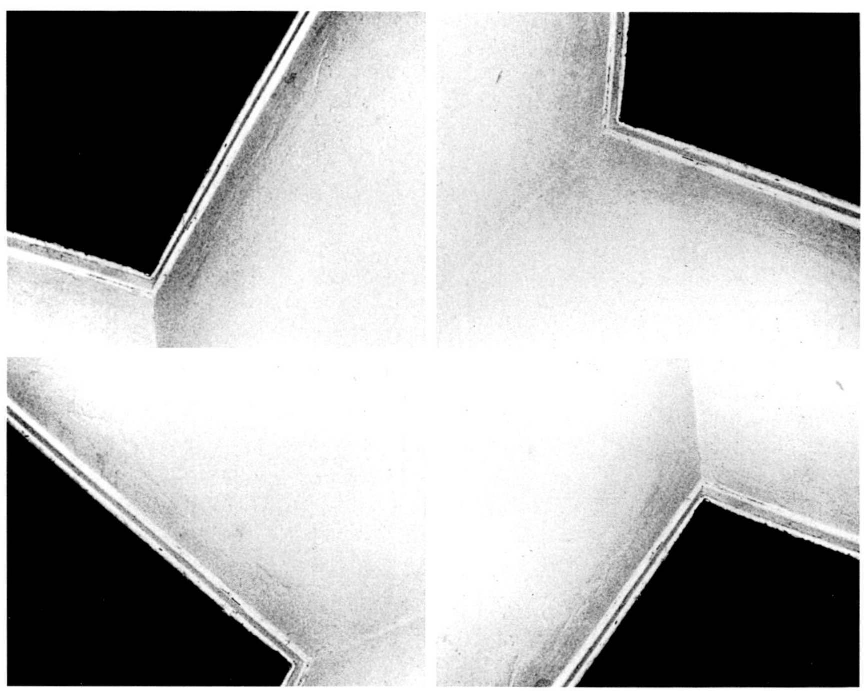

traditional perspective and contradicts these suggestions."[39] Returning to Kahn's journal, we read his thoughts on this effect: "Competing for the same space that the viewer occupies, so that they become (perhaps) real, visual (physical) alternatives to the space of the 'real' room."[40]

Kahn's Duchampian concern with erotic punning carried through to the *Triptychs* and *Quadrants*. Cropped, grainy images of meeting points between bare walls or between bare walls and bare ceilings begin to resemble the creases and folds of unclothed bodies. *Quadrant* 1 (pl. 57), for example, channels the perverse energy of Duchamp's infamous *Fountain*, a mass-produced urinal, which, when set on its back, ambiguously resembles a female nude, while the pattern of drain openings suggests a triangle of pubic hair. *Quadrant* 1 also resonates, albeit distantly, with Gustave Courbet's scandalous *Origin of the World* (1866), painted roughly a century earlier, with its up-close, cropped image of female genitalia.[41] In Kahn's *Triptychs* and *Quadrants*, women and rooms once again exchange qualities. Walls become like skin and carpets like hair. Art critic William Wilson picked up on this fact in a review of Kahn's first exhibition of multi-panel images, observing that they "achieve the oddly sensuous fantasy of classic Weston nude close-ups with their etched folds."[42] However, Kahn's objective was not to convey a Weston-style anthropomorphism but rather to construct a larger metaphor concerning the way the mind works and, specifically, the way the mind "puts together its fragmented perceptions into whole constructs."[43] But in the *Triptychs* and *Quadrants* this process of connecting perceptions is thwarted by the discontinuity between individual images, which renders the "gestalt" unstable and the "whole constructs" friable and temporary. Unconscious slippage persists as rooms start to look a little bit like female bodies and female bodies begin to resemble surrounding windows, furniture, and other inanimate things. In fact, Kahn settled on *Hollywood Suites* as an apt title precisely because of the homonym when spoken out loud, between the rooms and the women he photographed in them (Suites/Sweets).[44] In other words, he framed the entire project in terms of an elementary flipping back and forth between associations.

In what Kahn termed the "last phase" of *The Hollywood Suites*, he used color film to capture nearly identical views down hallways in the four-story apartment buildings in which he was working (see fig. 34).[45] Starting at the top floor, he moved quickly down the stairs, pausing to take photographs from the same vantage point on each subsequent floor. The vacant hallways are illuminated by Kahn's on-camera flash, but the light reaches only so far. In some, a reflective sheen on the painted doors at the end of the hallways breaks up the darkness, bouncing a bit of the flash's light back at the camera. Sheen and reflected light appear everywhere in *The Hollywood Suites*, as in a photograph of a pair of gleaming high-heeled shoes placed casually on a Naugahyde couch (fig. 35), or in a cropped view of a nude woman reclining in a chair, lustrous patterns of reflected light traversing the metal buttons, the taut leatherette surface, and her own skin (app. 58). Flash-induced radiance rebounded from nearly every surface of the rented apartments, from the shiny vinyl curtains and bathroom tiles to the glossy wallpaper masking broken or missing mirrors. Reflected light is a byproduct of the photographic encounter, a fugitive phenomenon that responds to and tracks the shifting angles of the photographer's on-camera flash. Like grain, sheen dissolves and unifies the subjects Kahn photographed in a single, mobile field of shifting desire, elevating them to an alternate plane of consciousness in which anecdote fades and substitution and displacement become the rule. The gleaming doors at the end of the long recessive

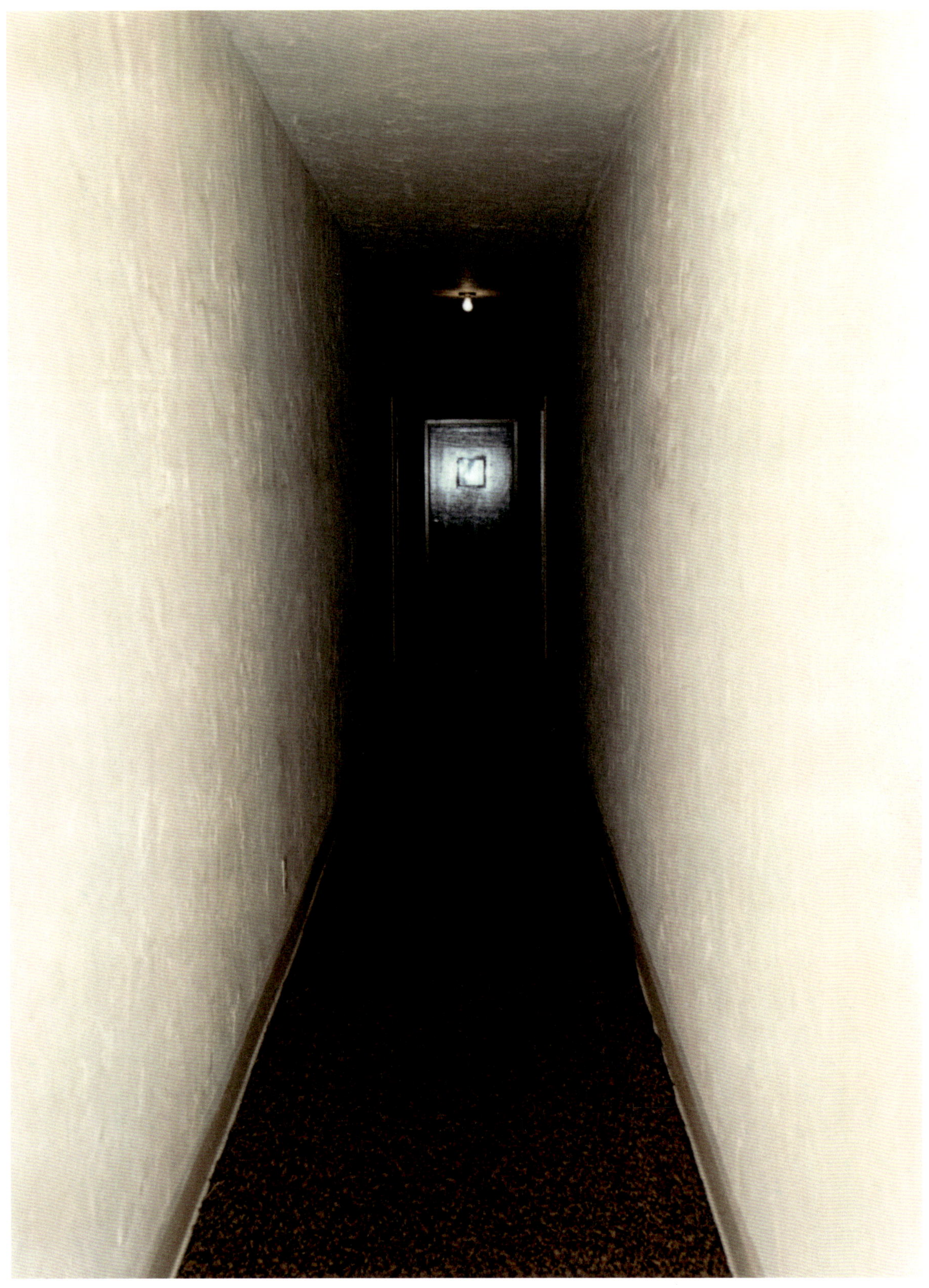

34
STEVE KAHN
Corridor 2, 1979–1980 (printed 2014).
Archival pigment print. 30 x 24 in.
Stephen H. Kahn Trust

35
STEVE KAHN
Nude 31, 1974–1975. Gelatin silver print.
Mary and Dan Solomon Collection, Los Angeles

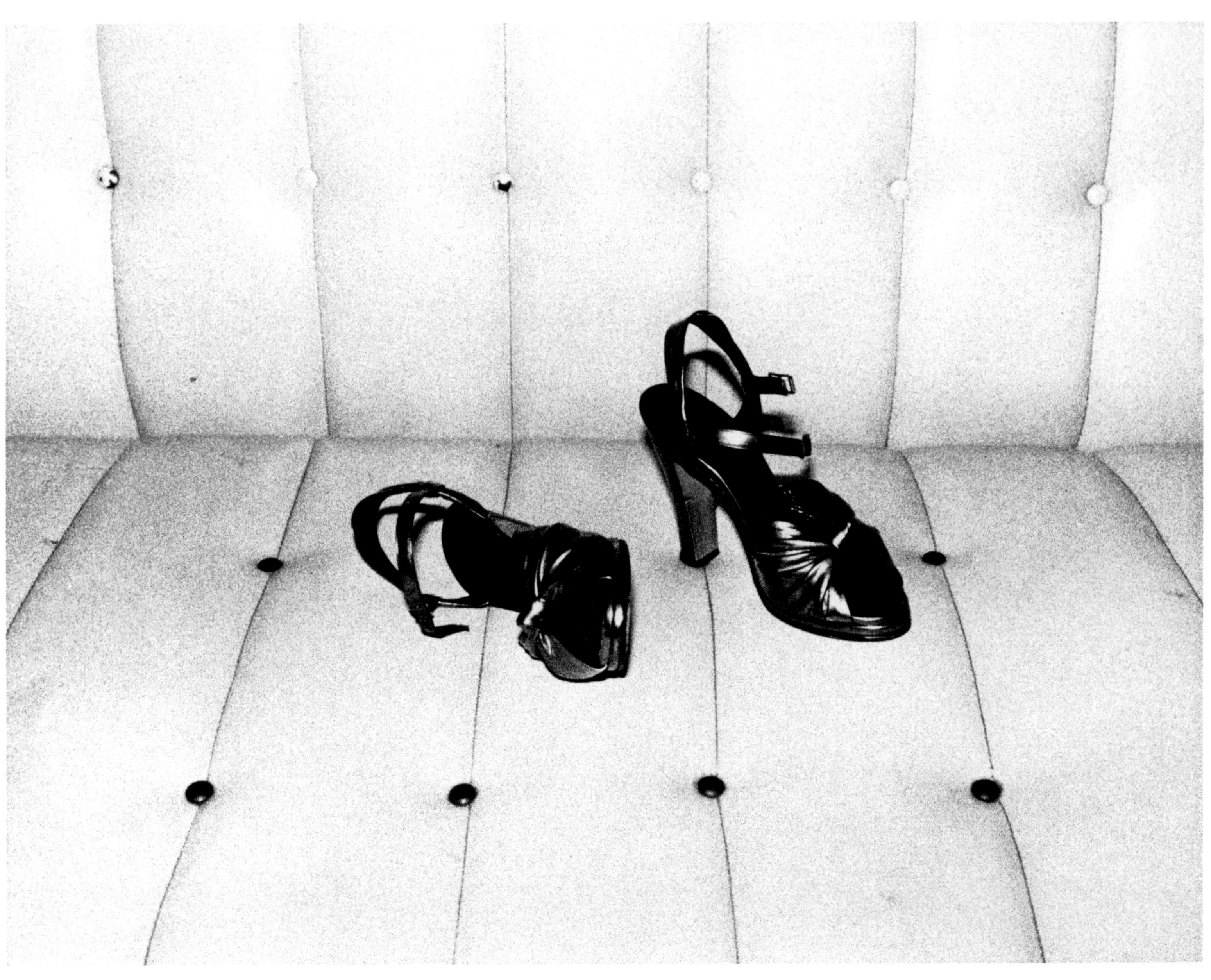

passages imply that it is not just the camera that looks but also the building that returns the camera's gaze, reversing perspectives and lending an uncanny presence to the eerie corridors.

The *Corridors*, like the *Triptychs* and *Quadrants*, were multi-image ensembles, always shown in groups of four, a quantity determined by the number of floors in the photographed buildings. The successive images demand comparison in order to tease out subtle differences, similar to the perceptual method recommended for viewing the *Windows* and *Portraits*. Kahn's ambitions, even in color, remained focused on freeing up the gaze to surf across images, comparing and associating alternate like and unlike things in the second-order realm of photographic representation. As the end point of *The Hollywood Suites*, the *Corridors* lend yet more credence to Kahn's statement, cited at the outset, that his aim was to explore how rooms, and now hallways, could resonate subjectively and how subjectivity itself could begin to feel like confinement and enclosure. "How one takes on the nature of the other," Kahn remarked. Or, as he also phrased his aims: "Using the world around me as a metaphor for the feelings and emotions within."[46] Photography supplied Kahn with the tools to develop this principle of equivalence and reversibility into a system with "relationships and cross references, etc."—a system called *The Hollywood Suites*.

I would like to thank Jim Ganz, Daniel Solomon, and Victoria Gannon for their feedback on this essay. I owe a special debt of gratitude to Steve Kahn, who first invited me to write about his art, and who spent many precious hours discussing it with me.

1 Apps. 5, 6, and 7 represent the first session associated with *The Hollywood Suites.*

2 Melinda Wortz, "Introduction," *Interchange* (Los Angeles: Mount Saint Mary's College, 1978), 11.

3 Kahn, "Notes for The Hollywood Suites" (artist statement, 2012), Stephen H. Kahn Trust.

4 Kahn, in conversation with the author, October 13, 2017.

5 See James A. Ganz, "*The Hollywood Suites:* Origins, Creations, Interventions, and Generations," in this catalogue.

6 Kahn, "Notes."

7 Kahn, "Notes."

8 Ganz, "The Hollywood Suites."

9 Ganz, "The Hollywood Suites."

10 Kahn, in discussion with unknown, [1977?], pp. 4–6, Stephen H. Kahn Trust

11 Kahn, *Journal entry, June 1, 1976,* Journal 1, pp. 62–63, Stephen H. Kahn Trust.

12 Kahn, "Notes."

13 Kahn, *Journal entry, March 5, 1975,* Journal 1, p. 16.

14 Kahn, "Notes."

15 Frederick Wight, *Transparency, Reflection, Light, Space: Four Artists* (Los Angeles: UCLA Art Galleries, 1971).

16 On his rejection of "photographing people journalistically" see Kahn, *Journal entry, March 22, 1978,* Journal 1, p. 141.

17 Kahn, *Stasis* (Malibu, CA: Steve Kahn, 1973).

18   Kahn, *Journal entry, May 31, 1976,* Journal 1, p. 55.

19   On Kahn's concern to use the camera to make art, see *Journal entry, March 22, 1978,* Journal 1, p. 142.

20   Kahn, *Note inserted in journal, no date,* Journal 1, after p. 185.

21   See Lewis Baltz, *The New Industrial Parks Near Irvine, California* (Göttingen, Germany: Steidl, 2005); and Virginia Heckert, *Some Aesthetic Decisions: The Photographs of Judy Fiskin* (Los Angeles, J. Paul Getty Museum, 2011).

22   Kahn, *Journal entry, June 29, 1975,* Journal 1, p. 22.

23   Kahn, cited in Wortz, "Introduction," 11.

24   The darkness is likely the result of a light-absorbing fabric that Kahn hung behind the opening.

25   Kahn, "Notes."

26   Kahn, *Journal entry, June 1, 1976,* Journal 1, pp. 58–59.

27   Kahn, *Journal entry, September 23, 1975,* Journal 1, pp. 24–25.

28   Kahn, *Journal entry, November 26, 1976,* Journal 1, p. 89.

29   Kahn, *Journal entry, November 26, 1976,* Journal 1, p. 90.

30   Pierre Cabanne, *Dialogues with Marcel Duchamp,* tr. Ron Padgett (New York: Thames and Hudson, 1971), 88.

31   Kahn, *Journal entry, November 26, 1976,* Journal 1, p. 87.

32   Kahn, *Journal entry, November 26, 1976,* Journal 1, p. 87.

33   Kahn, *Journal entry, August 30, 1976,* Journal 1, p. 72.

34   Kahn, *Journal entry, May 31, 1976,* Journal 1, p. 57.

35   Kahn, *Journal entry, [March 1976?],* Journal 1, p. 39.

36   Kahn commented on "the strength of Minimalism" in his journal (see *Journal entry, September 23, 1975,* Journal 1, p. 25; *Journal entry, May 31, 1976,* Journal 1, p. 57; and *Journal entry, November 26, 1976,* Journal 1, p. 90). He also referred to what he termed Mel Bochner's "measurement piece" (*Measurement Room* [1969]) as an influence on his never-realized project to create a video as part of *The Hollywood Suites* (*Journal entry, April 3, 1978,* Journal 1, p. 143).

37   Kahn, *Journal entry, April 5, 1976,* Journal 1, p. 40.

38   Kahn, *Journal entry, August 5, 1978,* Journal 1, p. 153.

39   Wortz, "Introduction," 11.

40   Kahn, *Journal entry, June 1, 1976,* Journal 1, pp. 61–62.

41   In an entry dated November 26, 1976, he described his quadrants as "vaginal cavities" (Journal 1, p. 87).

42   William Wilson, "Art Walk," *Los Angeles Times* (Feb. 25, 1977).

43   Wortz, "Interchange," 11.

44   In an entry dated August 3, 1976, Kahn jotted: "possible title for nudes: Hollywood Suites, with play on Sweets/Suites" (Journal 1, p. 69).

45   Kahn, "Notes."

46   Kahn, *Note inserted in journal, no date,* Journal 1, between pp. 8 and 9.

DISPARATE ELEMENTS BROUGHT TOGETHER
STEVE KAHN'S TRIPTYCHS AND QUADRANTS

CONSTANCE M. LEWALLEN

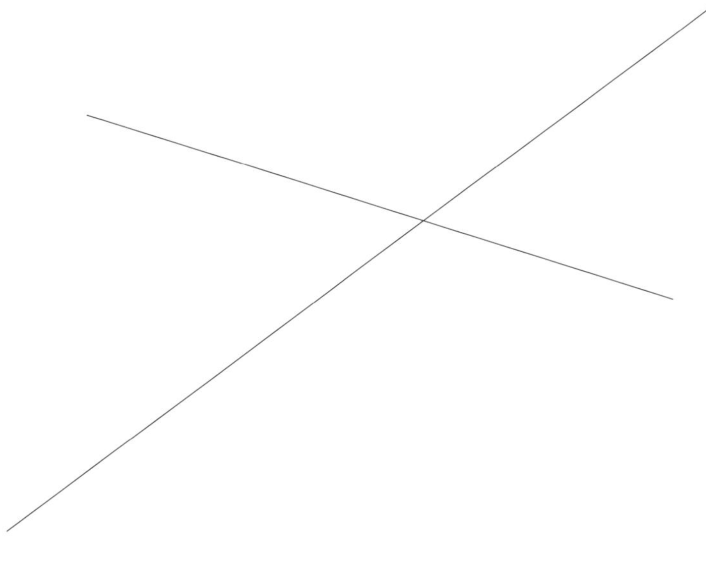

36
Unknown photographer
Steve Kahn at Broxton Gallery, 1977.
Stephen H. Kahn Trust

IN THE WINTER of 1977, Steve Kahn exhibited his *Triptychs* and *Quadrants* at the Broxton Gallery on La Cienega Boulevard, in Los Angeles (where I was working as assistant to the owner, Larry Gagosian; see fig. 36). Broxton was one of the first galleries to exhibit "straight" photographers like Lee Friedlander, Ralph Gibson, and Robert Frank alongside Conceptual artists who used photography as part of a larger project, such as John Baldessari, Bruce Nauman, and William Wegman. It was an apt venue for Kahn, whose work by then had moved from the former category to the latter.[1]

Kahn started out in Los Angeles in the 1970s as a street photographer doing commercial work on the side. It was a brief project intended for a bondage magazine—photographing models in seedy, rent-by-the-day Hollywood apartments—that improbably led him to create the *Triptychs* and *Quadrants,* a series of extraordinary large-scale black-and-white photographic works (pls. 53–57 and figs. 32, 33, and 40). As Kahn explained, when a model didn't show up one day, he photographed the shabby room instead—walls, windows, mirrors, and doors—embarking on a series he would eventually title *The Hollywood Suites.* He found that the rooms devoid of human presence were nonetheless powerful conveyors of enigmatic narratives and emotions. As he wrote in a November 1975 journal entry, he was "using the world around me as a metaphor for the feelings and emotion within."[2] If the resulting images corresponded to his emotions, they might, by extension, inspire similar feelings in others.

Kahn was obviously familiar with the new uses of photography being adopted by Conceptual artists at the time. At the California Institute of the Arts (CalArts), just north of Los Angeles, faculty artists like Doug Huebler and John Baldessari had, starting in the late 1960s, pioneered the use of photography in conceptual work, and they were passing the practice down to students like

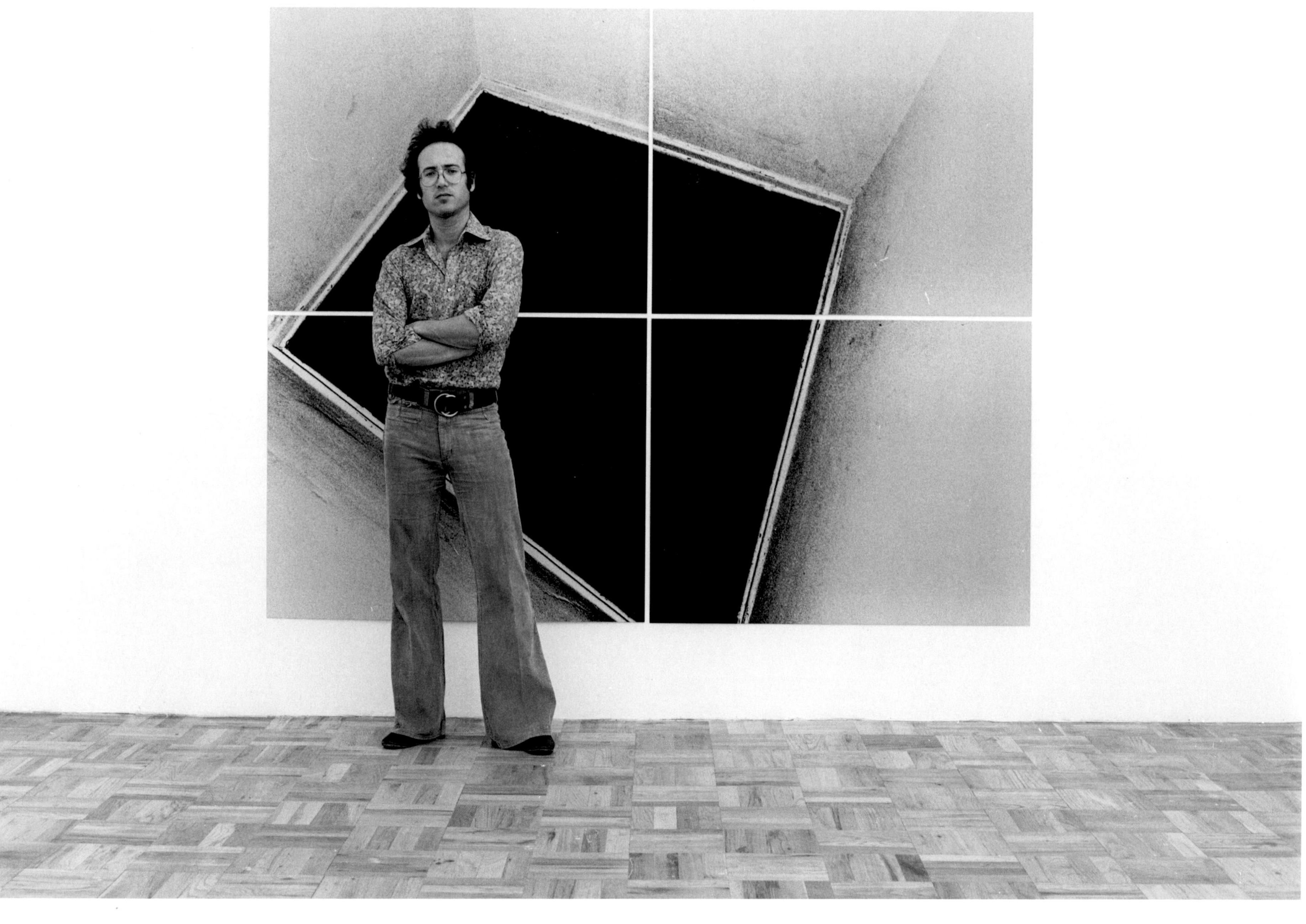

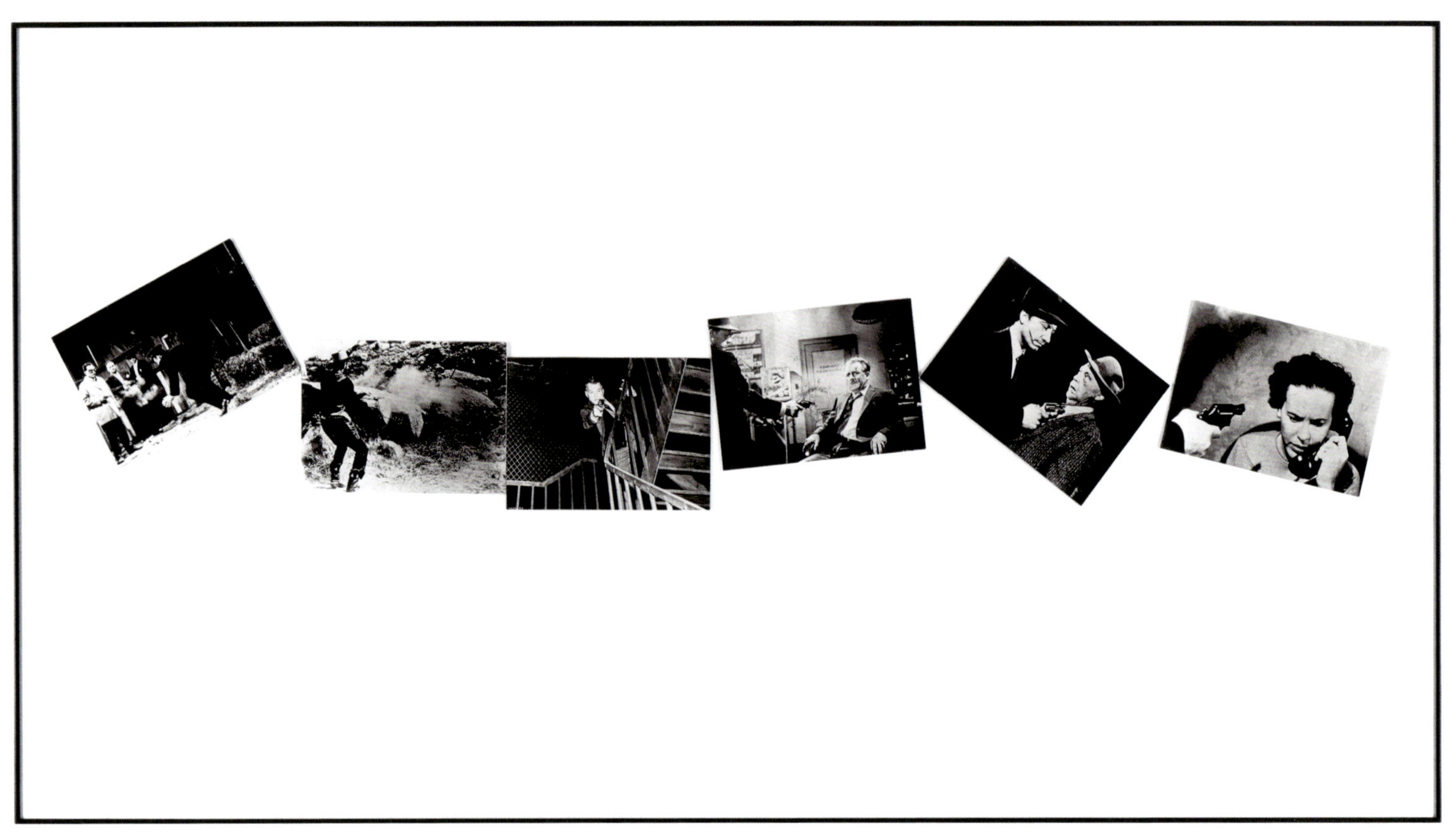

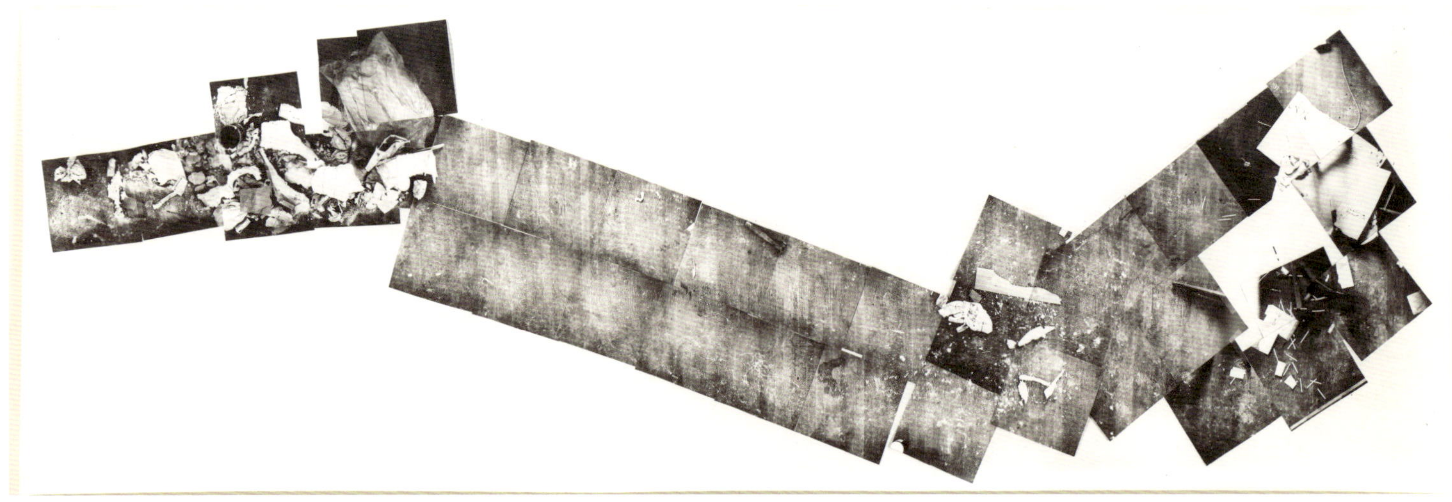

James Welling, Barbara Bloom, and a host of others. Kahn was even an instructor in the graduate program there during the 1978–1979 academic year.

In fact, like-minded artists everywhere at that time were using photography in new and varied ways, none of them respecting photographic tradition. Nor were they valuing the "fine print" (the composition and quality of the print); aesthetics were not the point. They even bridled at the label "photographer."[3] For some, the photograph was a convenient way to offer evidence of an ephemeral action, like a performance. A typical example is Vito Acconci's *Following* (1969), in which he trailed unsuspecting pedestrians through downtown New York streets and documented his furtive action with a gridded series of black-and-white photographs. The photographs were not the primary artwork—that was the street action—but simply a record of the activity. For other artists, the photograph served to communicate the idea at hand, convey information, or do both. Baldessari, for example, created semiotic games through provocative juxtapositions of photographs (see fig. 37). They were not even his photographs—he didn't see any point in taking a photograph himself if he could appropriate one that did the job.

Kahn's focus on room interiors accorded with contemporaneous interest in rooms not simply as containers for art but as artworks themselves. Southern California Light and Space artists like Robert Irwin and James Turrell were transforming rooms into immersive environments. Kahn was, of course, very familiar with these artists and on at least one occasion was hired to photograph Irwin's work. Rooms had become a distinct artistic genre, as evidenced by exhibitions such as the 1970 *Spaces* at the Museum of Modern Art and the 1976 *Rooms* at PS1, both in New York.

Kahn's photographs of empty rooms soon led him to an even more audacious project—rearranging photographs of interiors into abstract compositions such as the *Triptychs* and *Quadrants.* Again, Kahn was not the only artist to create photographic collages. Bruce Nauman's *Composite Photo of Two Messes on the Studio Floor* (1967; fig. 38), a montage of photos of detritus from what he was working on in his studio, provides a window into his process. Gordon Matta-Clark made composite photographs that not only documented the radical architectural deconstructions that he called "anarchitecture" but also conveyed the drama and energy of his action. The several such collages he made in relation to *Office Baroque* (1977; fig. 39), a cutting of an office building in Antwerp, are deliberately disorienting in order to "emulate their dynamic spatial and temporal qualities in unique photographs made by splicing and grafting negatives to create quasi-Cubistic images."[4]

In contrast to the composite photographs of Nauman, Matta-Clark, and others, Kahn's *Triptychs* and *Quadrants* are not records of an action. Composed of fragments of his architectural photographs, they are attempts, wrote the artist in May 1976, "to make another whole out of these distinct wholes."[5] *Quadrant* 1 (1976; pl. 57) consists of four individual photographs, rearranged so as to create an irregular quadrilateral. It takes a moment to notice the moldings along the edges before one realizes that one is seeing not a Minimal abstraction but photographs of architectural details. Minimal painting was on Kahn's mind. In the same May 1976 journal entry, he elaborates: "What I have done in the room triptychs is to make another whole out of these distinct wholes now rendered by visual-mental connection into parts . . . or more accurately creating a sense of physical dimensionality, each

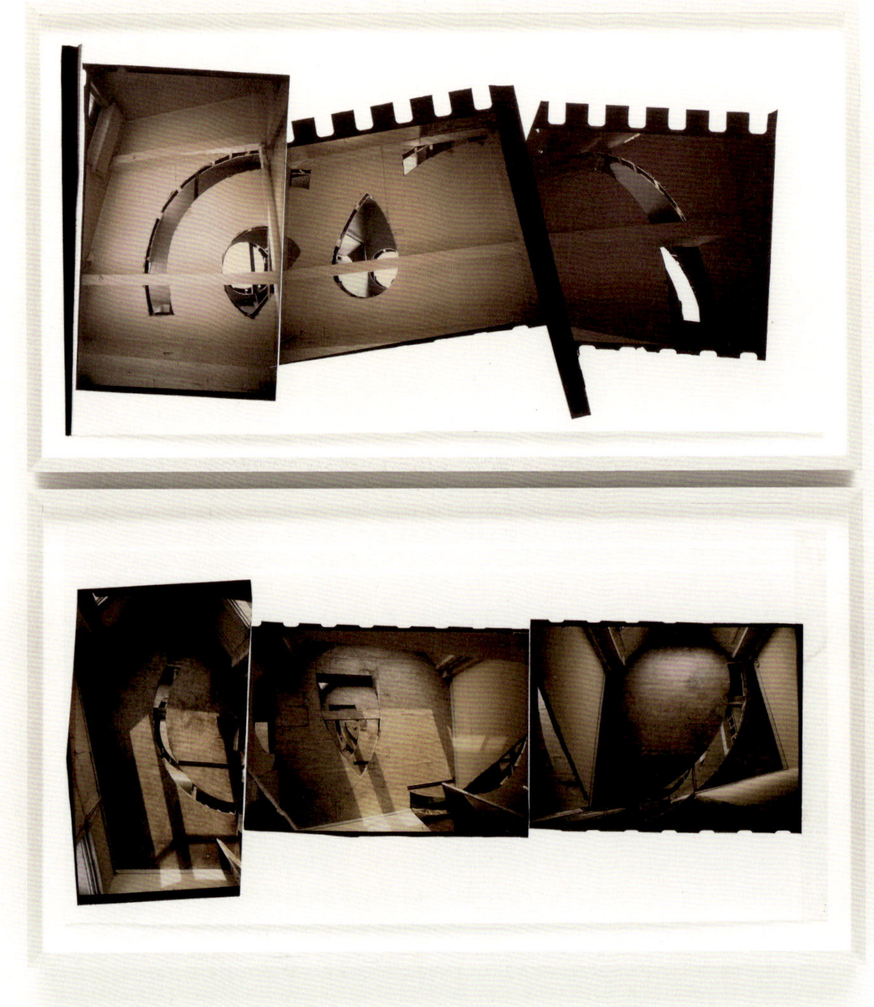

part adds dimension not necessarily relating the parts, the parts
coming together are non-relational (MINIMALISM) but they do
succeed in forming a gestalt with an extraordinary presence." This
same sentence could almost have been written by Minimalist painter
Frank Stella, who, along with other Minimalist artists, used the term
"non-relational" to distinguish his work from traditional European
geometric abstraction such as Constructivism. The parts in a Stella
painting (and in Kahn's work) act independently, connecting
additively rather than coexisting as components of a balanced
composition.

The scale of Kahn's photo constructions (he often
referred to them as murals) also relates them to painting. They are
very large. *Triptych* 10 (1976; fig. 40) is 28 inches high and 108
inches wide. As the title indicates, it consists of three photographs,
which are adhered to an aluminum panel. The zigzag composition
results from Kahn's juxtaposing photographs of corners of walls as
they meet the floor. In his journal, Kahn likened his horizontal
triptychs to landscapes; this is a possible reading, but they can just
as plausibly be seen as architectural conundrums. The space that
results from Kahn's reconstructions bends and distorts. The images
often seem to offer a way into a space while simultaneously
thwarting entry. If there is a door, it's shut, or one sees only the
top or bottom third of the room. In some *Triptychs* the
photographs are stacked vertically (pls. 54–56). Kahn
experimented with many permutations of both *Triptychs* and
Quadrants that variously bend and disrupt space. As he wrote, he
was "creating a formal arena for subjective experience."[8]

Newly discovered after having been packed away
for decades, Kahn's photo constructions retain their power.
Contemporary viewers will respond to them in their own ways.
Although the works don't seem as radical as they did when they
were first exhibited, they don't seem dated either. The territory

Kahn staked out is still fertile ground. For Kahn, writing in his journal in June 1978, they are explorations into "the meaning of life (certainly the meaning of mine). The interest [in] space as model for the mind carries itself into the gallery as arena set up for experiencing the results of these explorations. More than answering questions (which my work doesn't attempt to do) I explore, such that a piece of mine might be concerned with just bringing together different, possibly disparate elements in order to call attention to new relationships . . . shedding light on our incredibly complex lives in this culture."[9]

1   For more on this transition in Kahn's work, see Matthew Simms, "Steve Kahn: Displacements," in this catalogue.

2   Steve Kahn, *Note inserted in journal, no date*, Journal 1, between pp. 8 and 9, Stephen H. Kahn Trust.

3   Nancy Foote coined the term "anti-photographers" to describe these artists in her eponymous article in *Artforum* 15 (September 1976): pp. 46–54.

4   Nancy Spector, "Gordon Matta-Clark: *Reality Properties: Fake Estates, Little Alley Block 2497, Lot 42*, Guggenheim Collection Online, https://www.guggenheim.org/artwork/5210, accessed January 19, 2018.

Some of Matta-Clark's peers thought his photographs too arty, too "good," in Joseph Kosuth's words. However, for Matta-Clark, they were an apt analog to his cuttings; see: Pamela Lee, "Other Spaces: Proleptic Photography," in *Gordon Matta-Clark Moment to Moment*, ed. Hubertus von Amelunxen et al. (Vienna: Verlag fur Moderne Kunst, 2007), pp. 98–116.

5   Kahn, *Journal entry, May 31, 1976*, Journal 1, p. 57.

6   Kahn, p. 57.

7   Kahn, *Journal entry, October 6, 1977*, Journal 1, p. 122.

8   Kahn, *Note inserted in journal, no date*, Journal 1, between pp. 8 and 9.

9   Kahn, *Note pasted in journal, June 1979*, Journal 1, p. 174.

PLATES

1

PORTRAITS

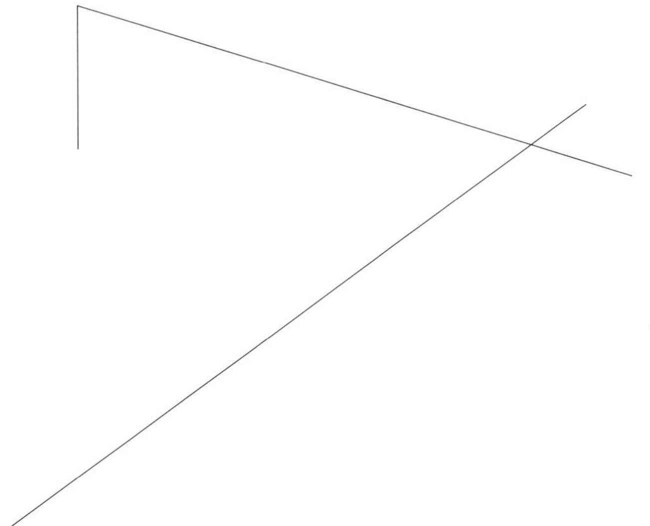

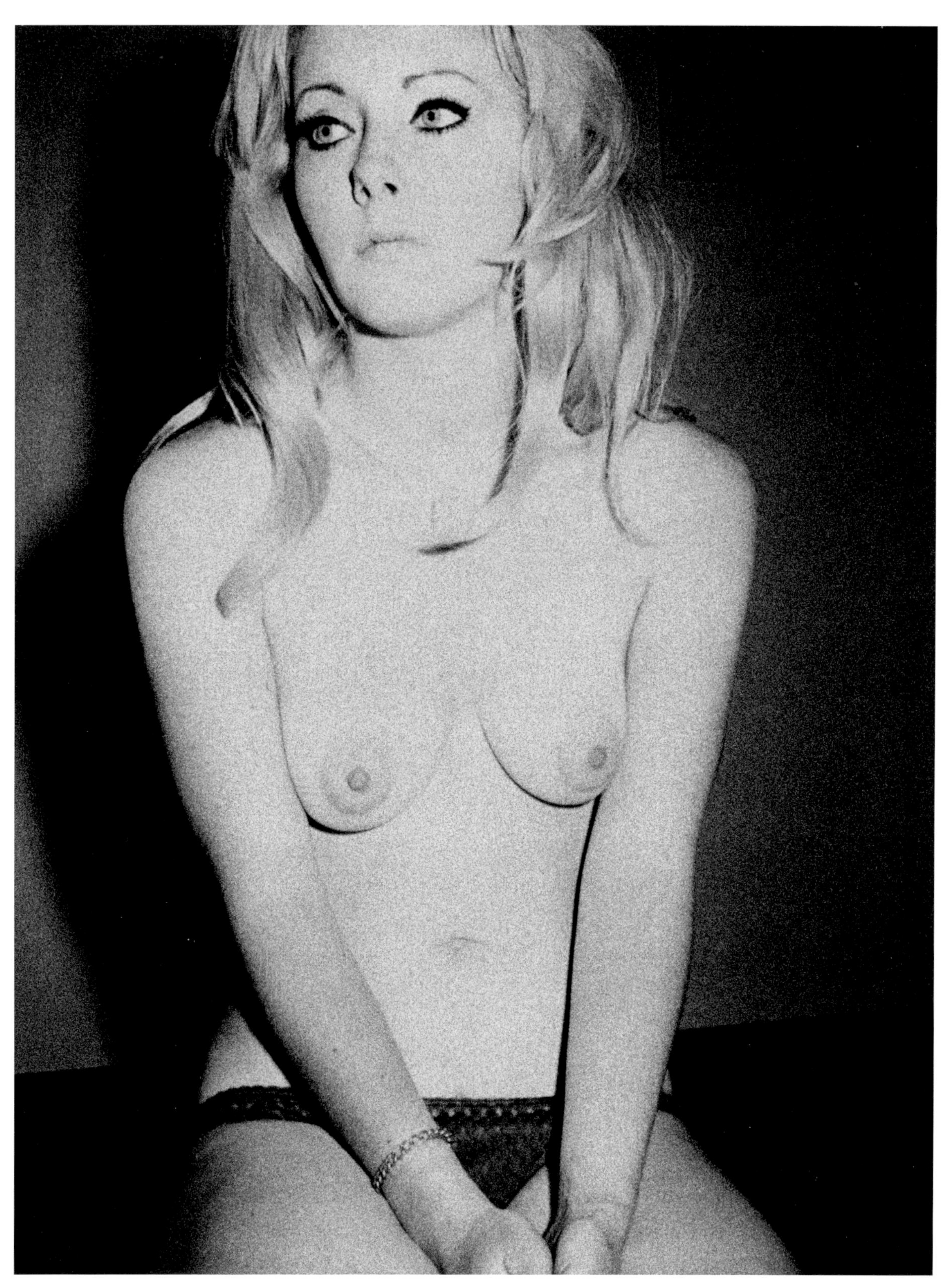

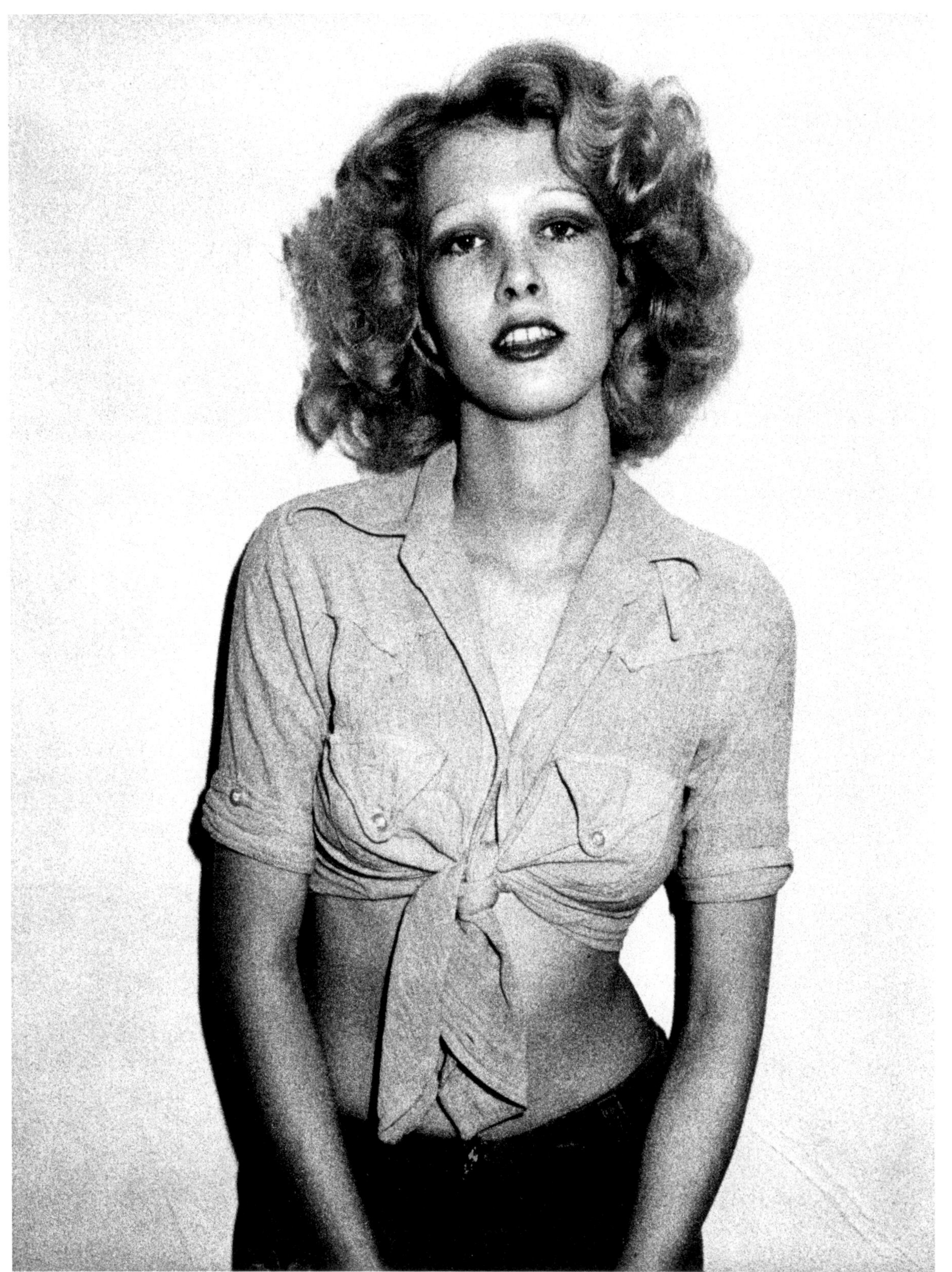

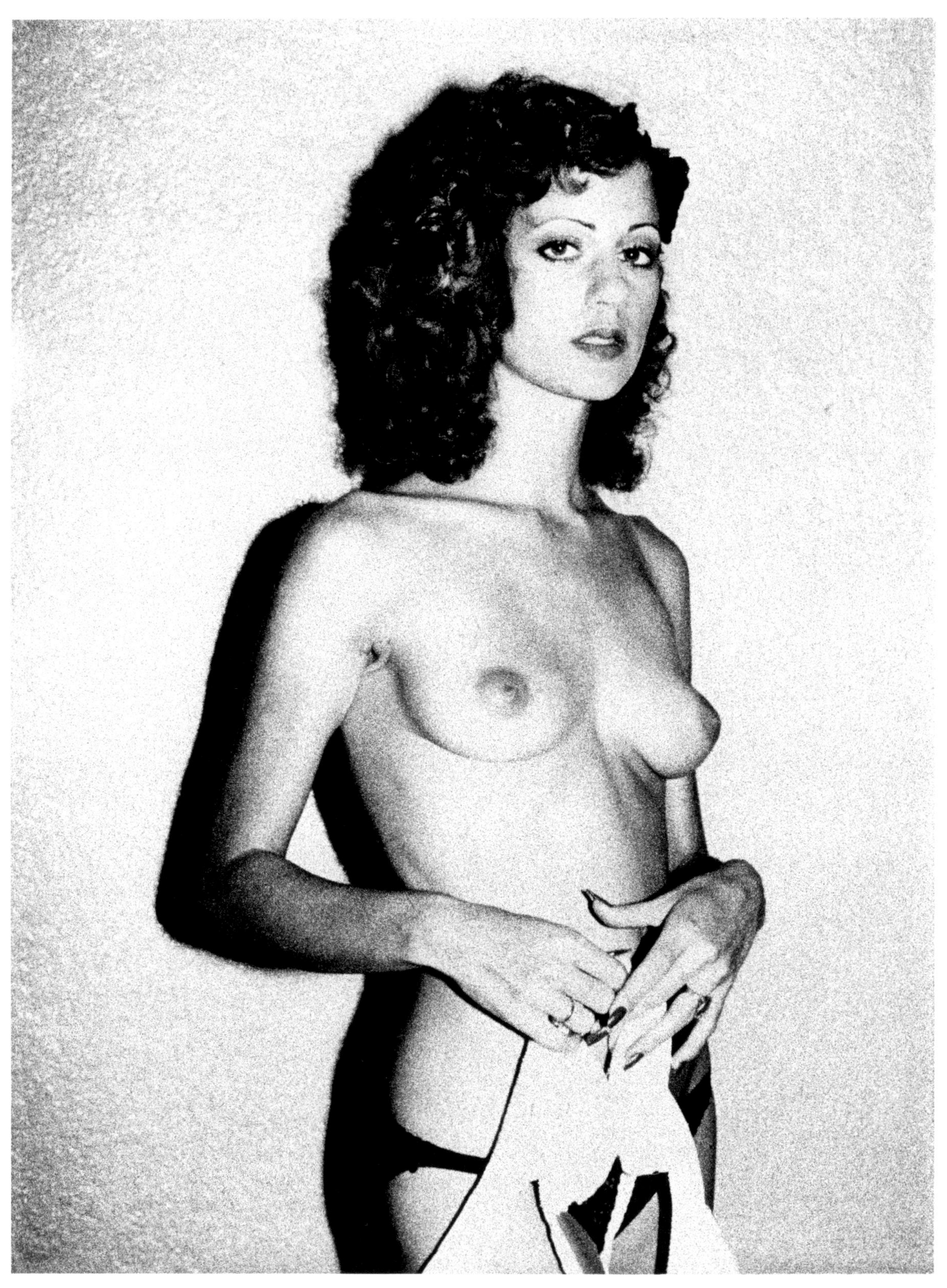

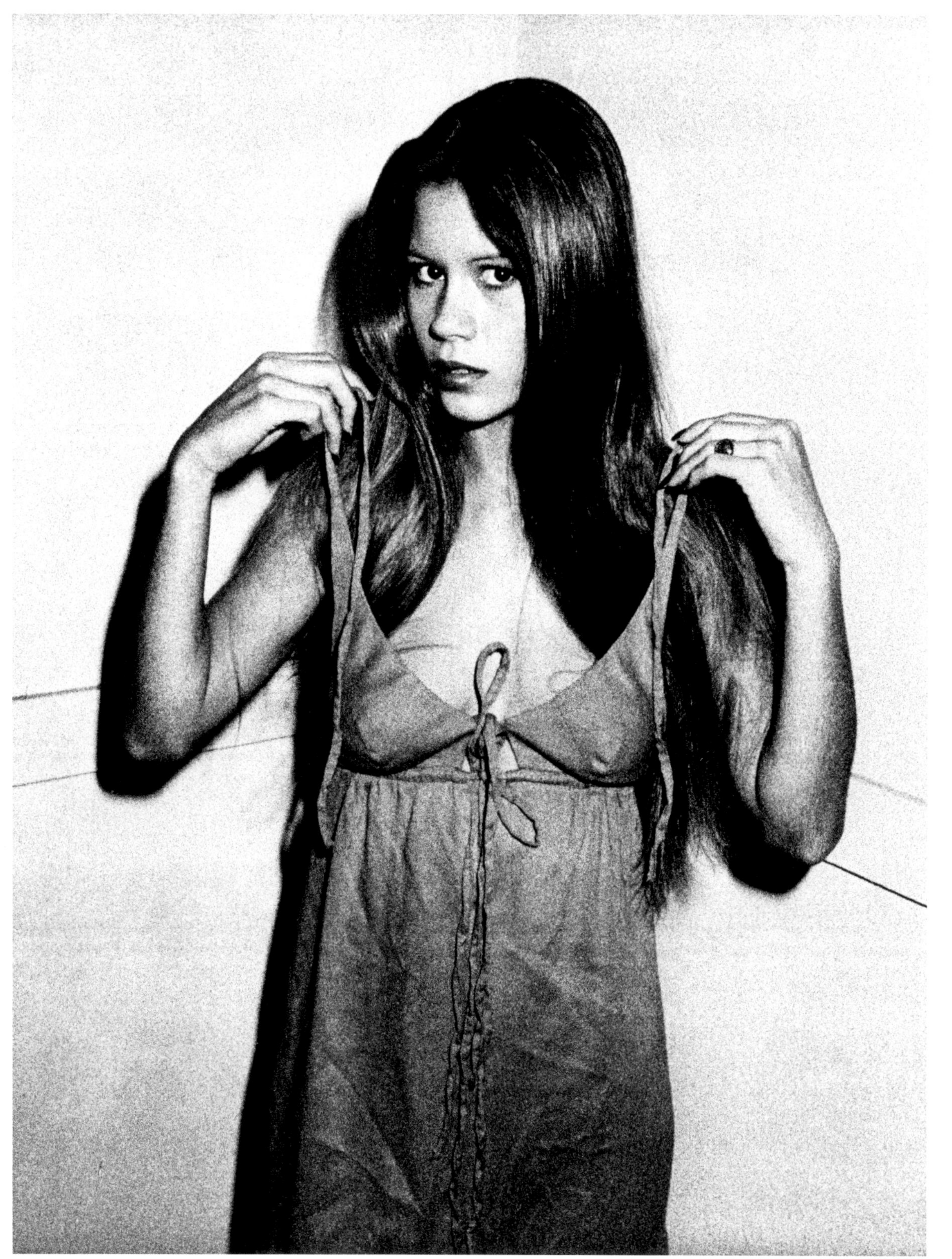

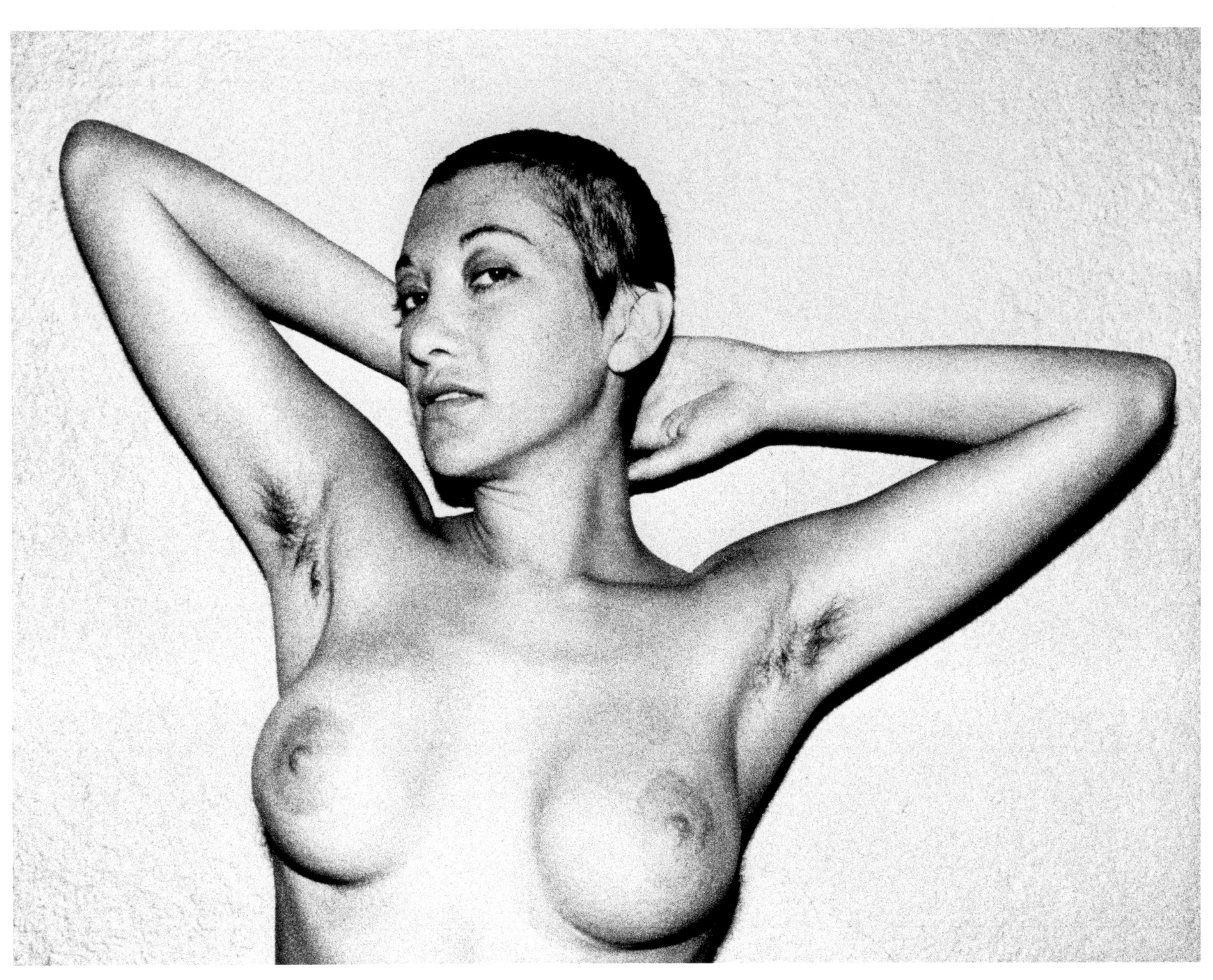

NUDES

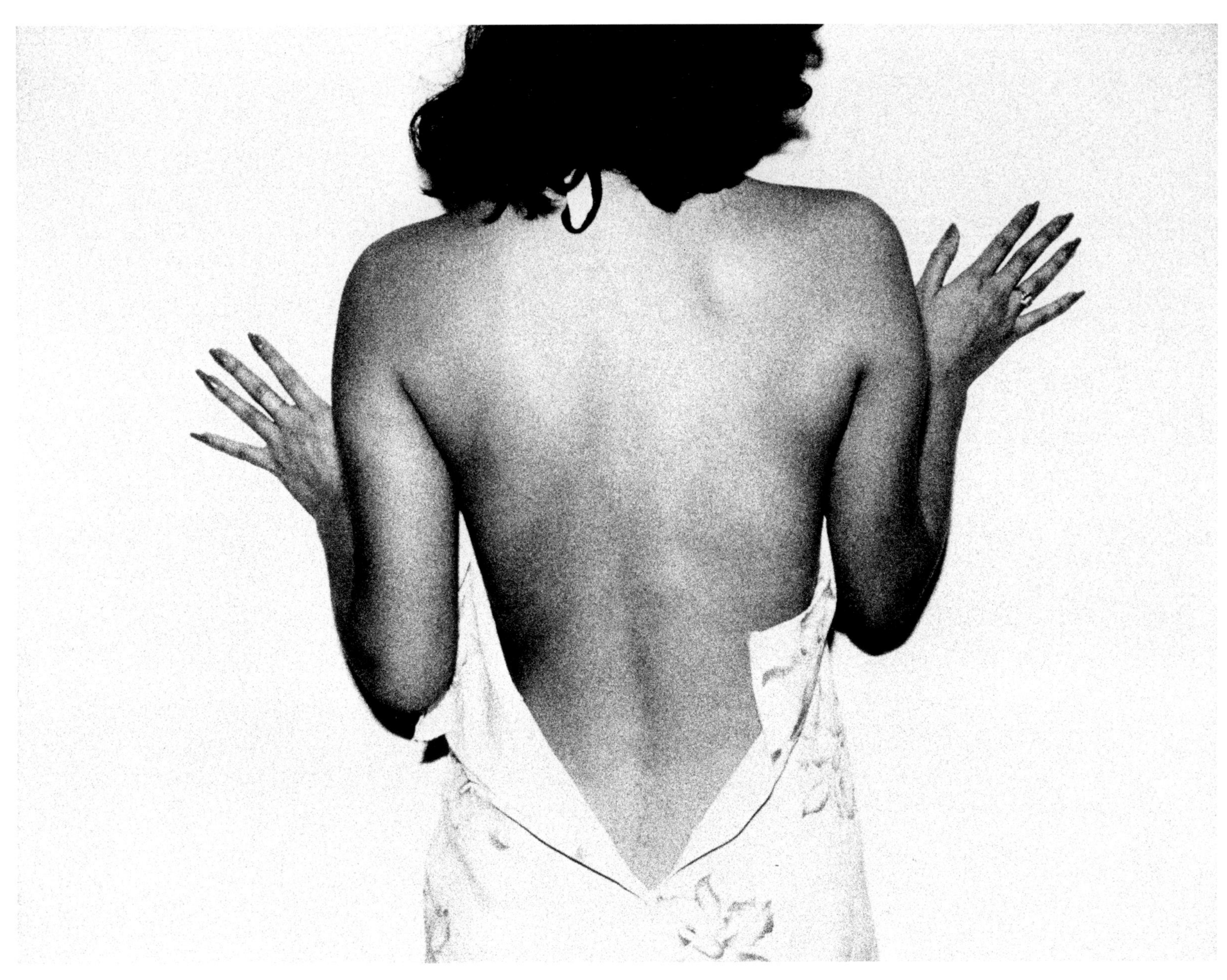

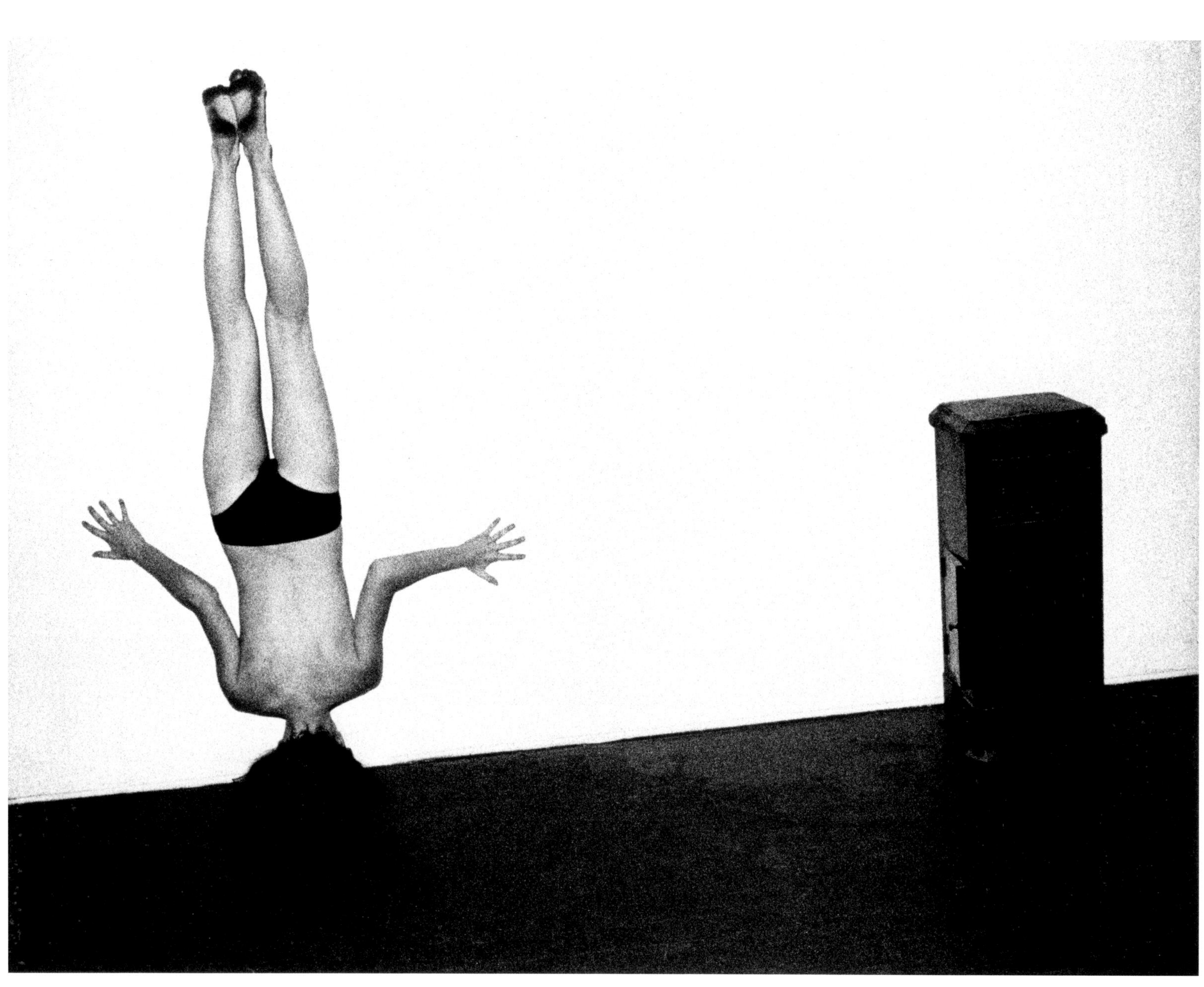

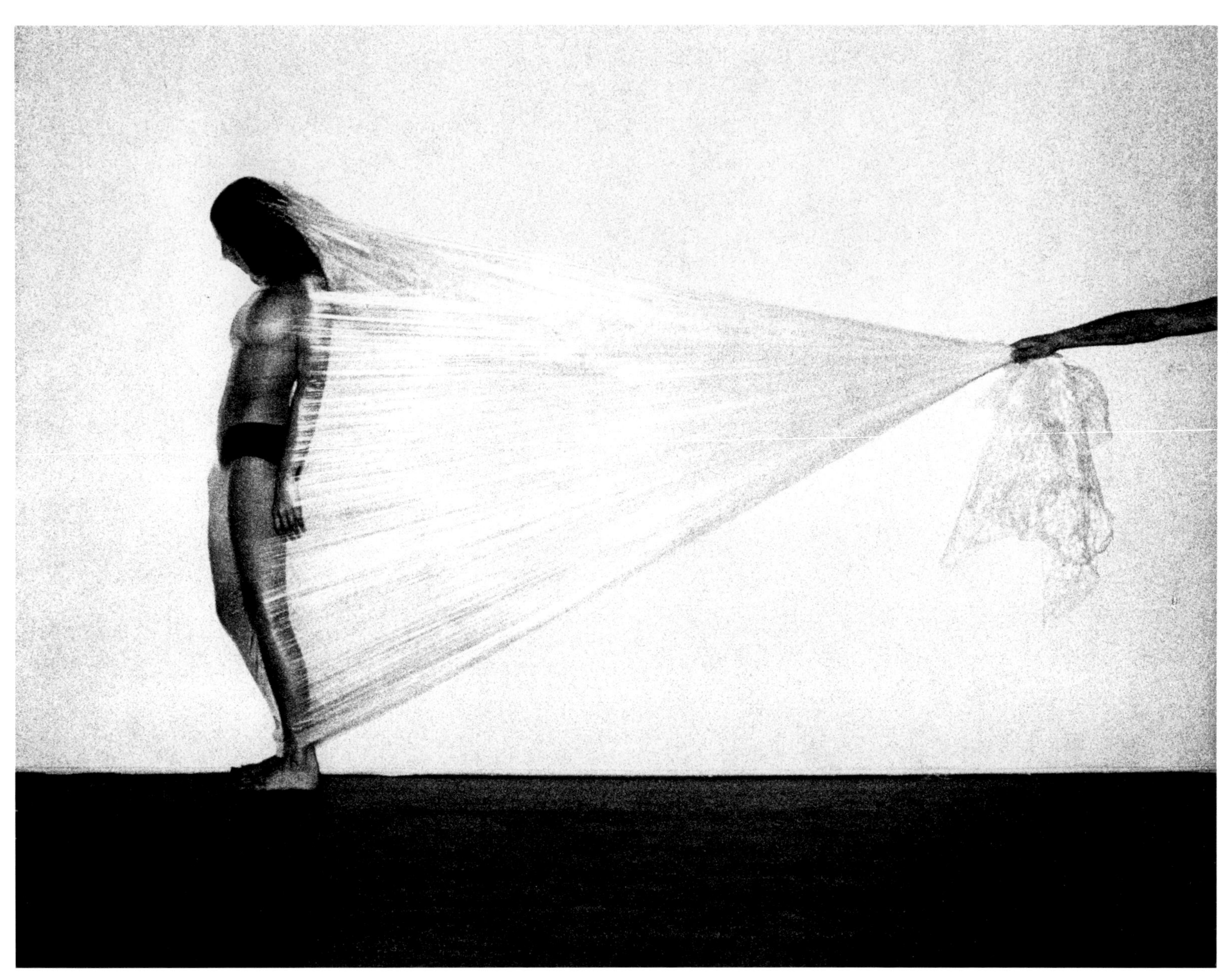

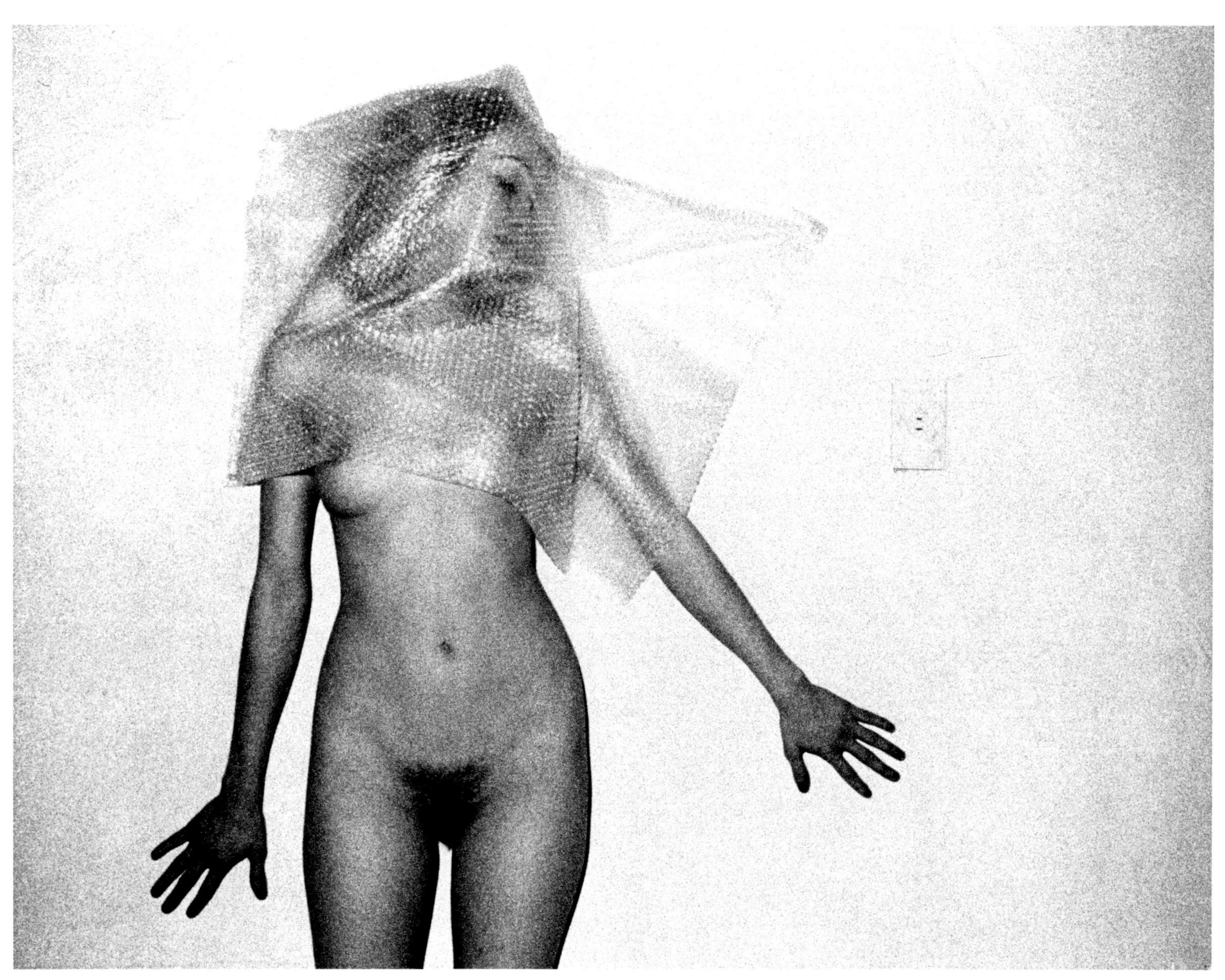

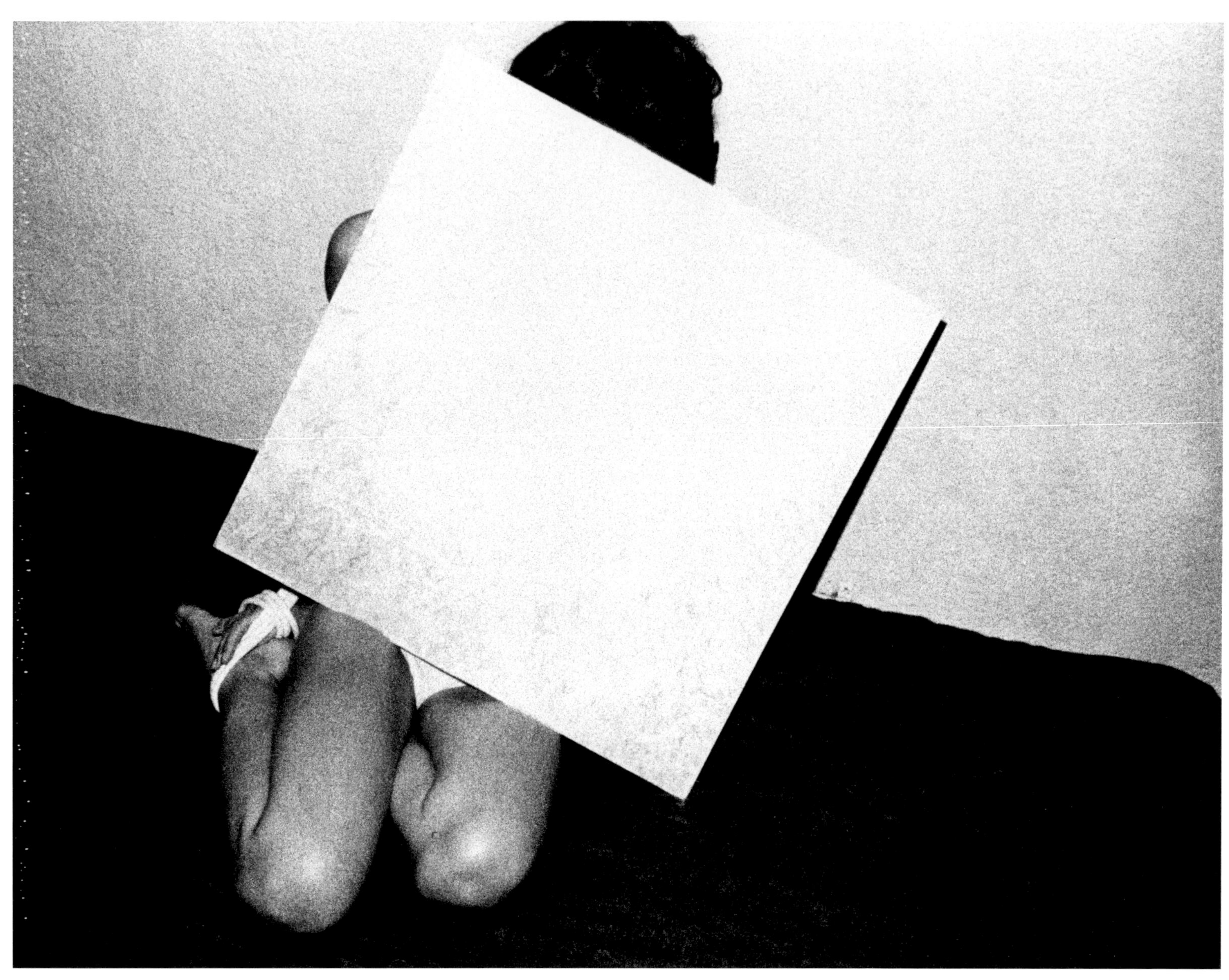

3   ROOMS

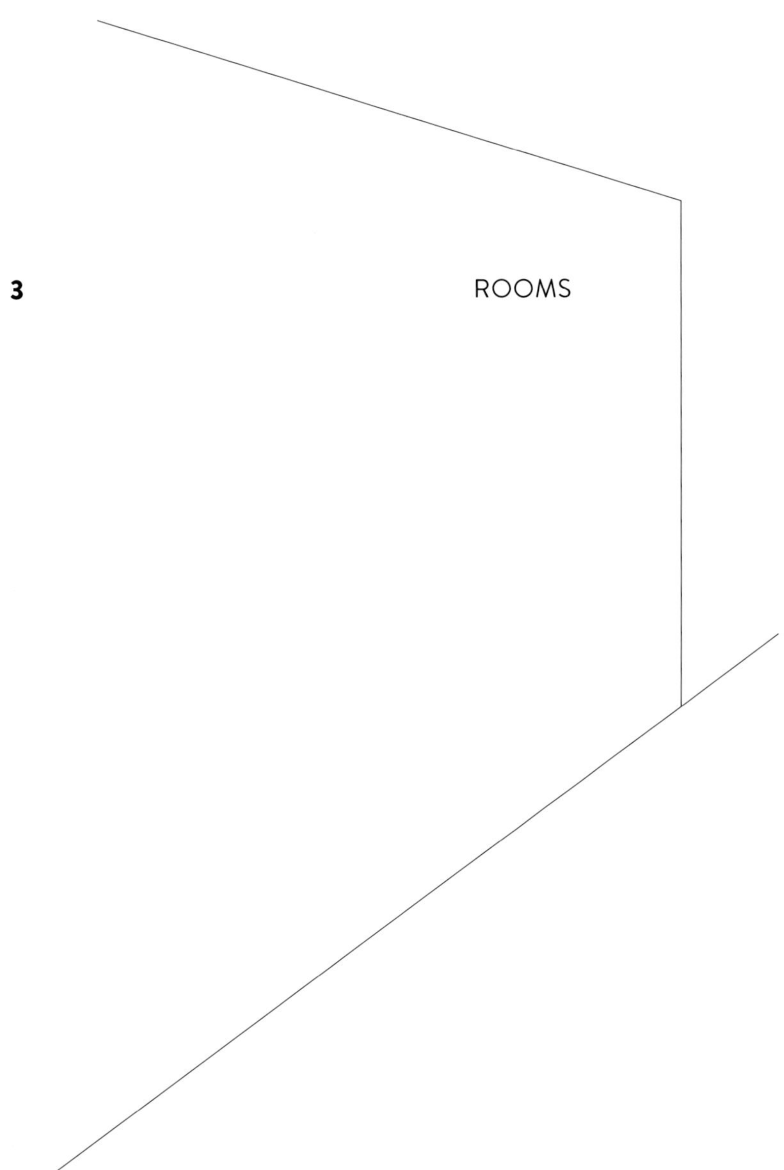

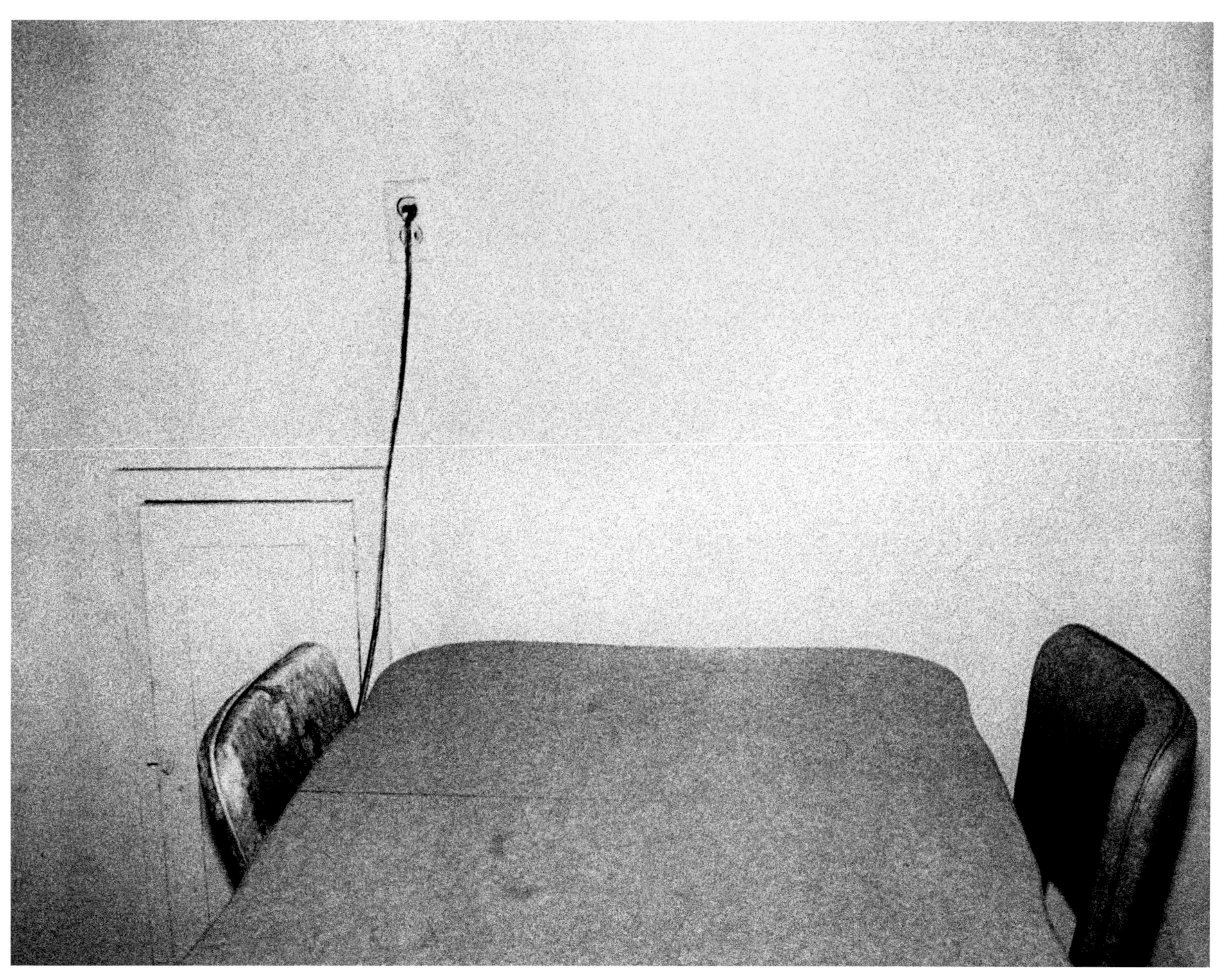

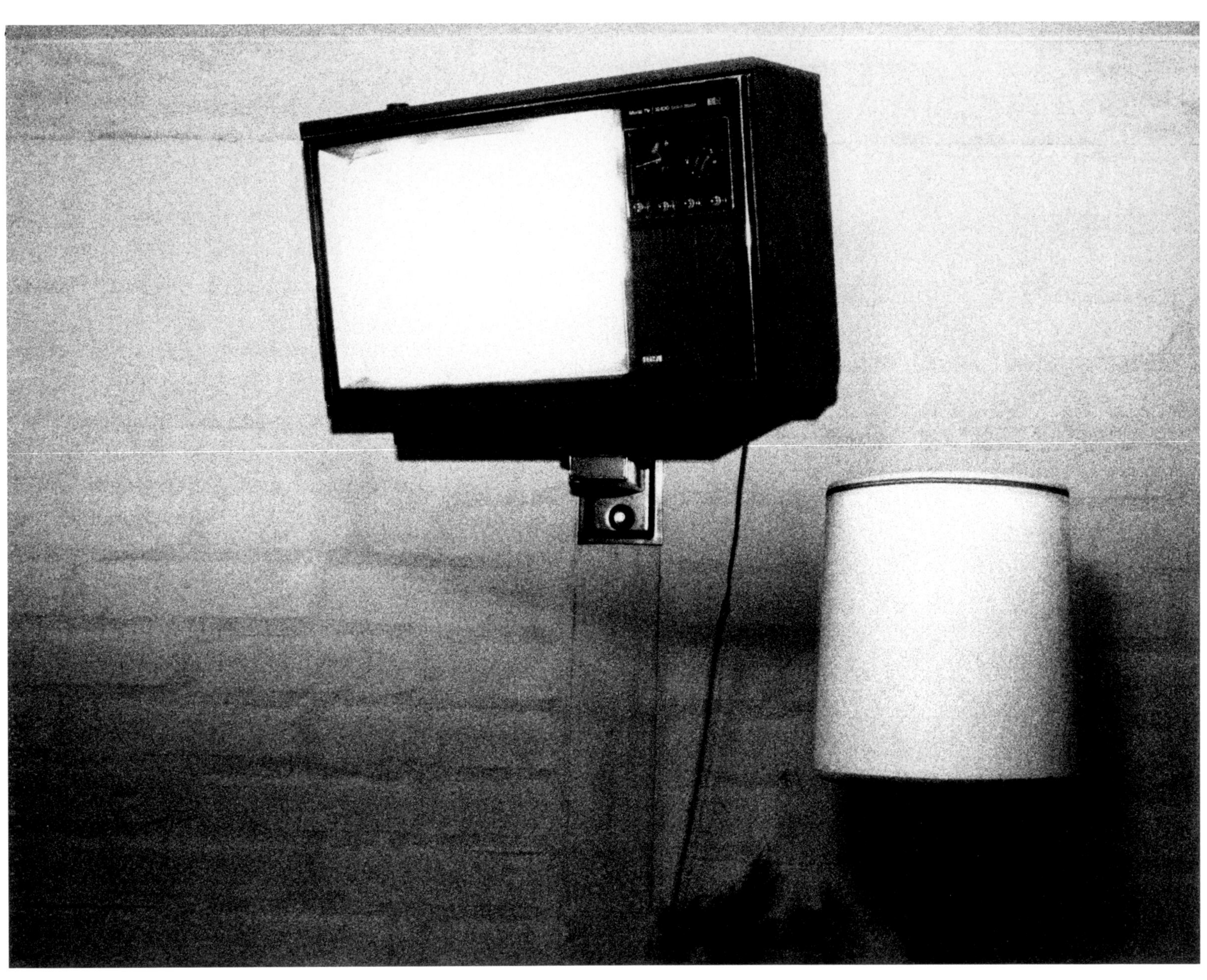

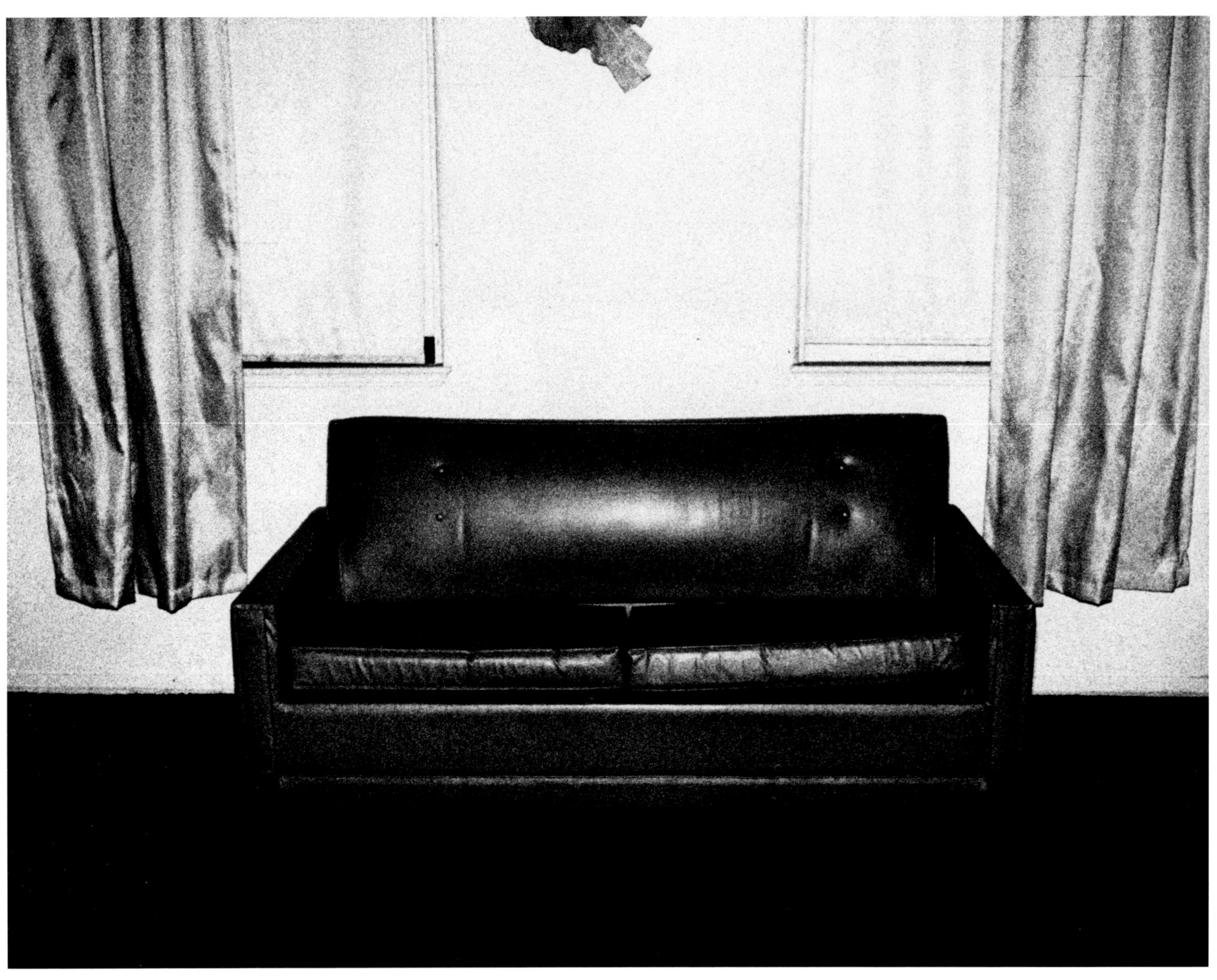

4

WINDOWS

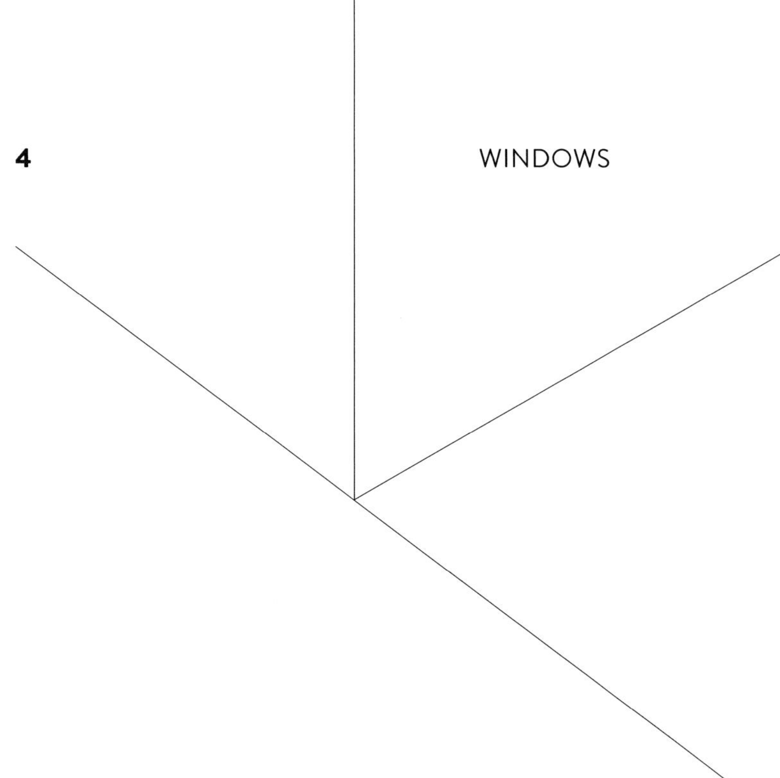

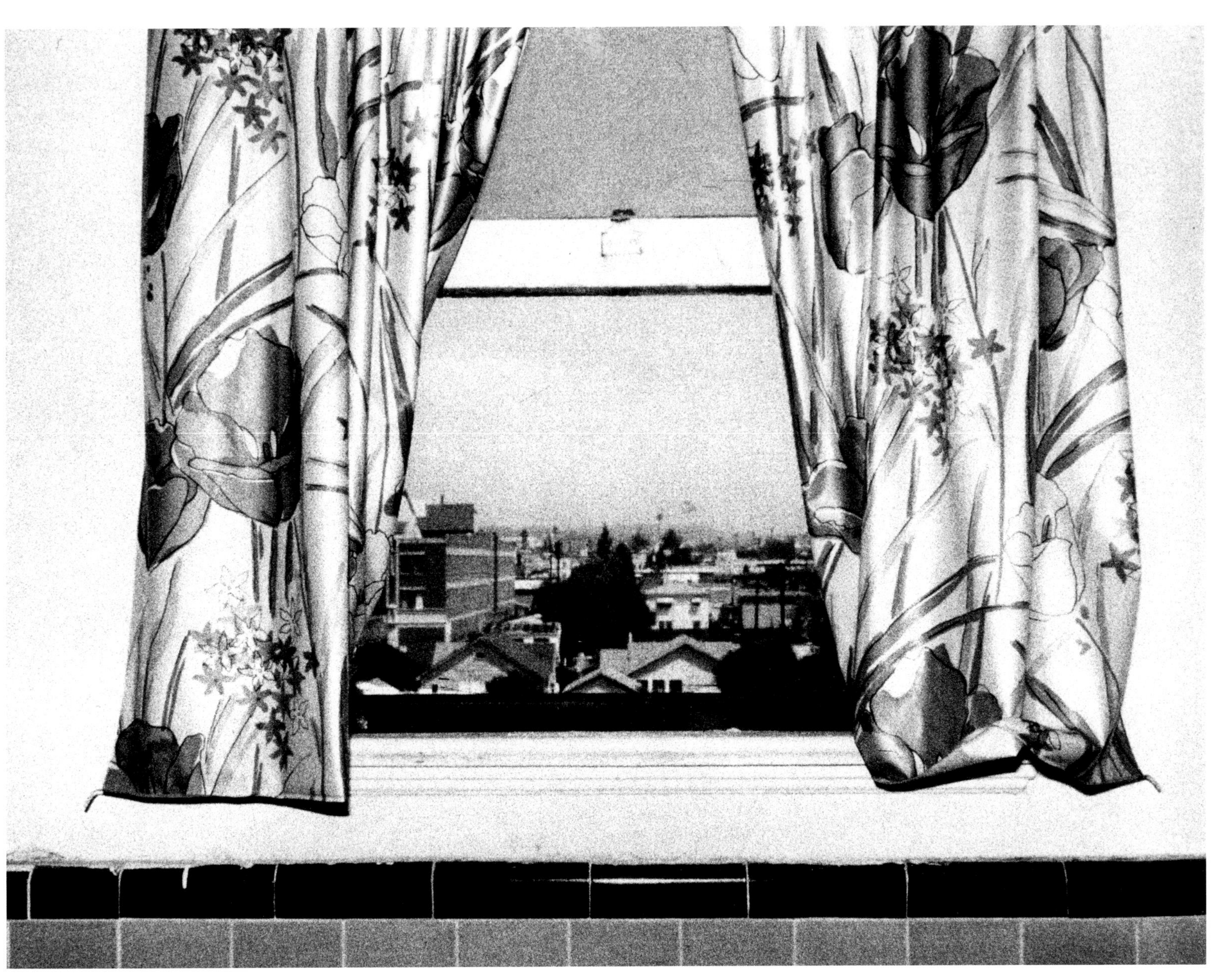

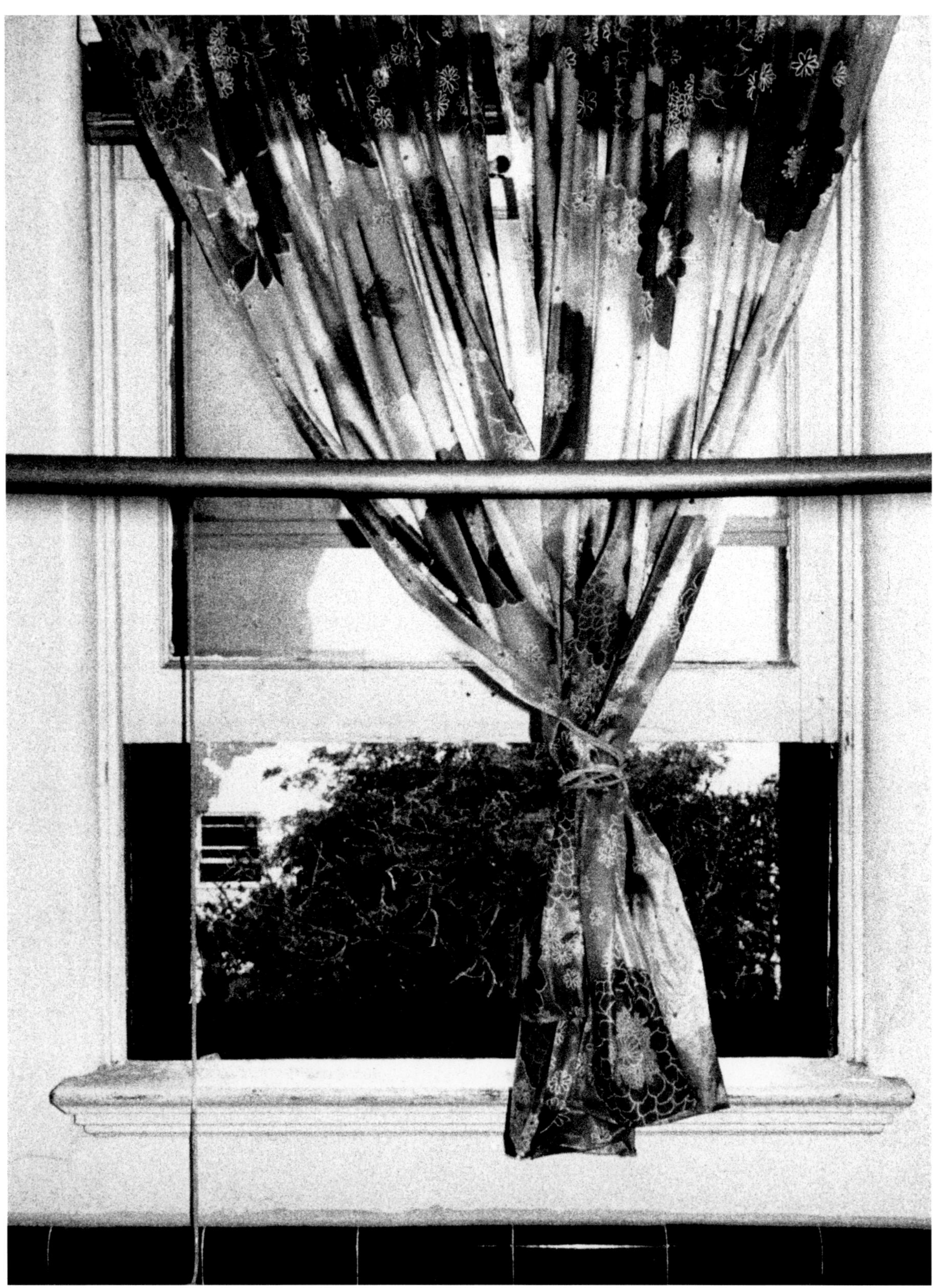

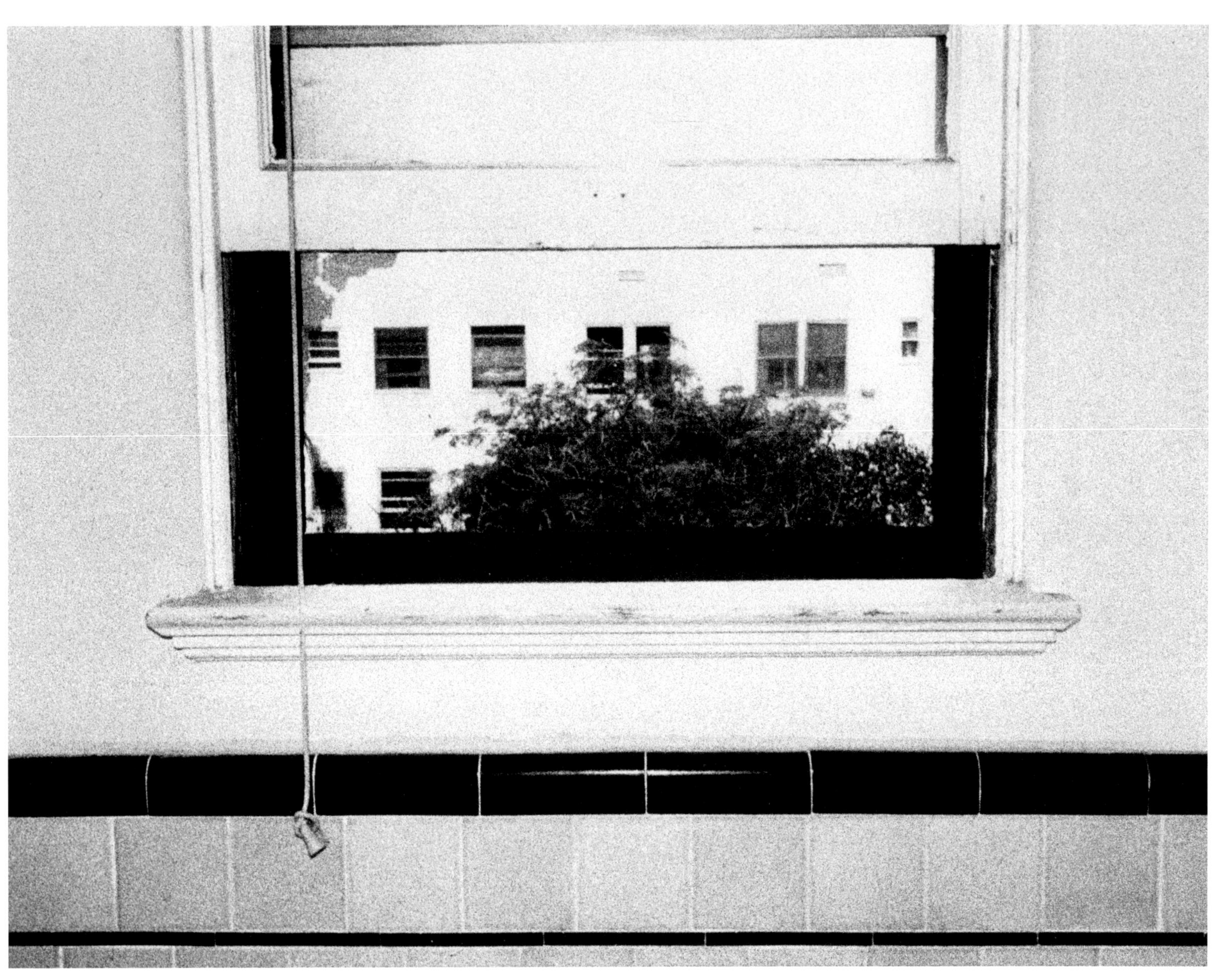

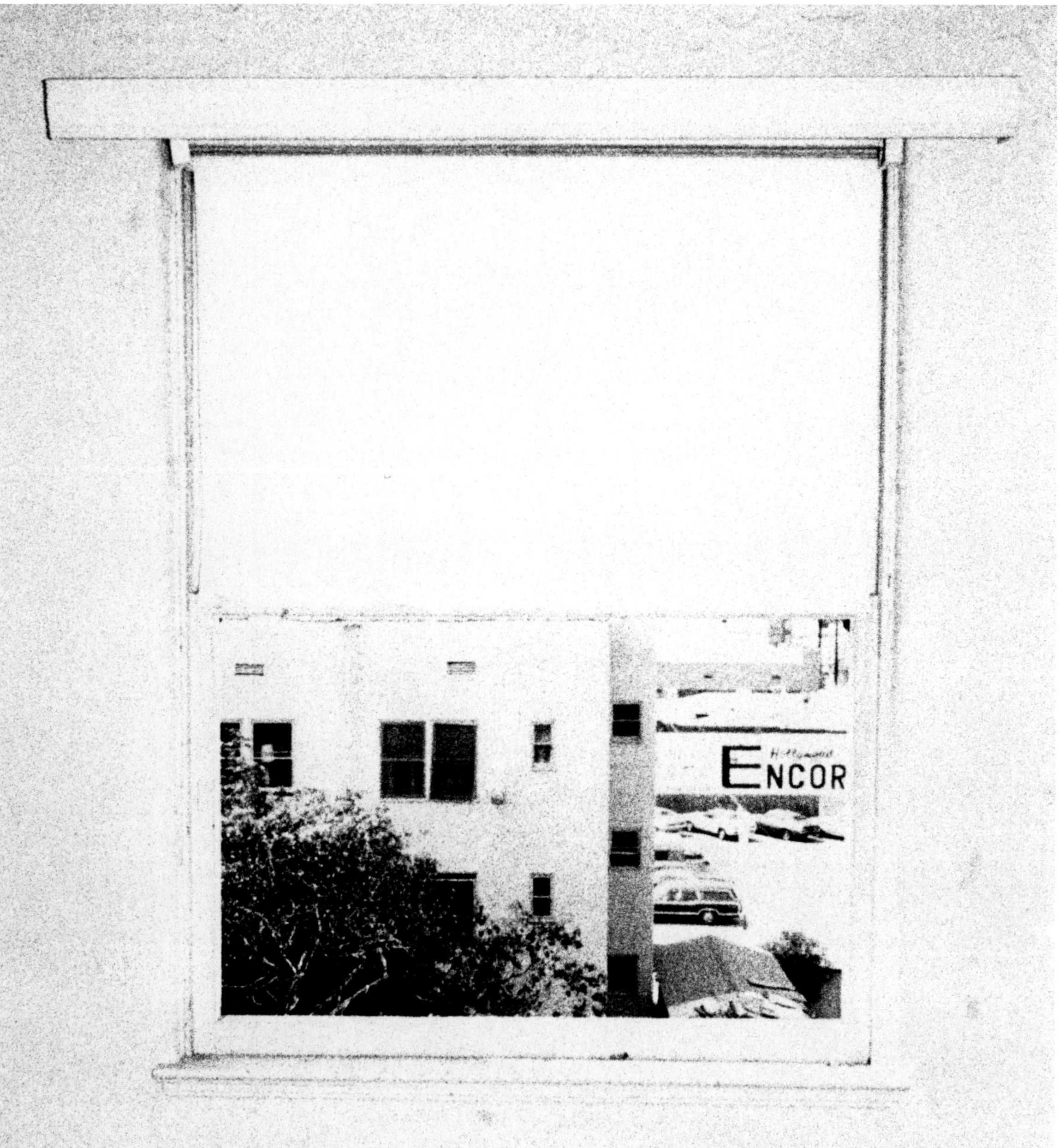

Hollywood
ENCOR

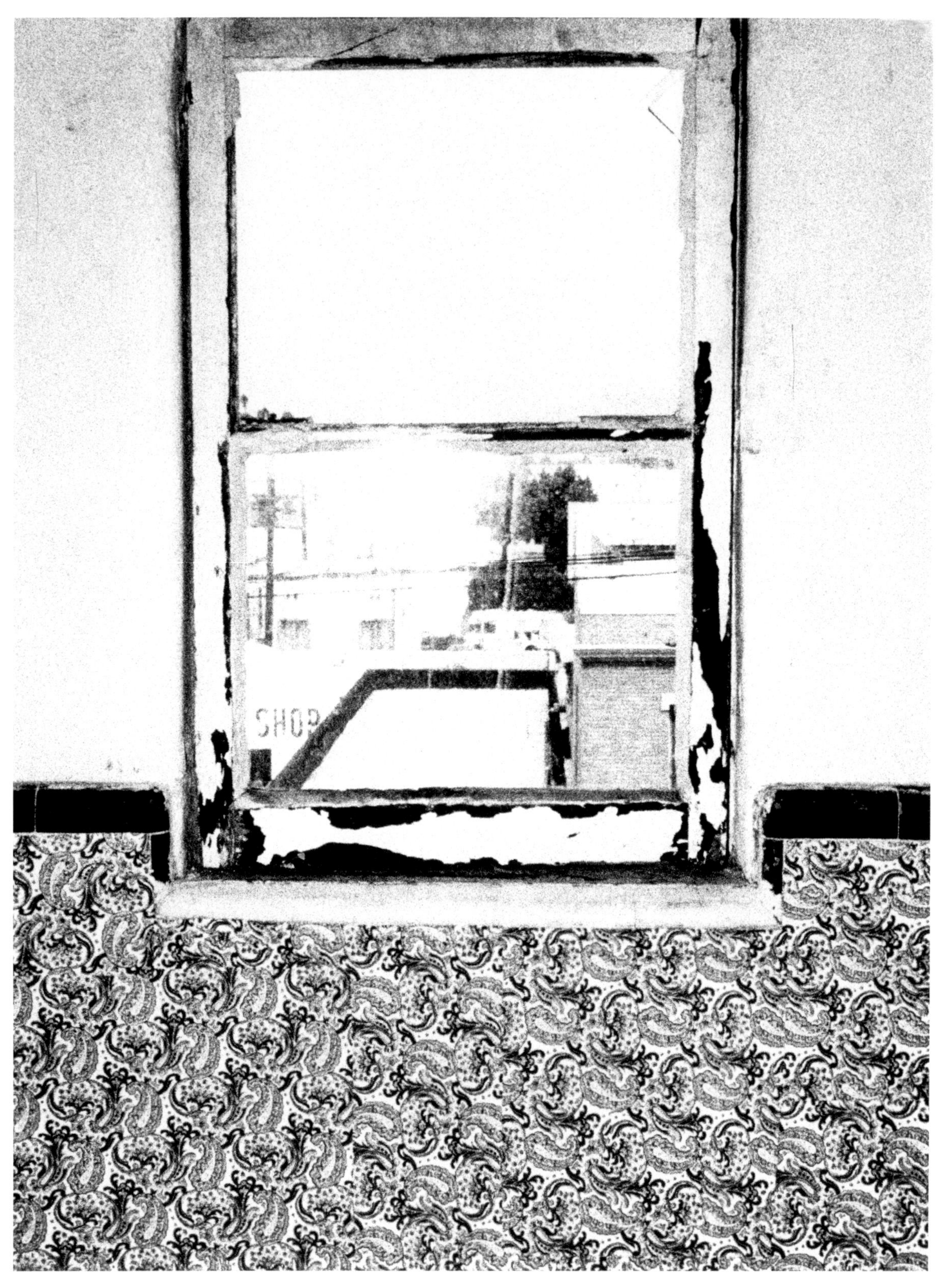

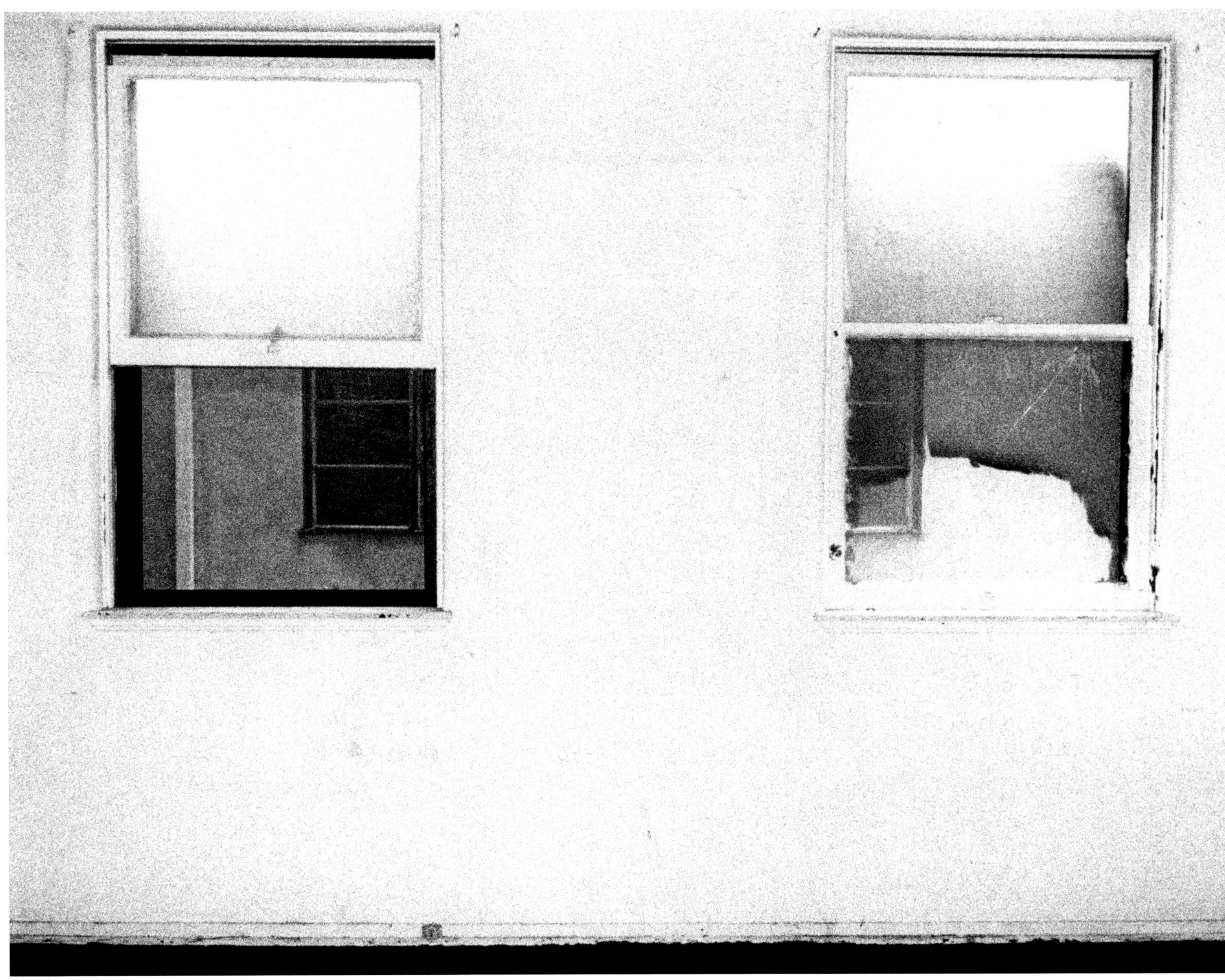

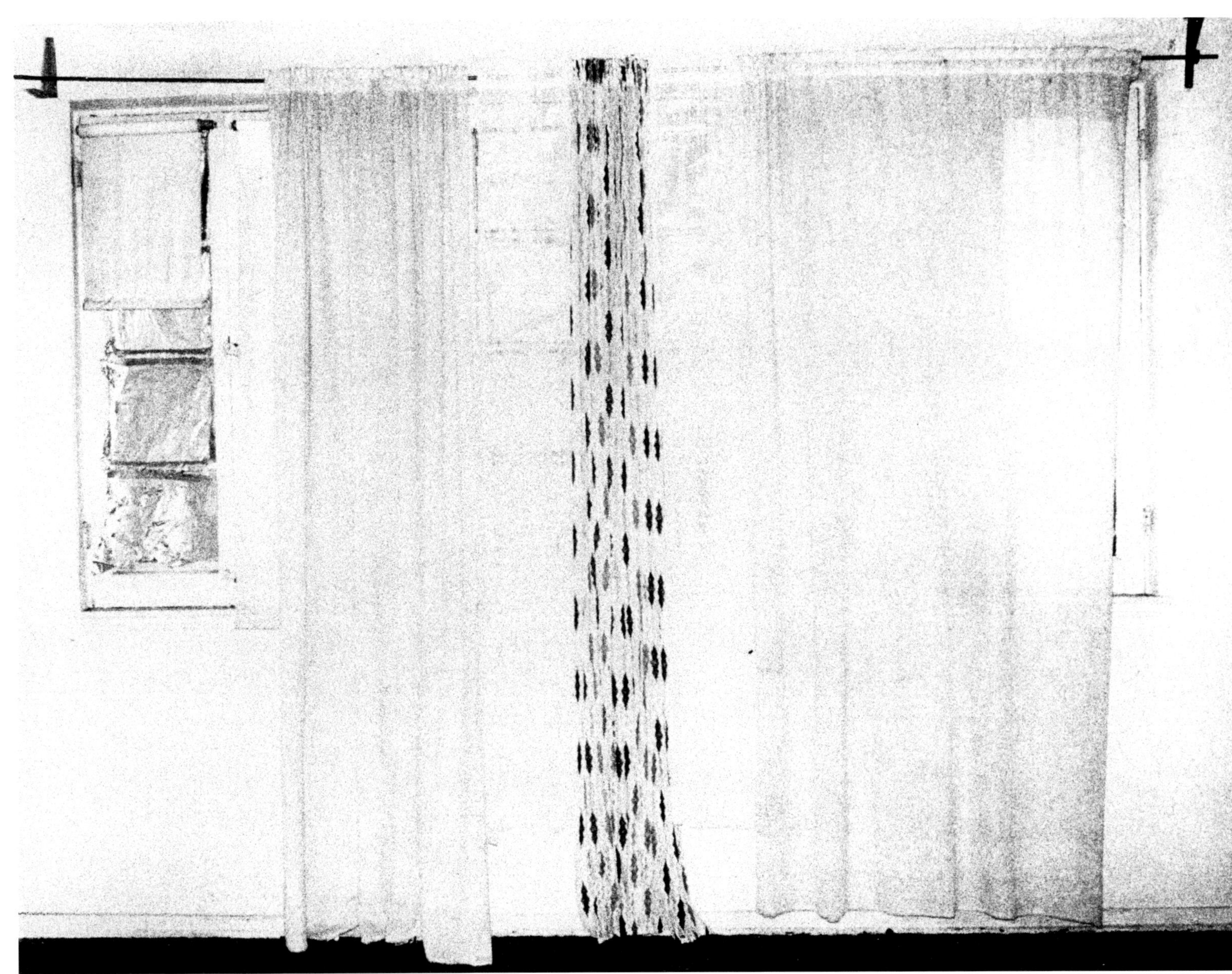

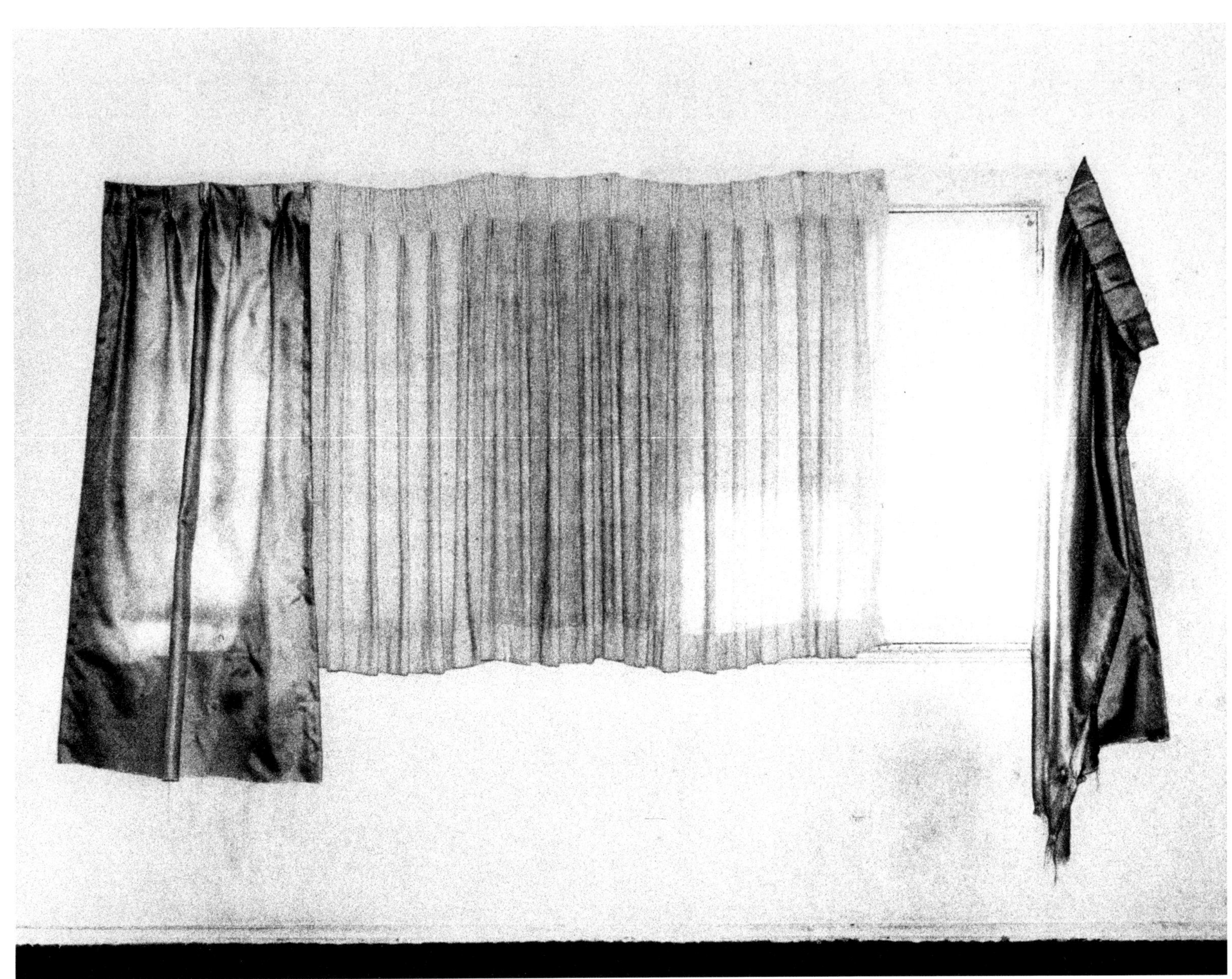

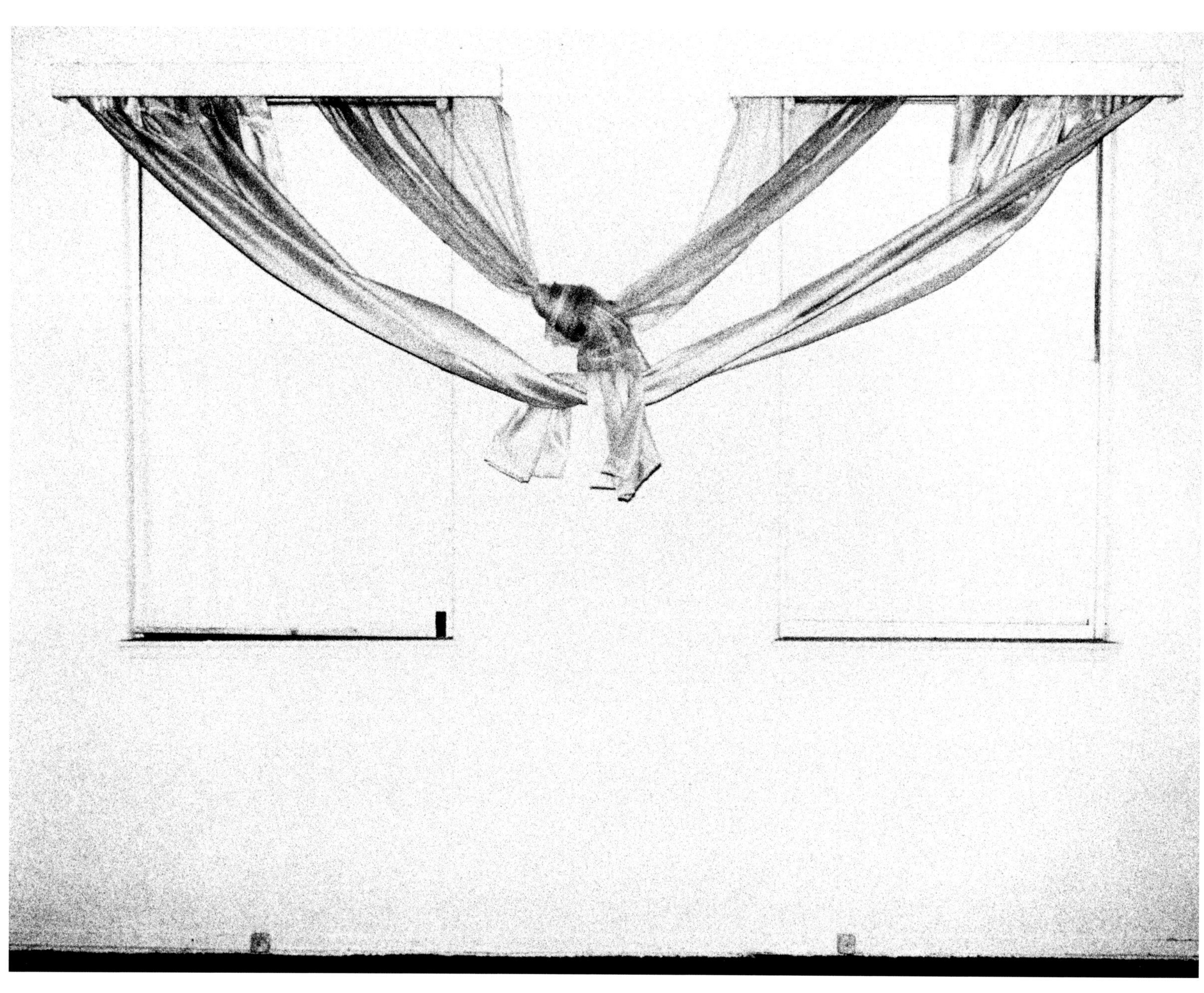

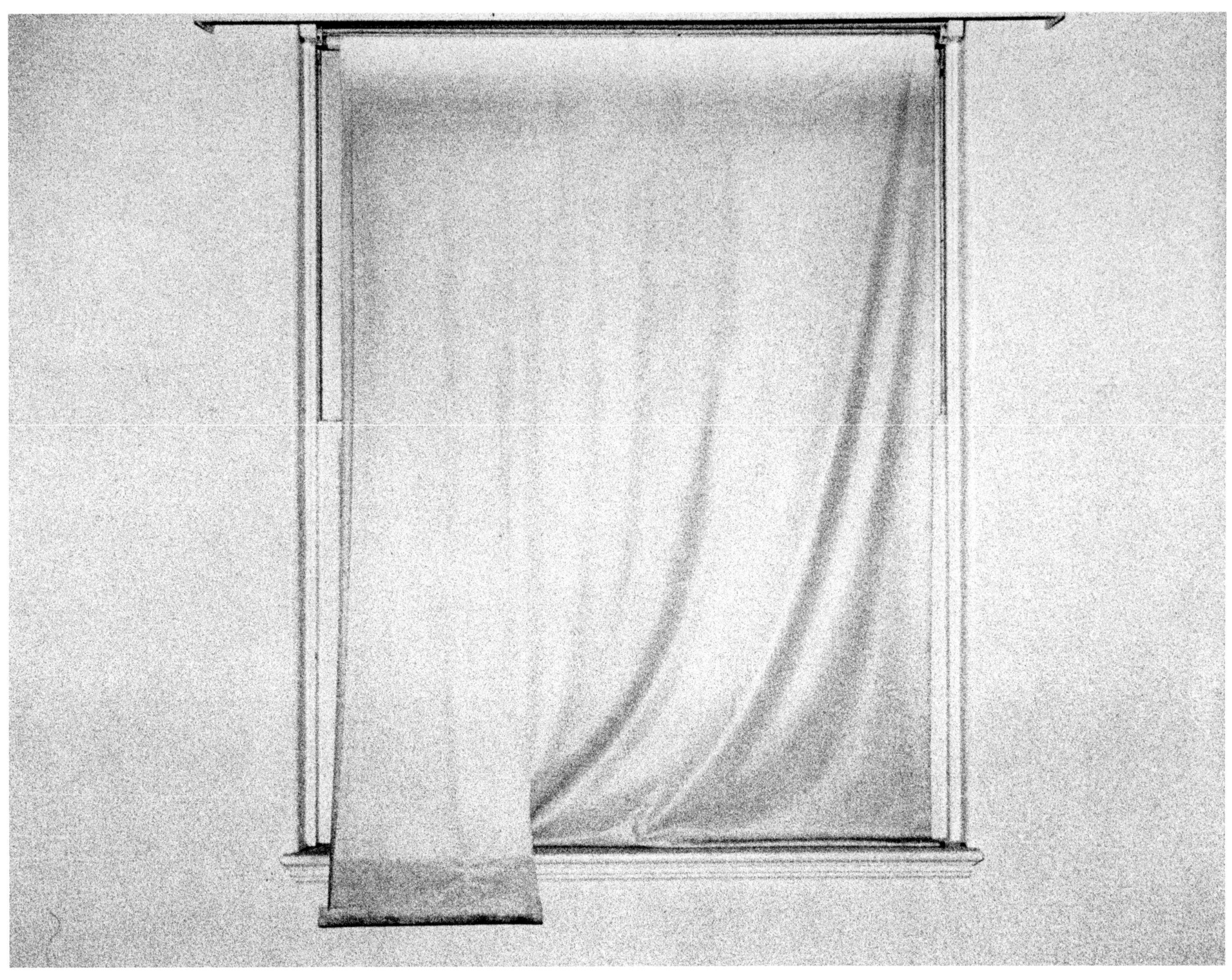

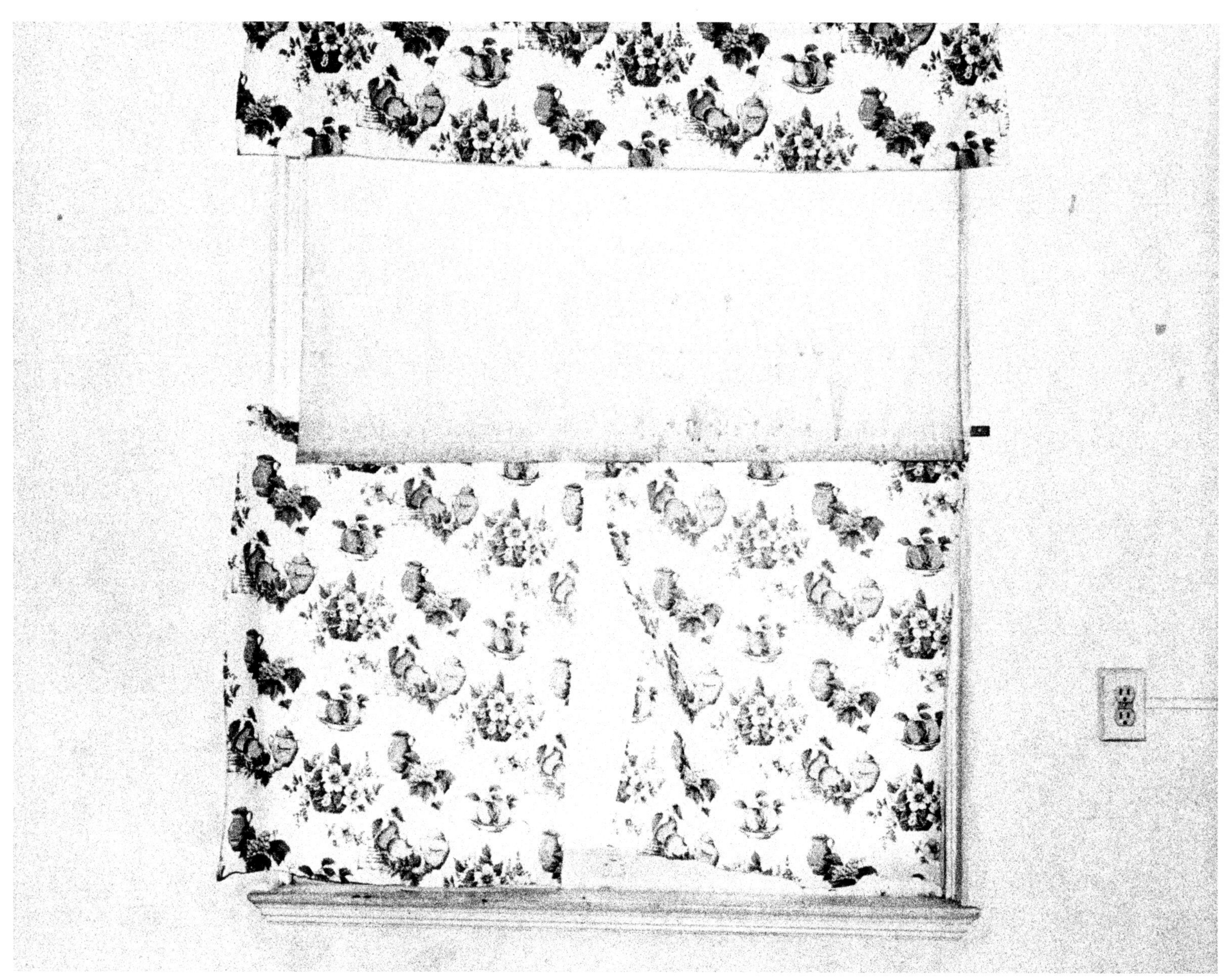

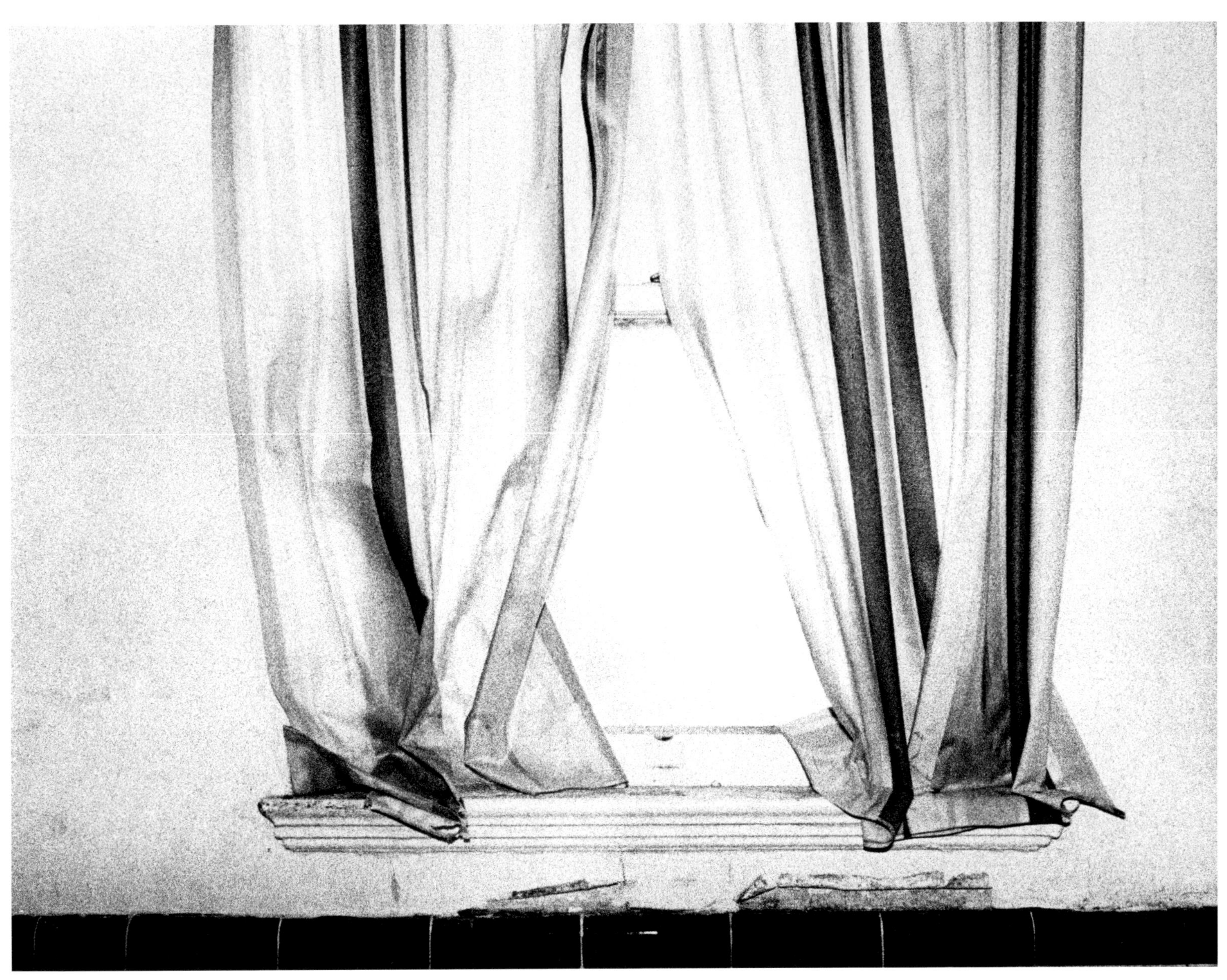

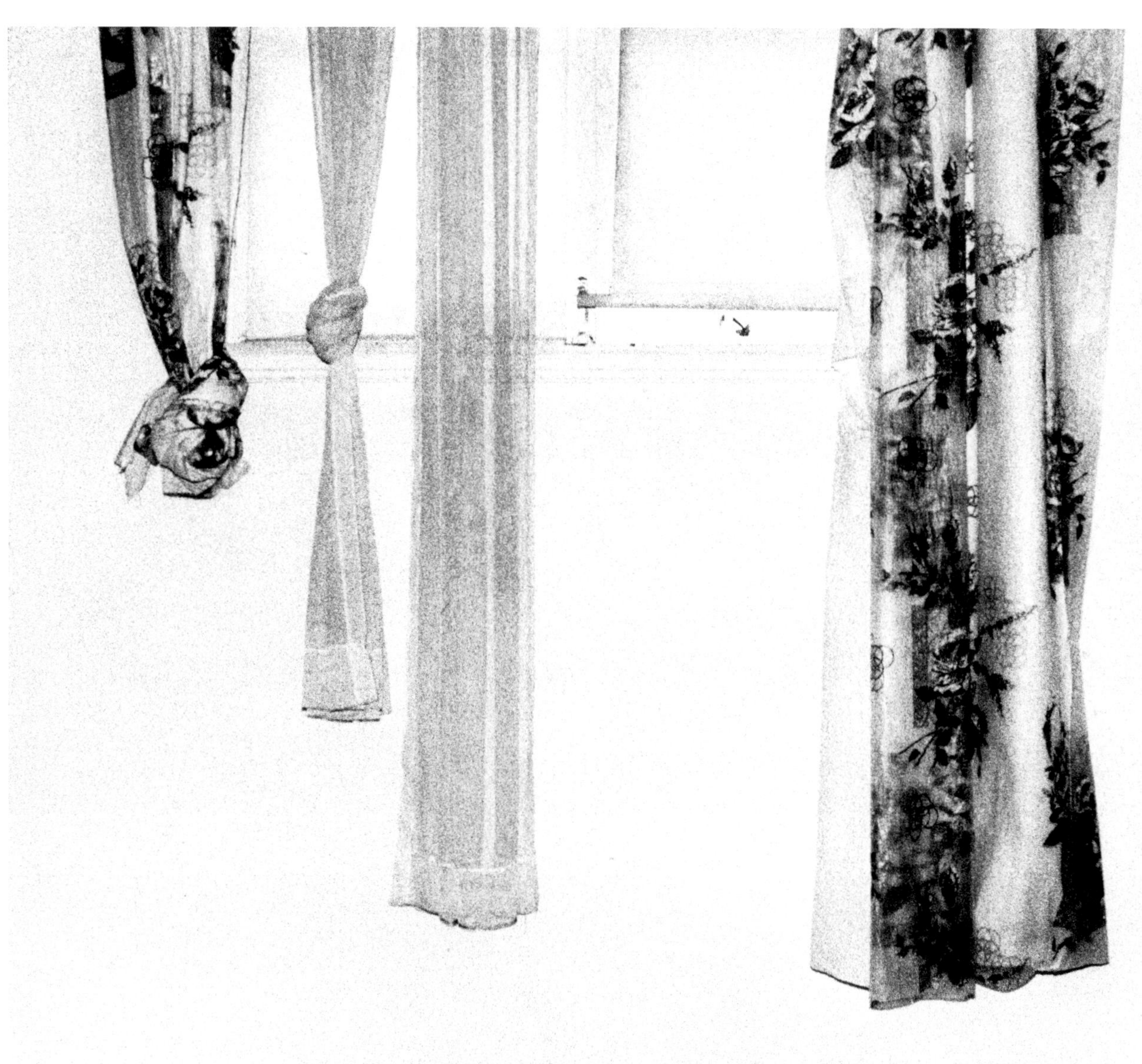

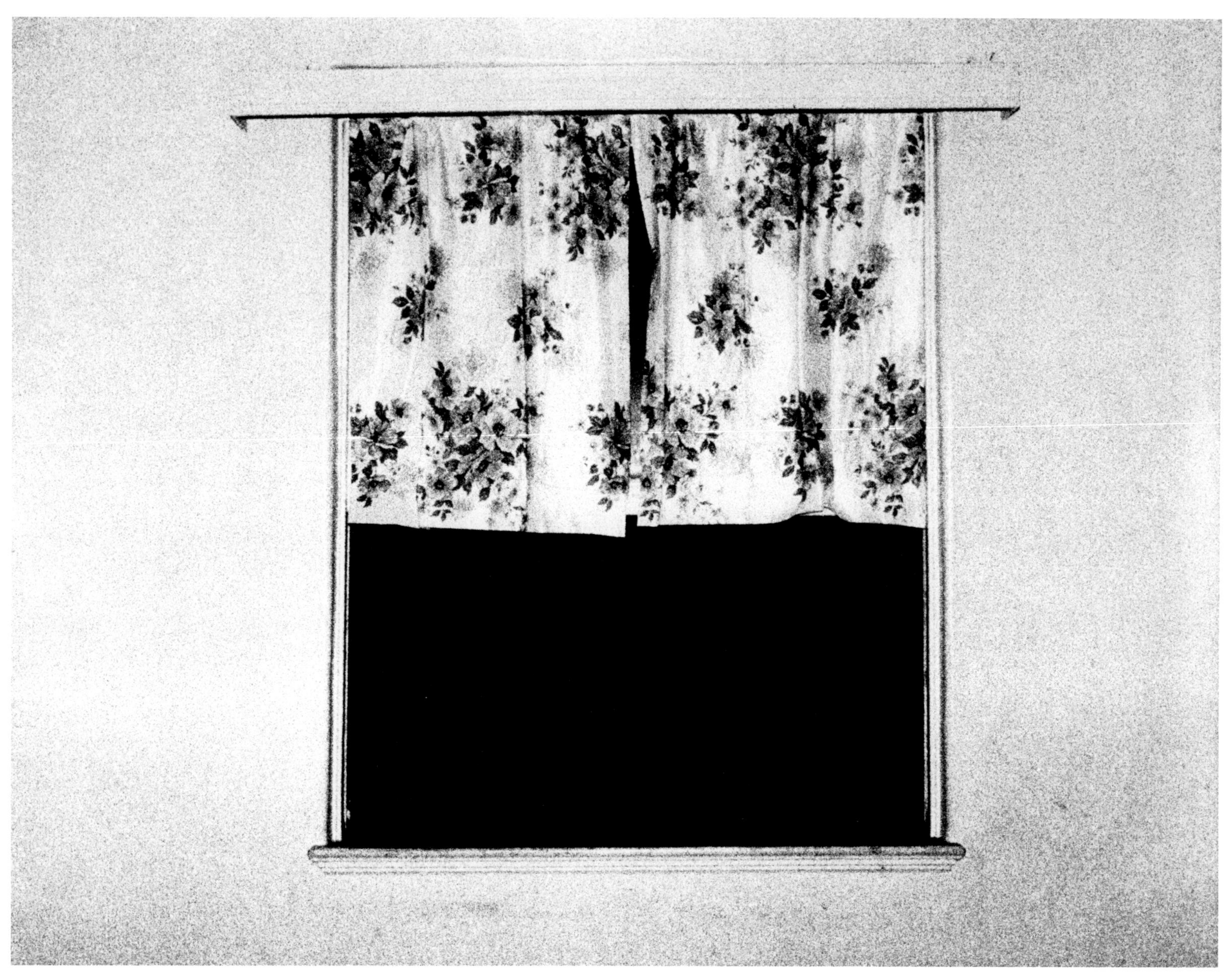

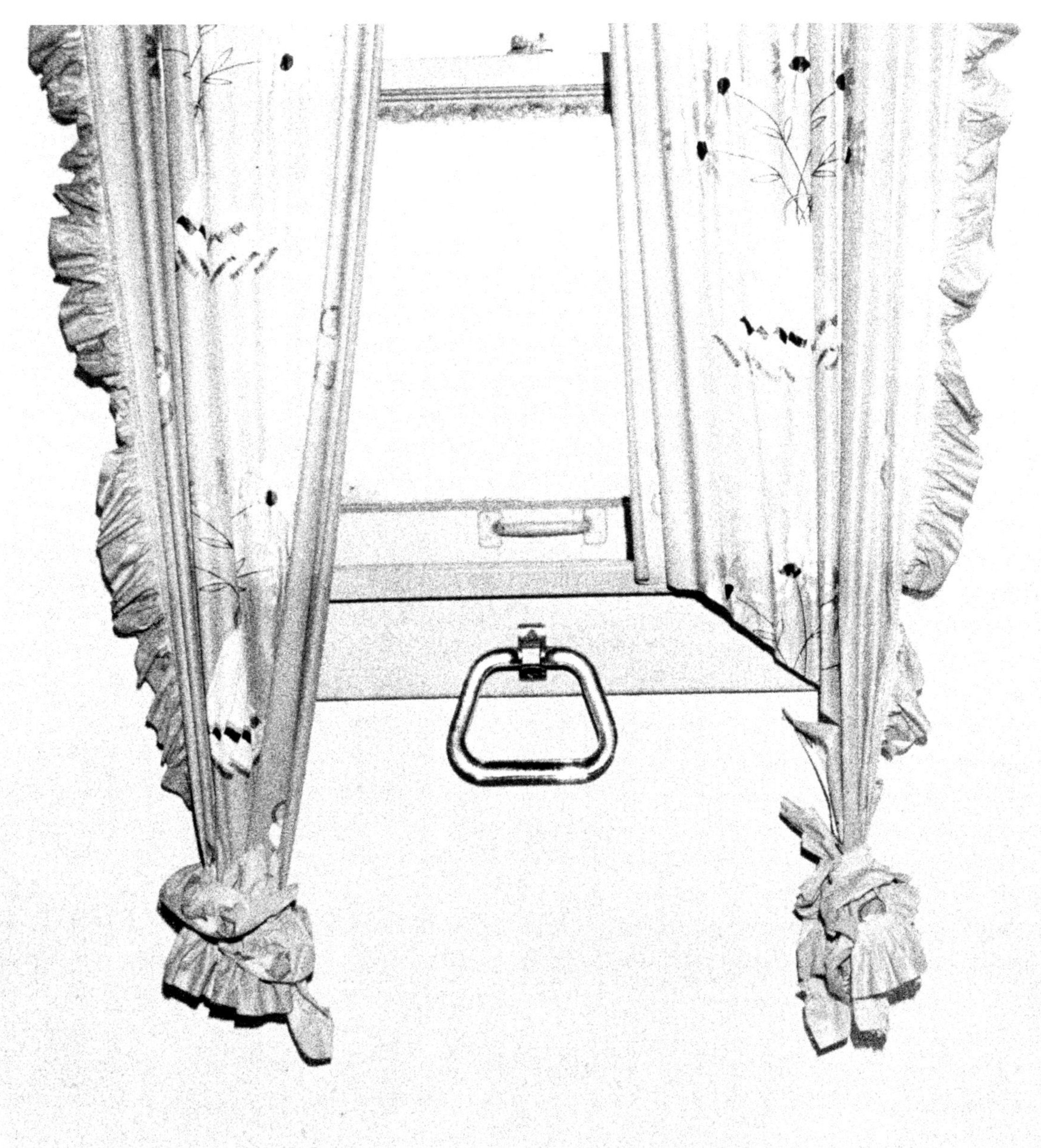

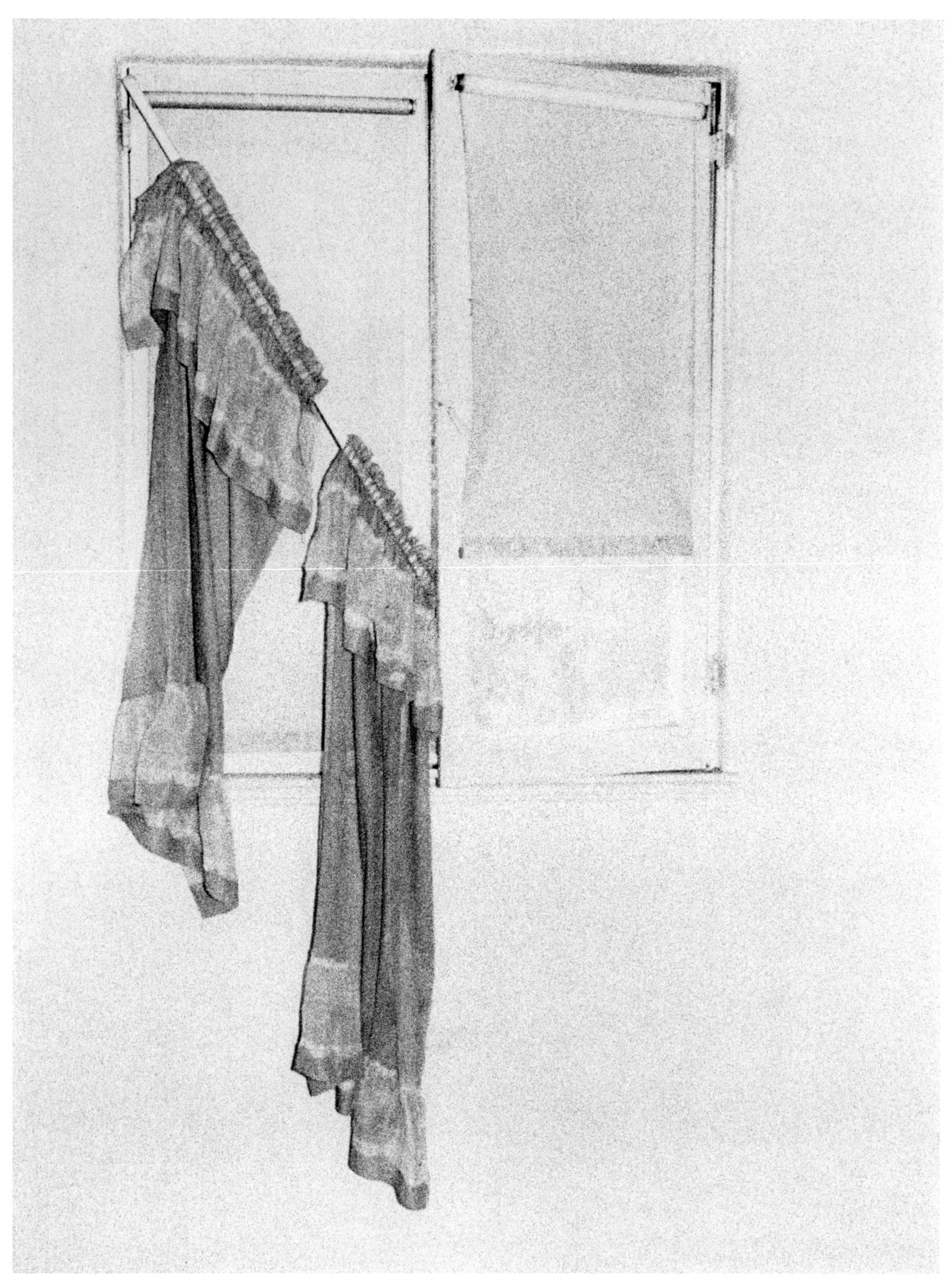

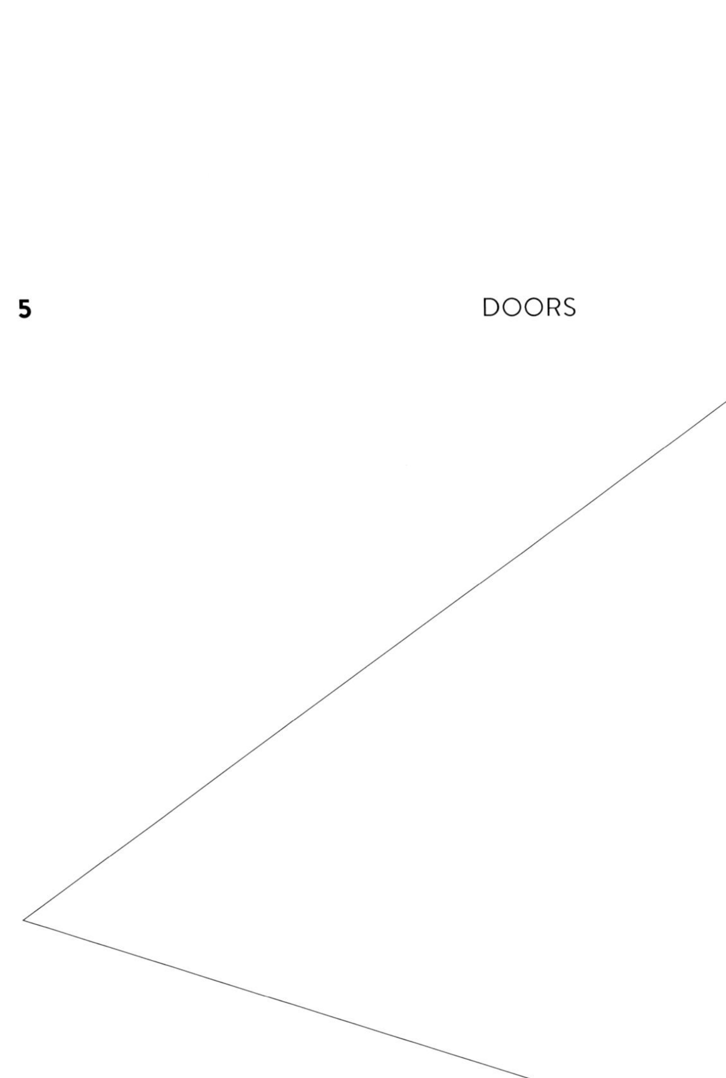

DOORS

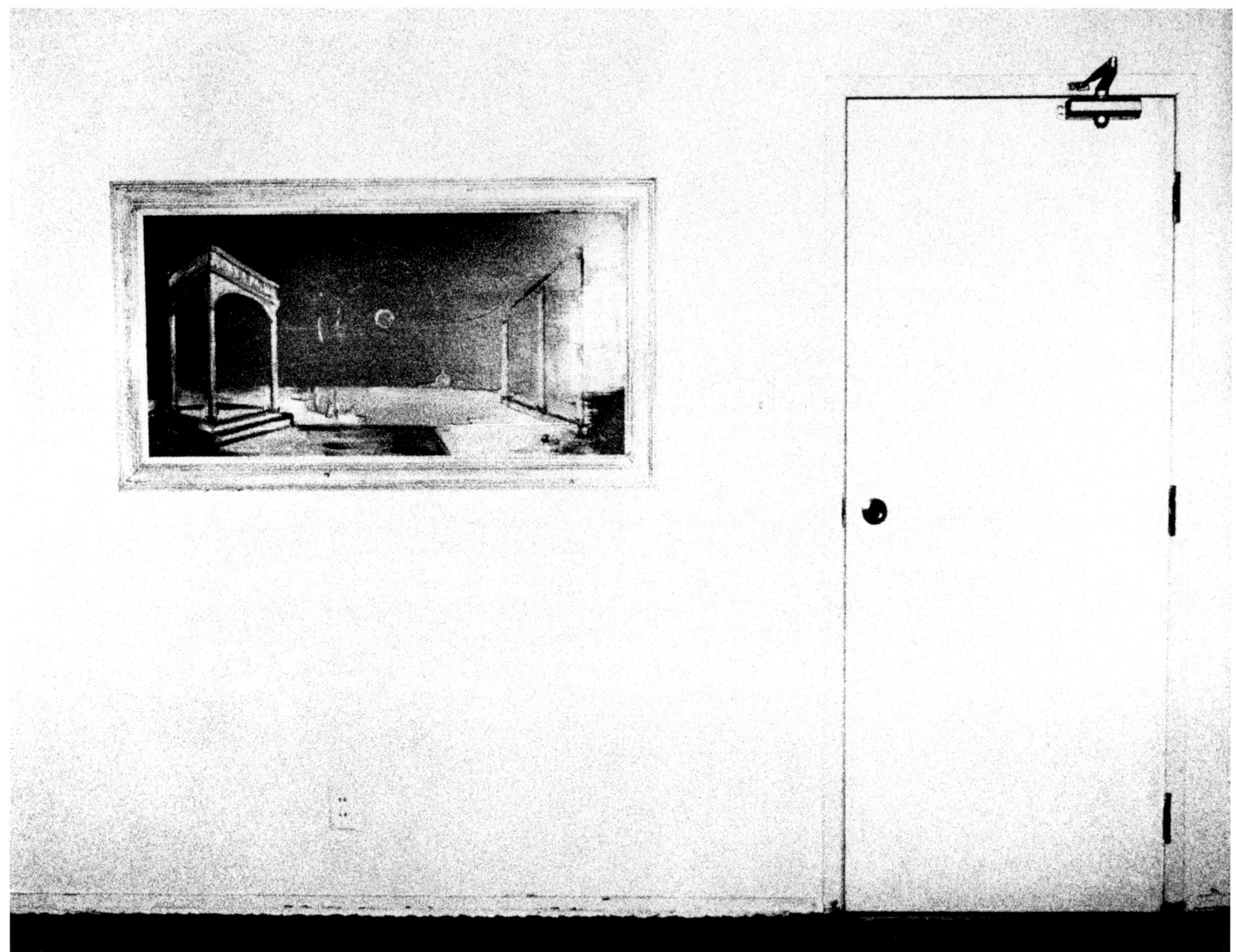

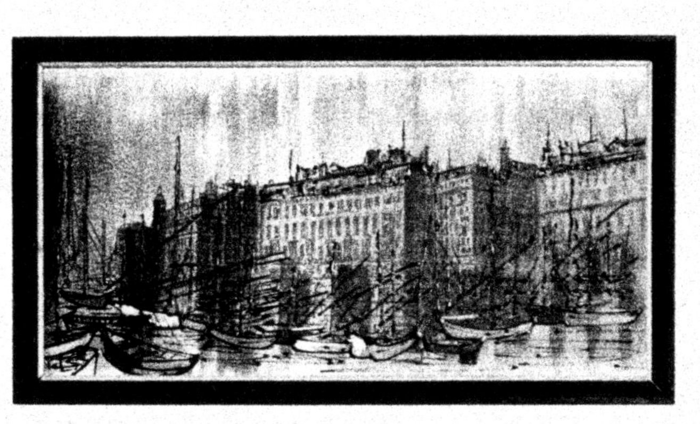

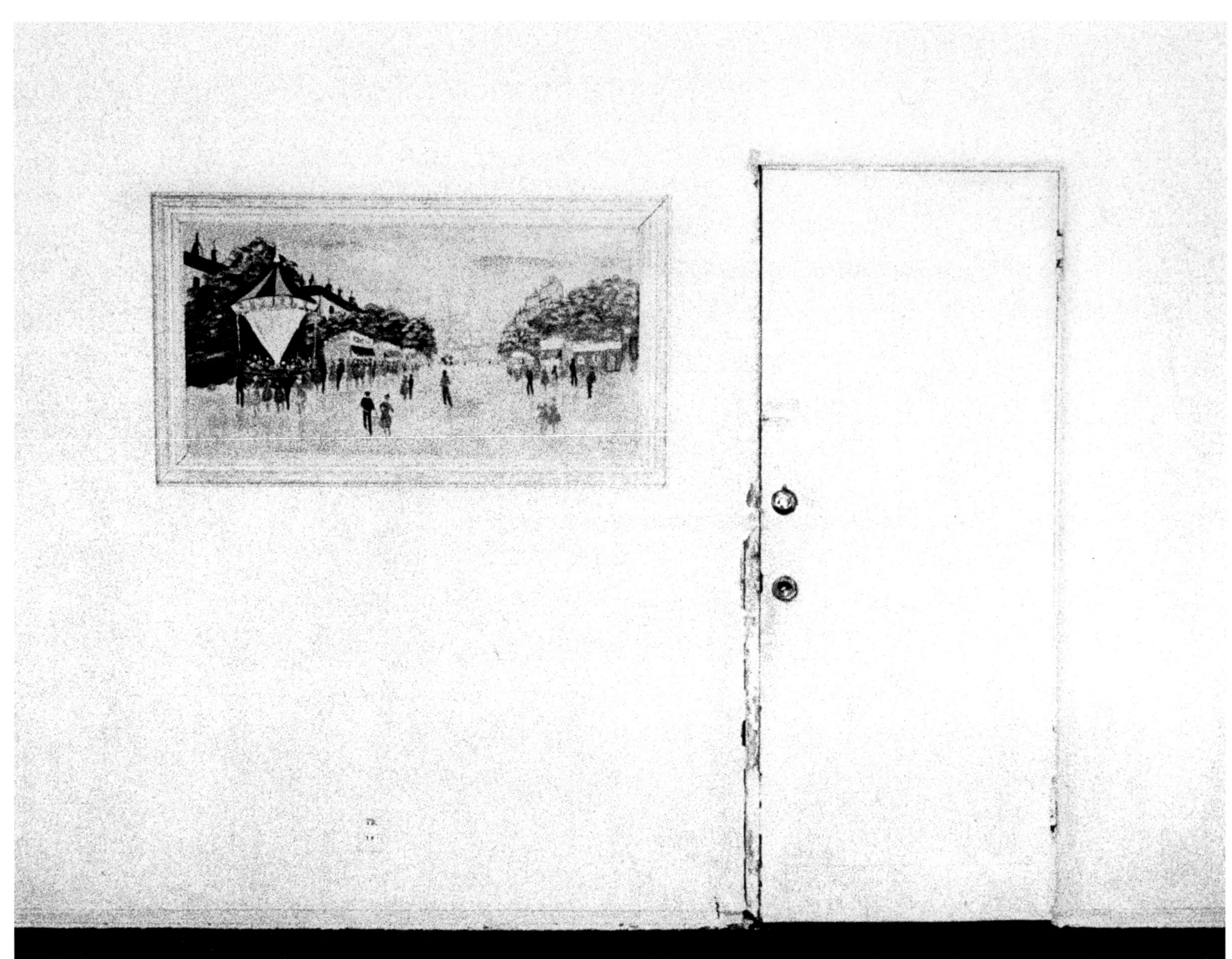

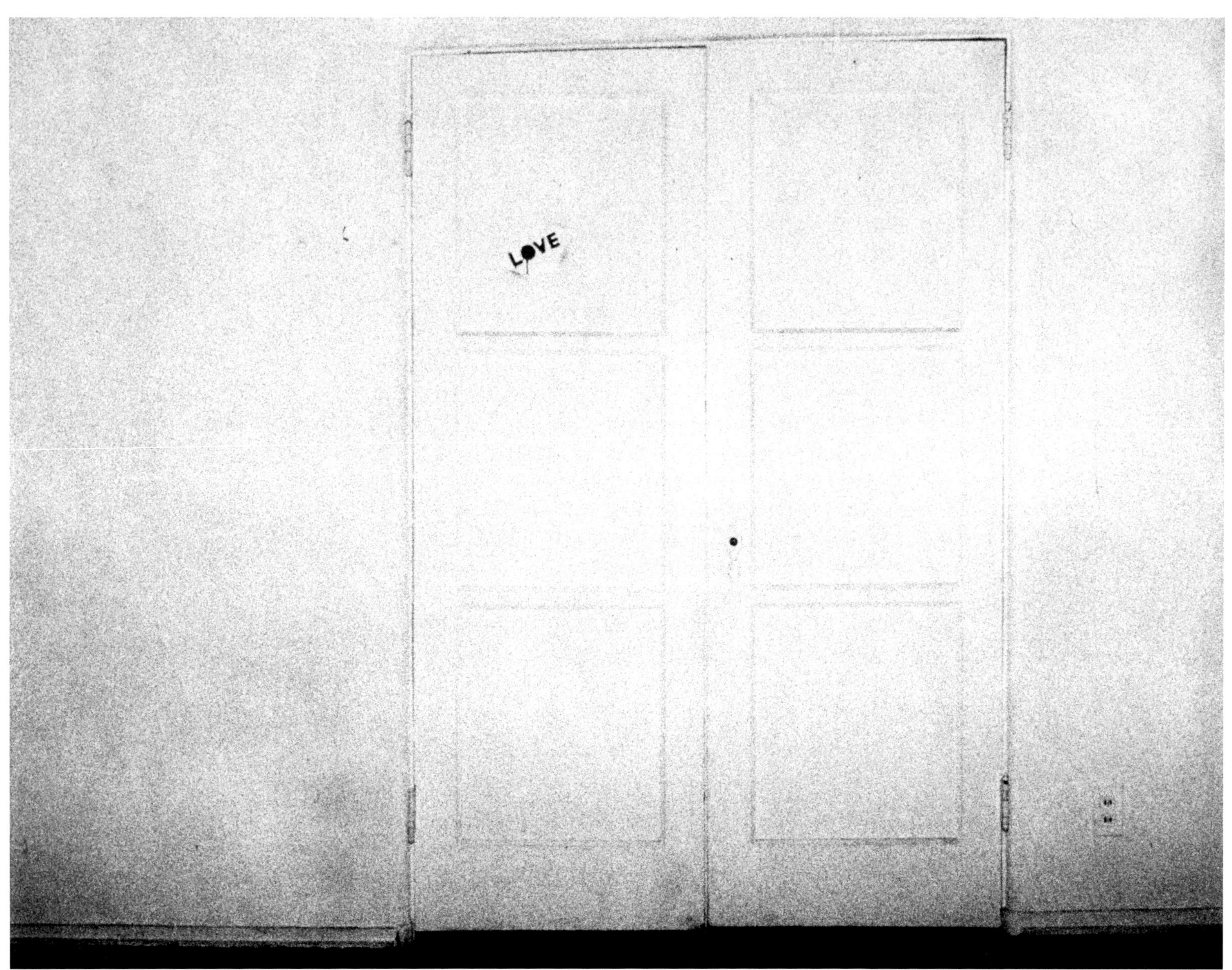
LOVE

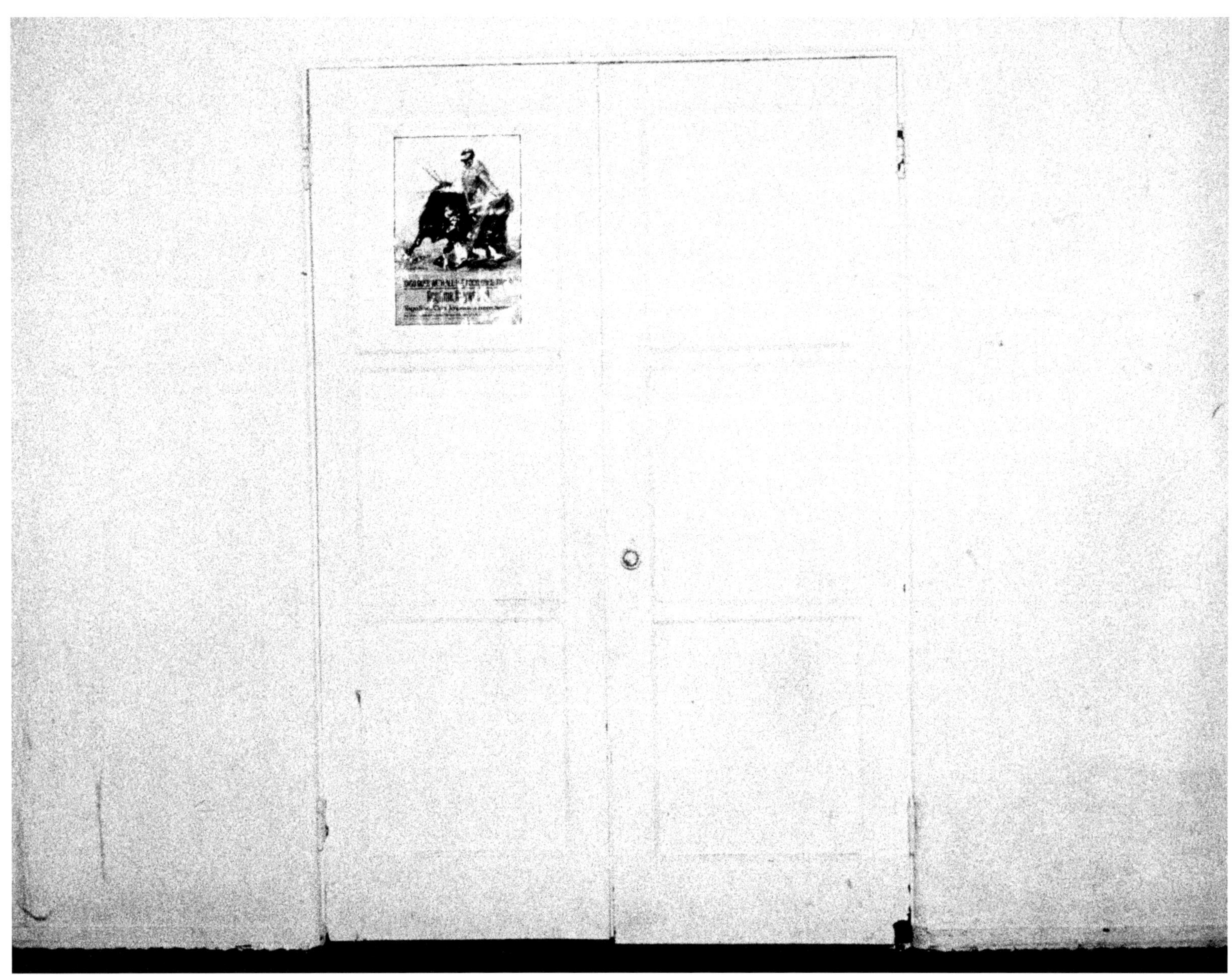

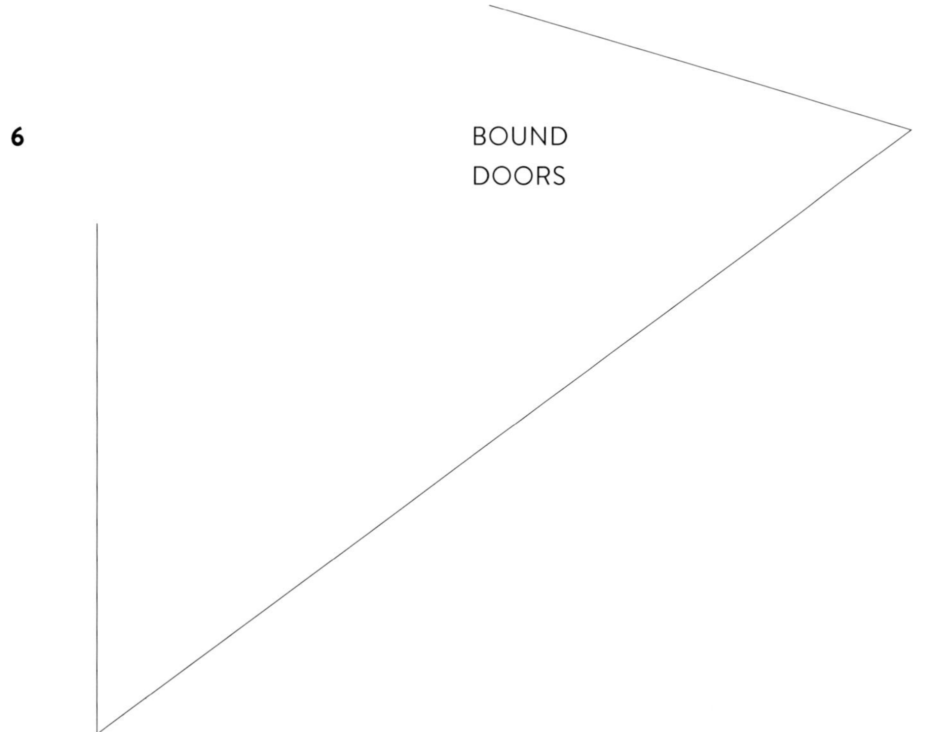

6

BOUND
DOORS

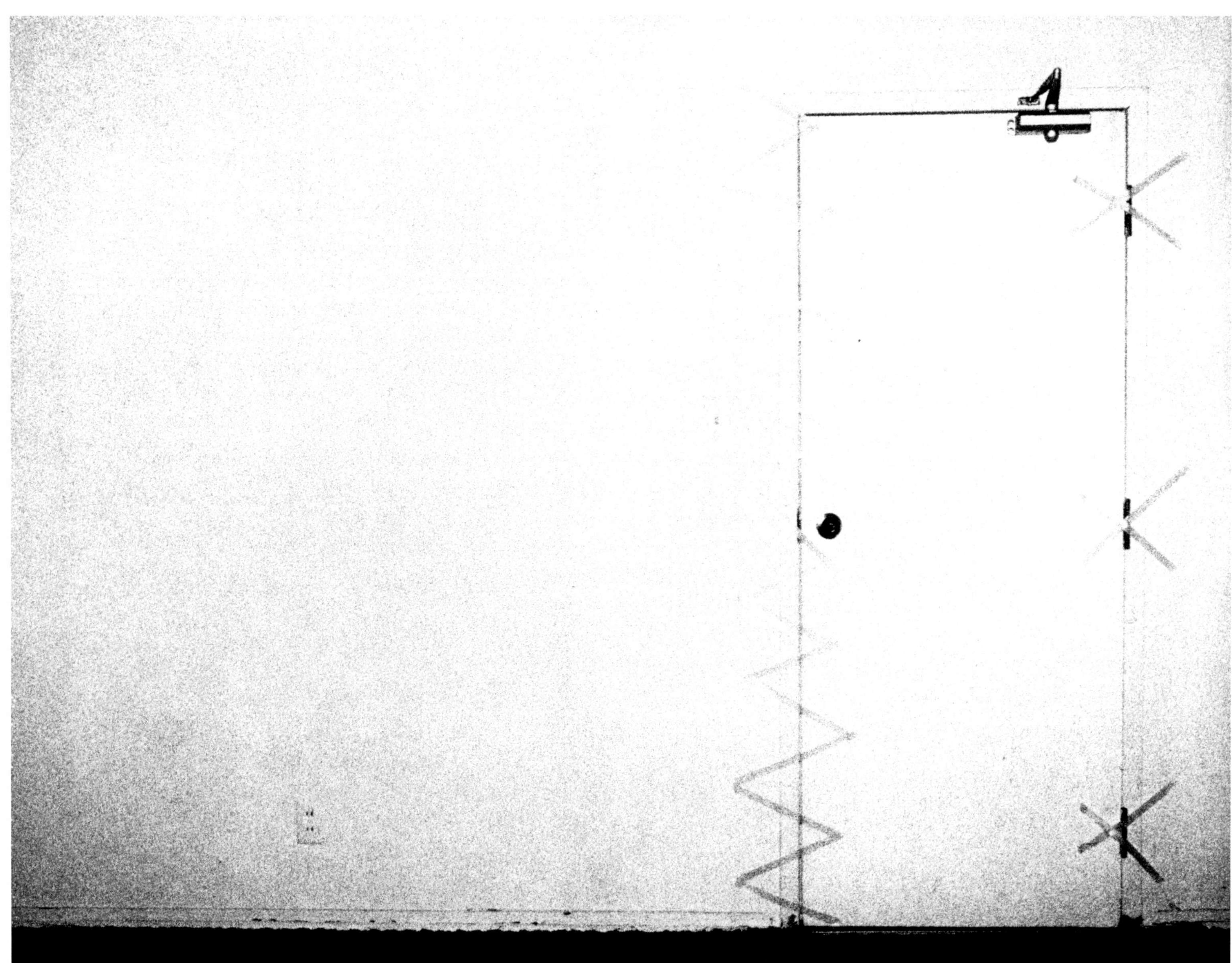

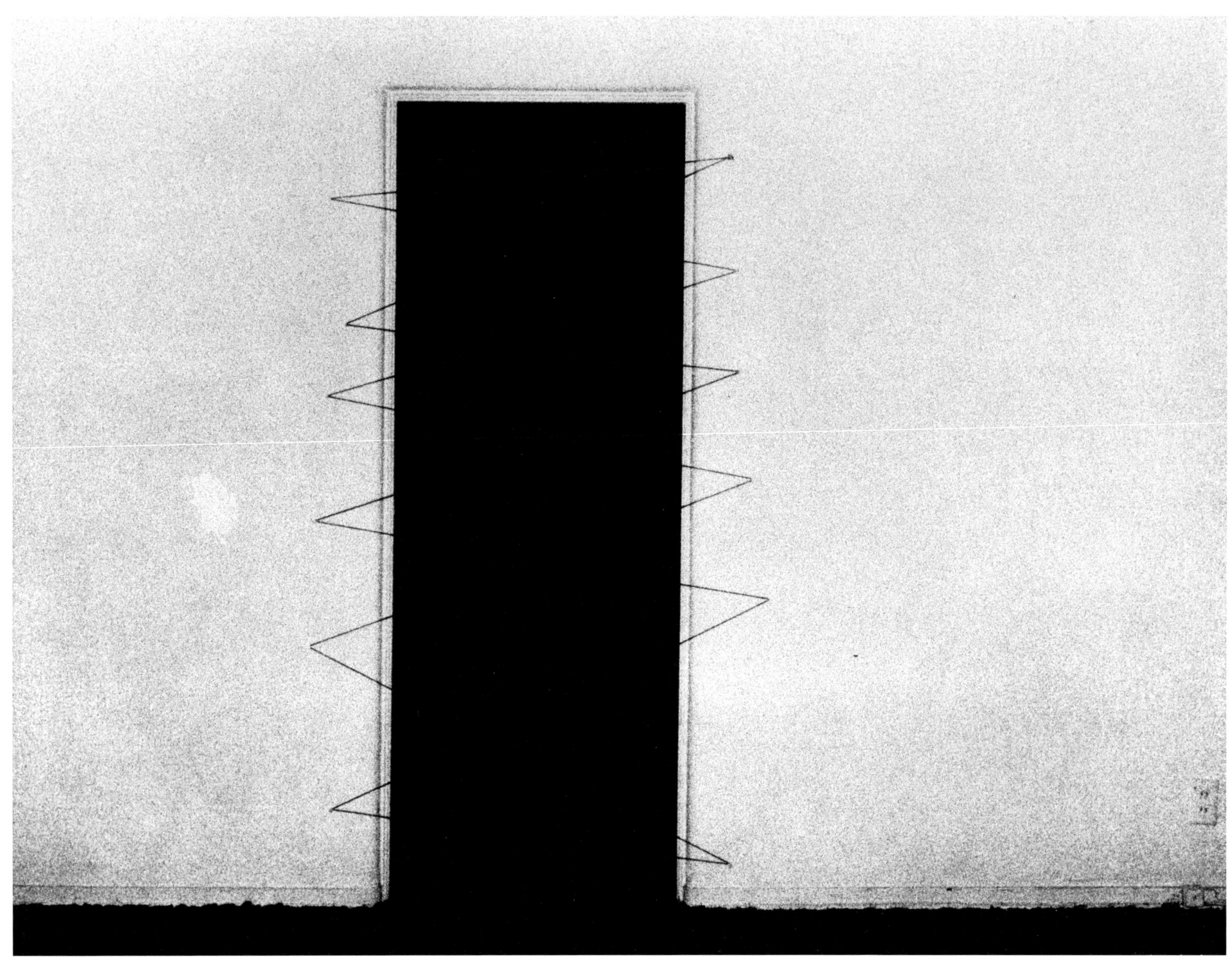

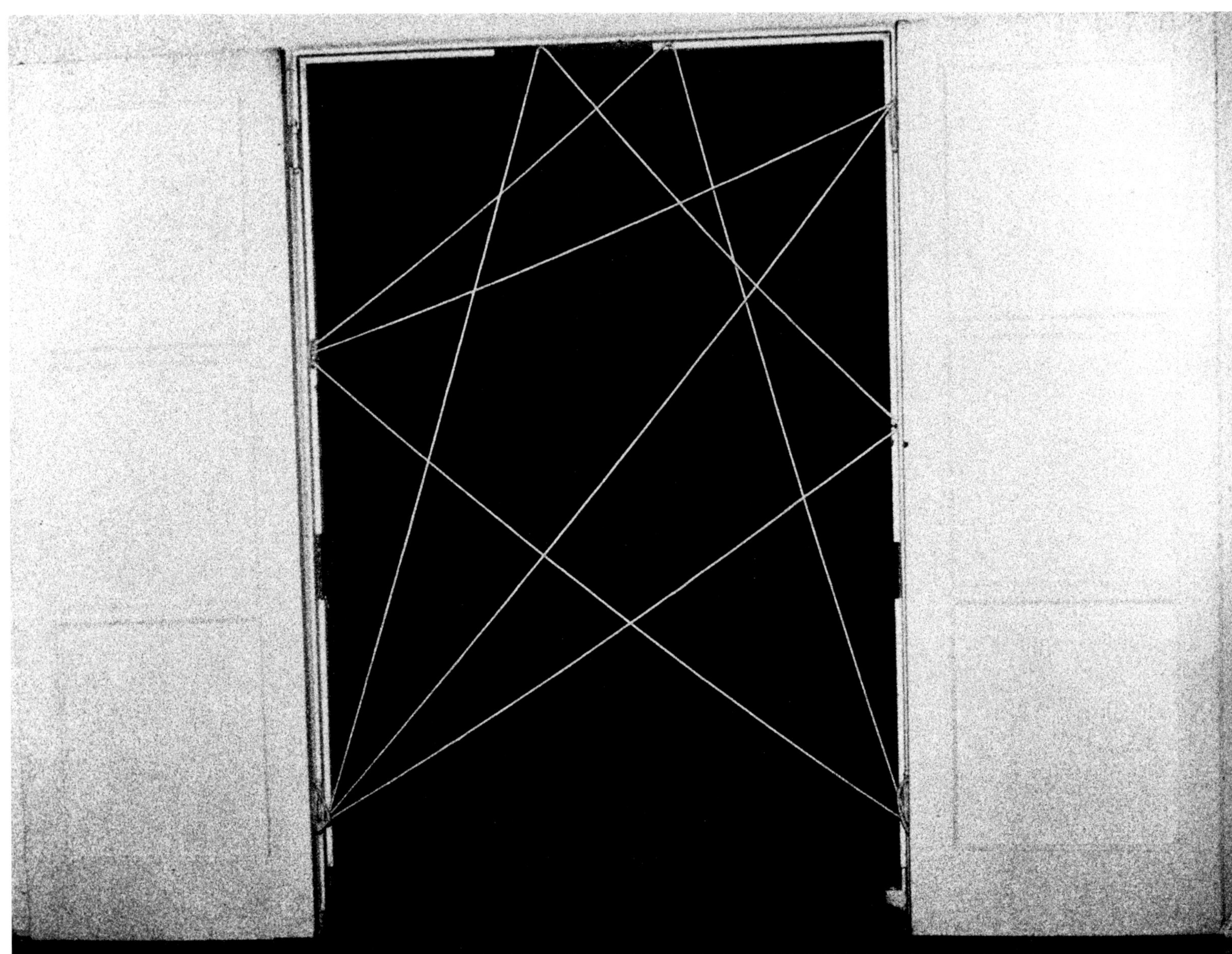

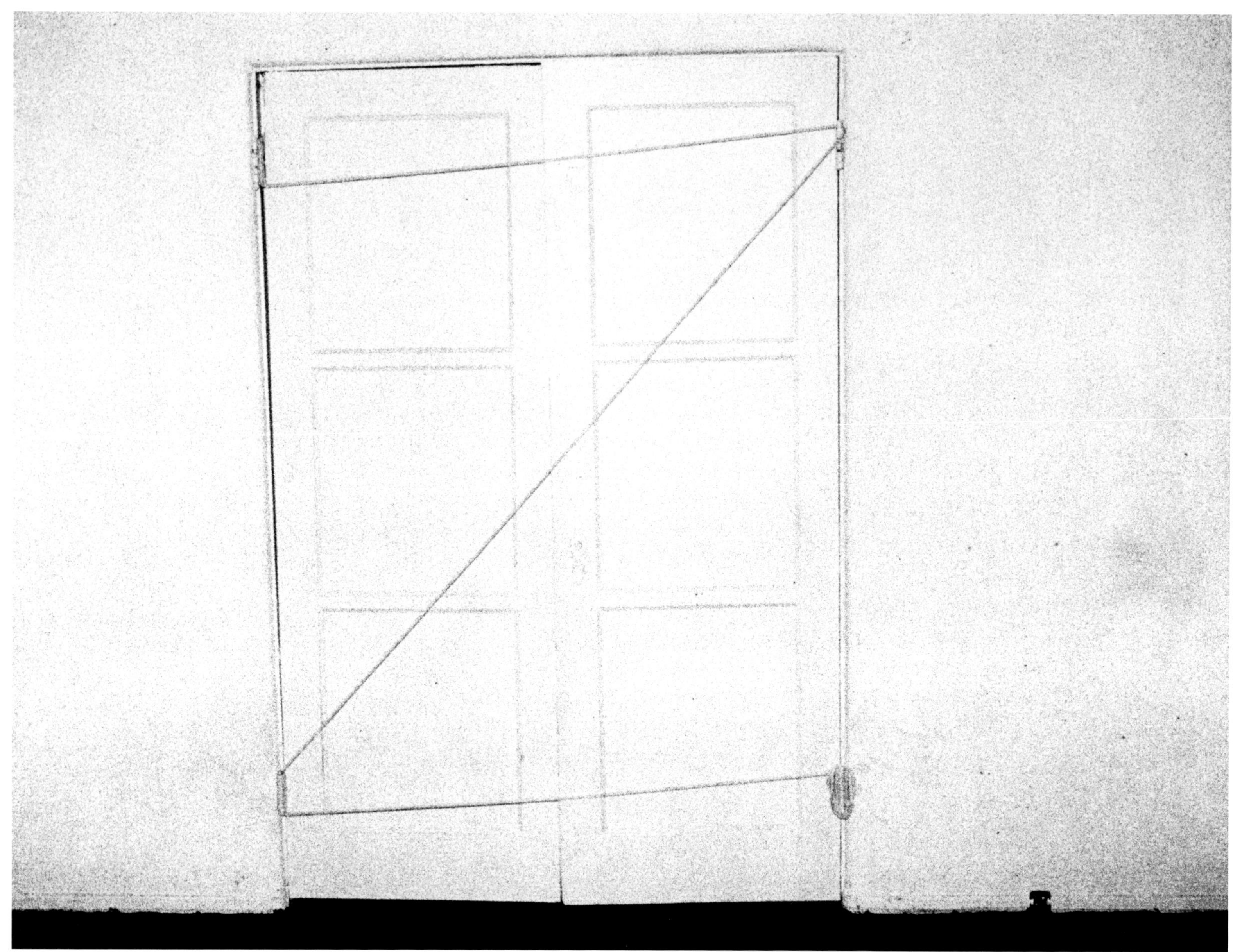

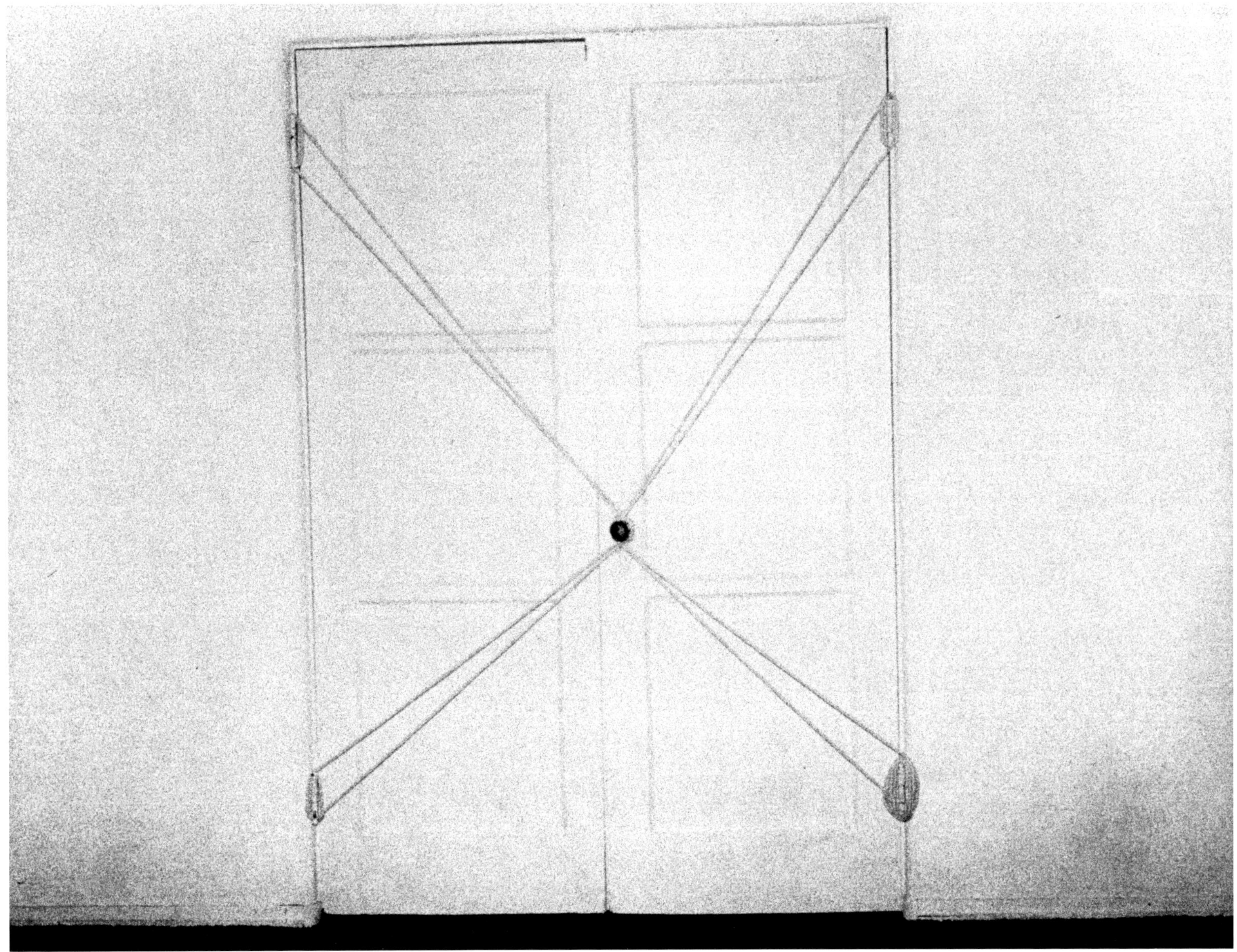

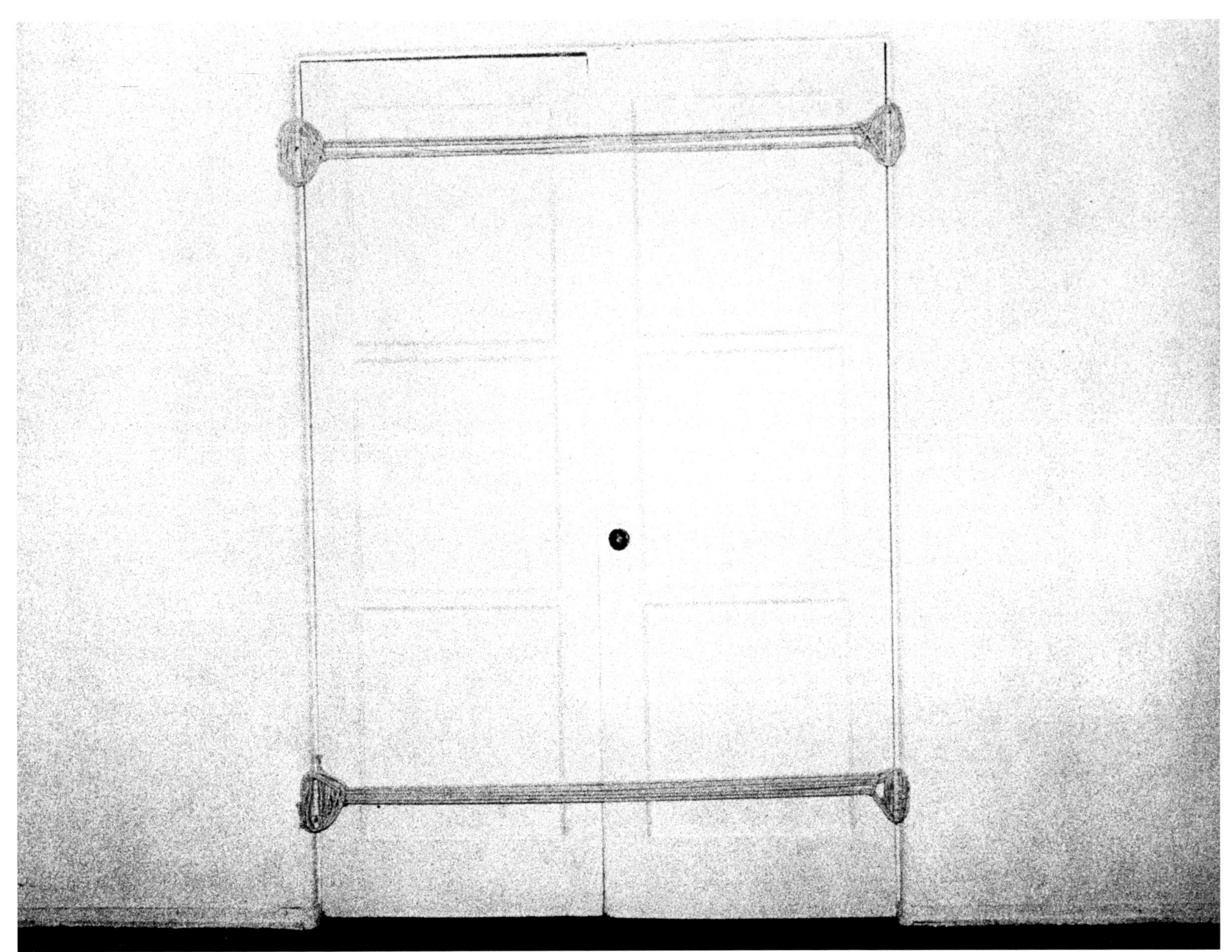

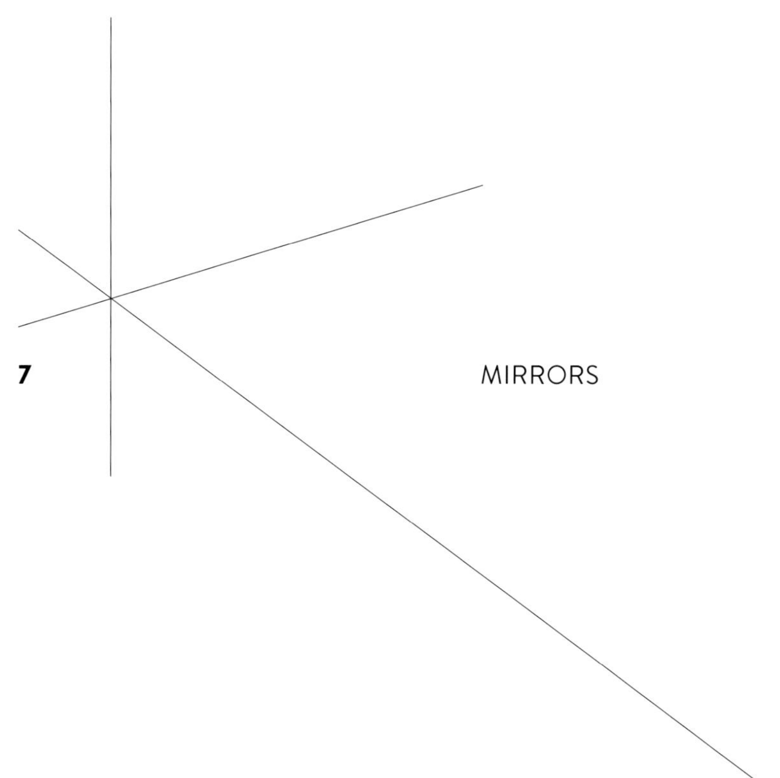

MIRRORS

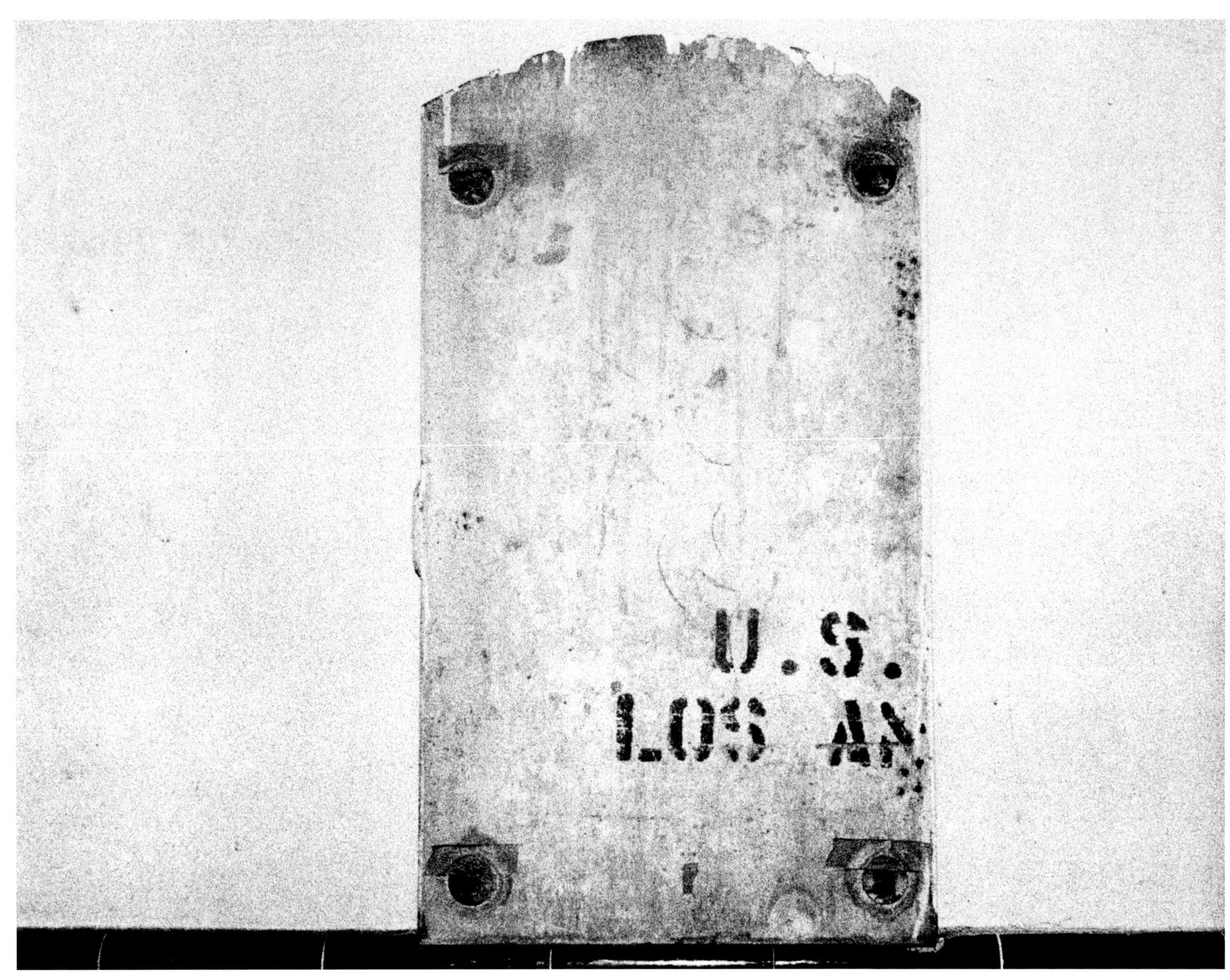
U.S.
LOS AN

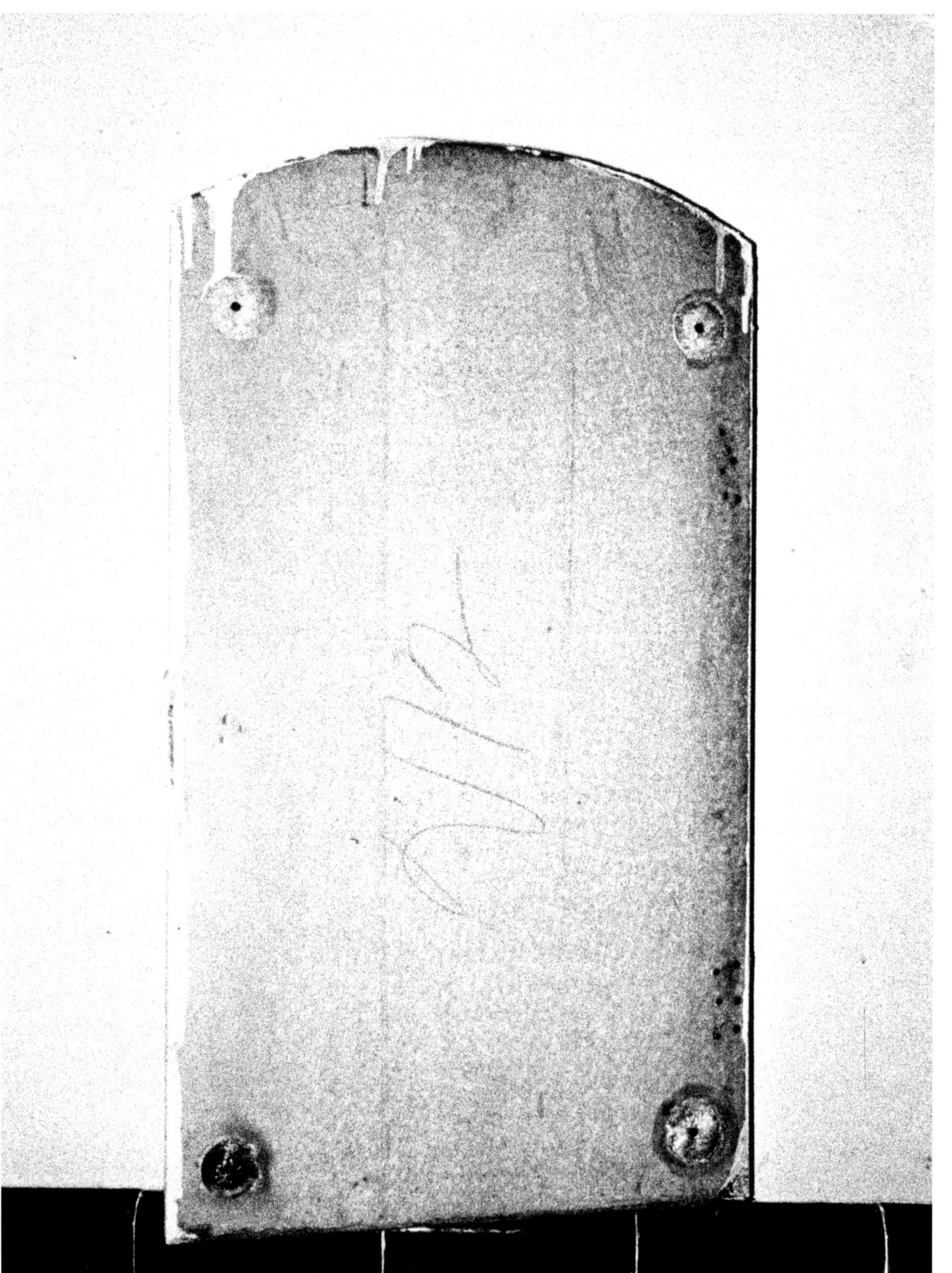

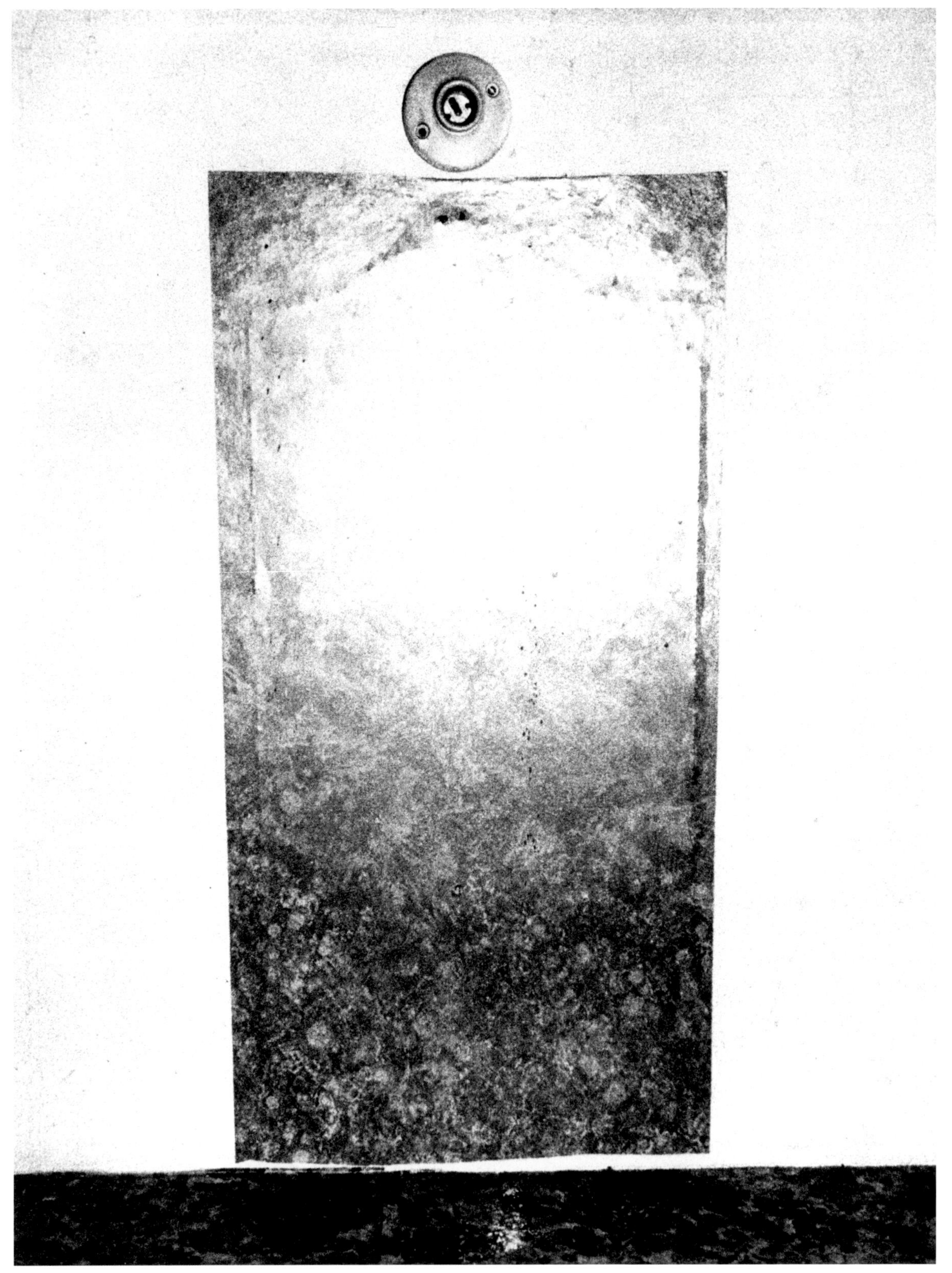

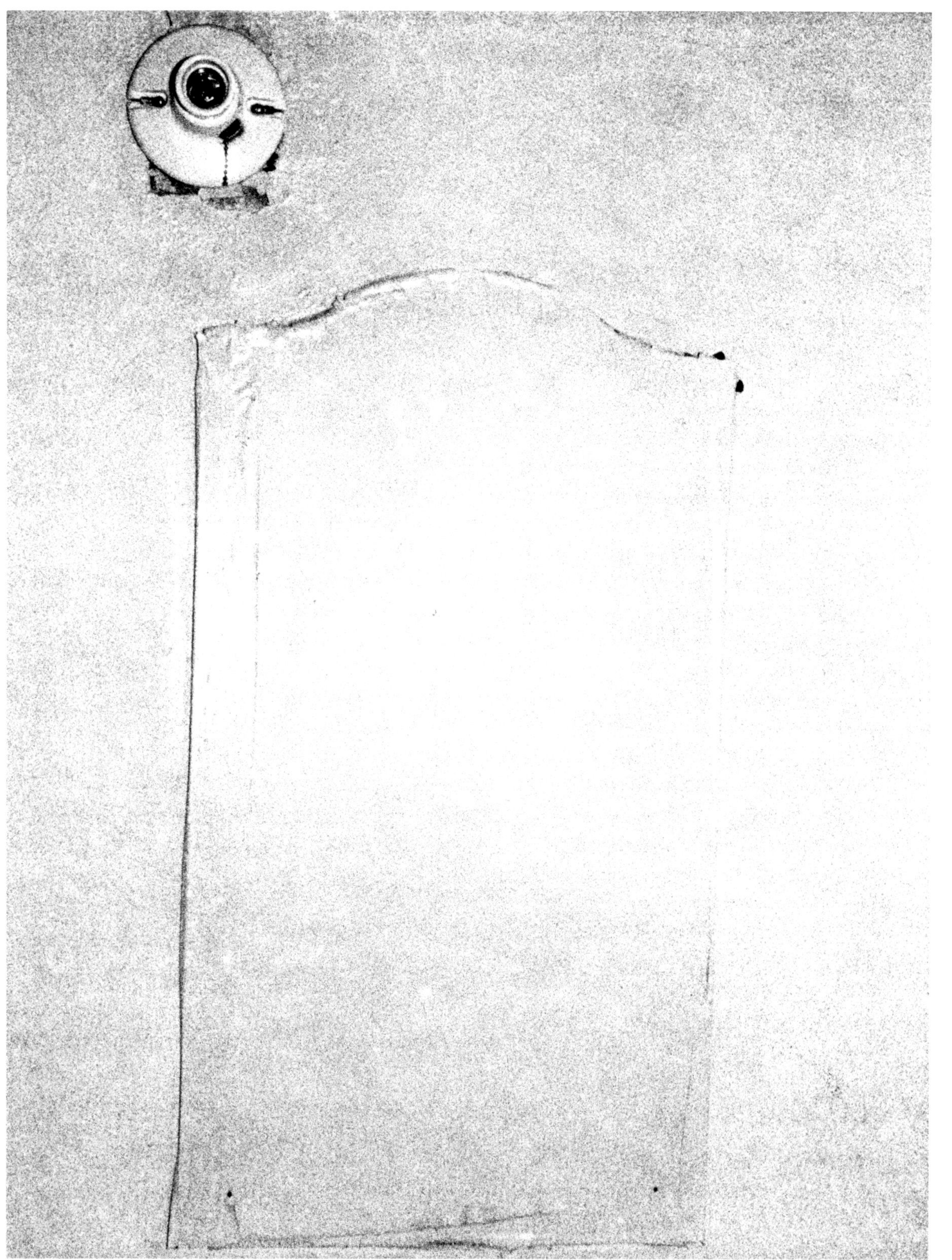

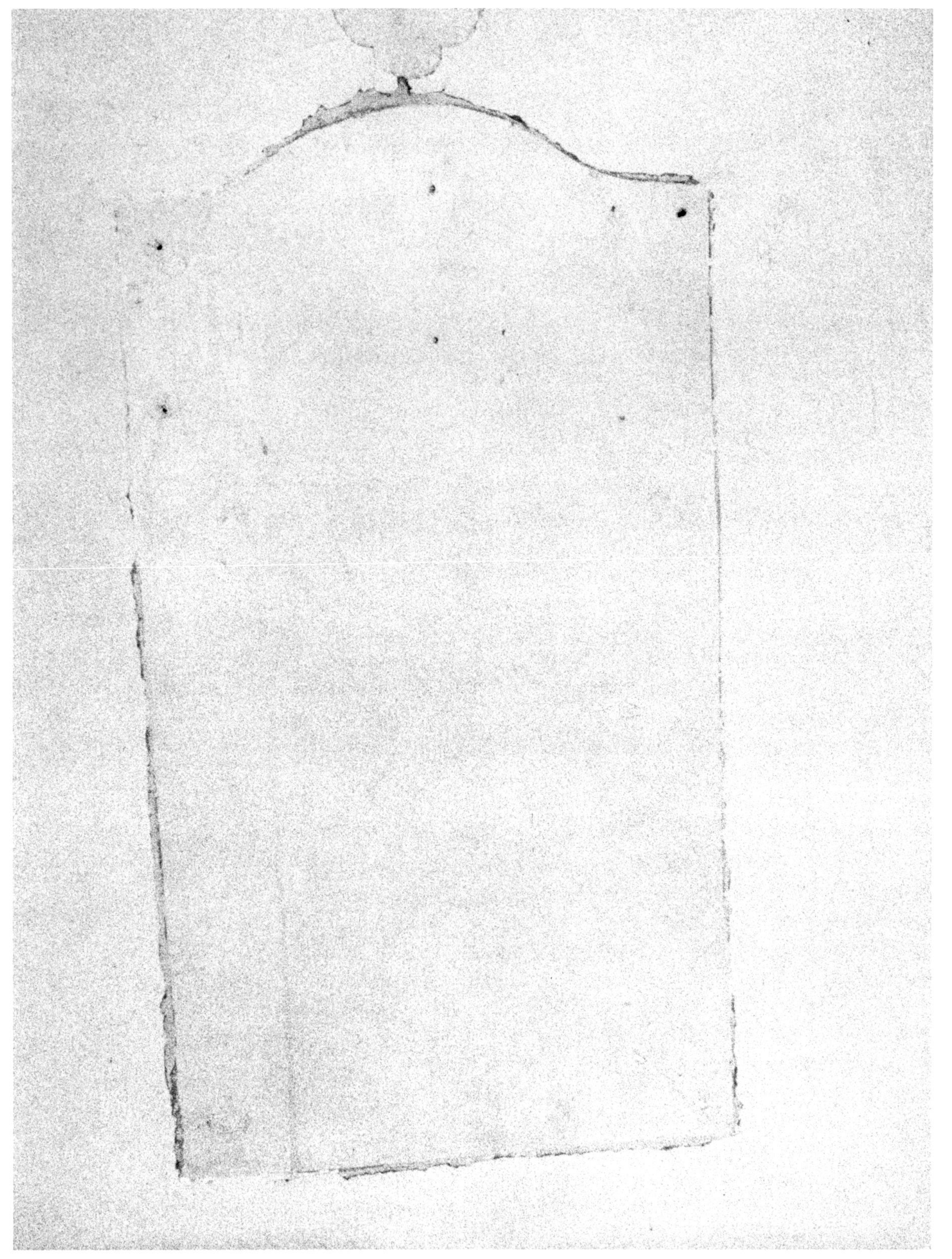

8 MULTIPART PHOTOGRAPHS

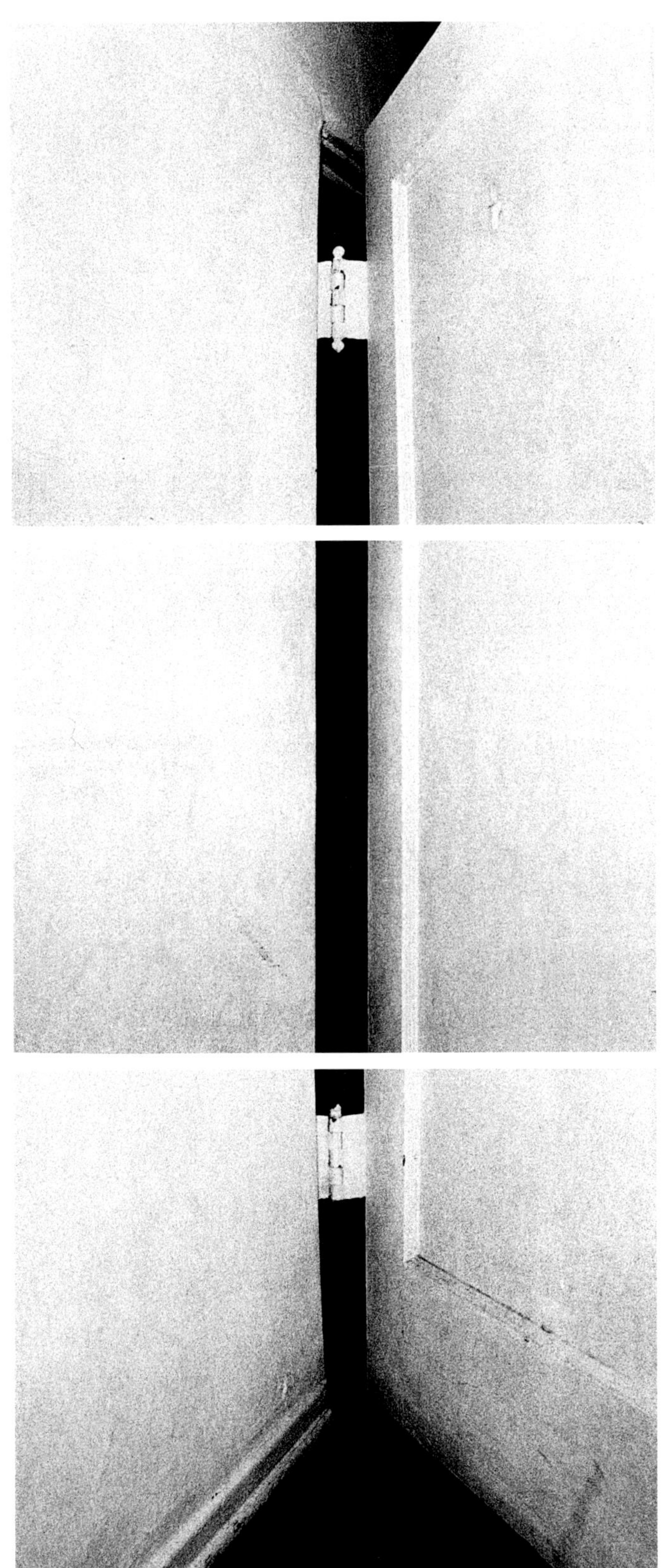

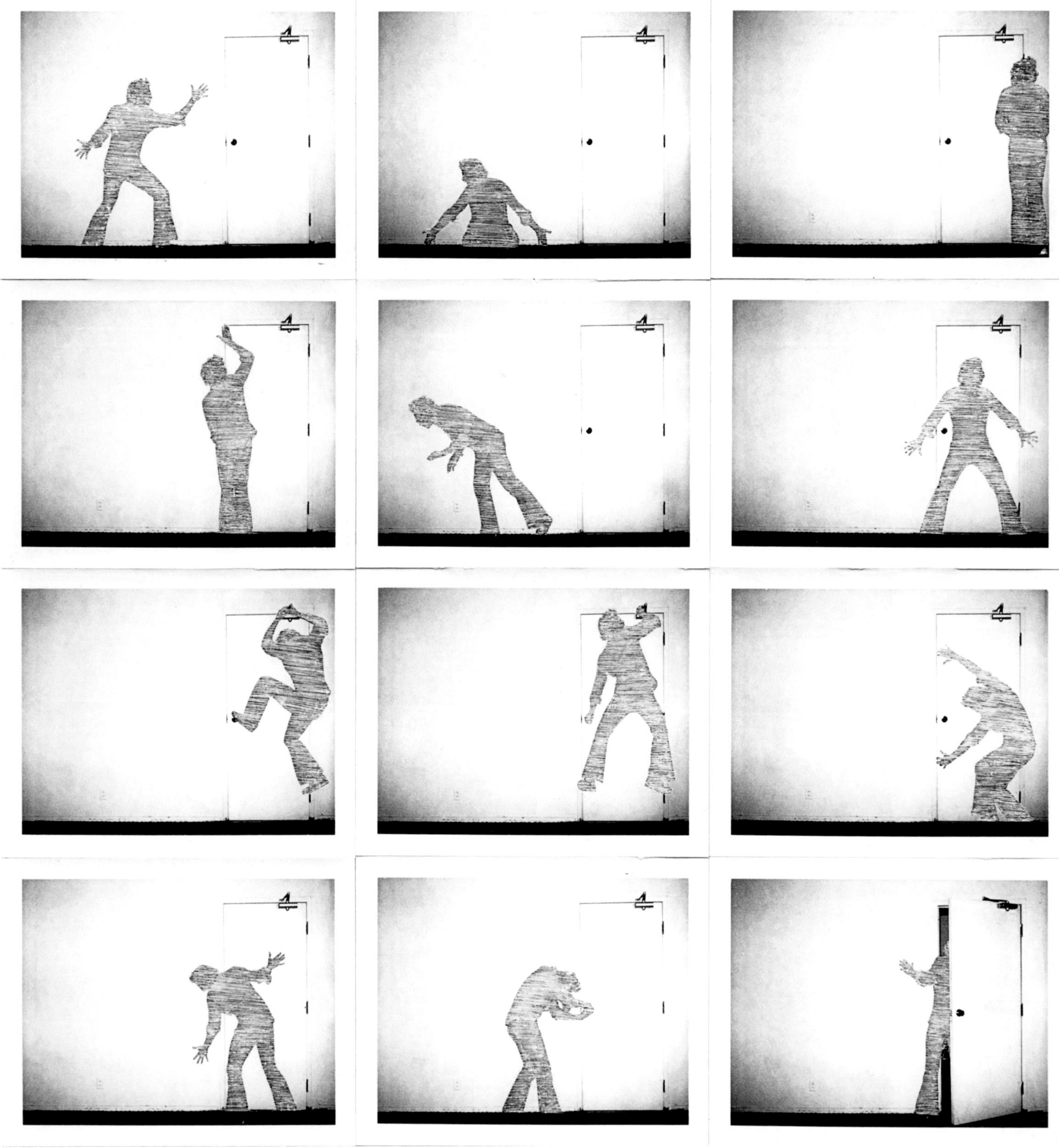

5

DOORS

PL 33
Door 1
1976

PL 34
Door 3
1976–1977

PL 35
Door 5
1977

PL 36
Door 2
1976

PL 37
Door 7
1977

PL 38
Door 6
1977

6

BOUND DOORS

PL 39
Bound Door 1
1975

PL 40
Bound Door 5
1976

PL 41
Bound Door 6
1976

PL 42
Bound Door 7
1976

PL 43
Bound Door 2
1975

PL 44
Bound Door 3
1976

PL 45
Bound Door 4
1976

7

MIRRORS

PL 46
Mirror 5
1977

PL 47
Mirror 1
1976

PL 48
Mirror 2
1976

PL 49
Mirror 3
1976

PL 50
Mirror 4
1977

PL 51
Mirror 6
1976

PL 52
Mirror 7
1977

8

**MULTIPART
PHOTOGRAPHS**

PL 53
Triptych 2
1976

PL 54
Triptych 14
1976

PL 55
Triptych 6
1976

PL 56
Triptych 15
1976

PL 57
Quadrant 1
1976

PL 58
Storm/Wall Diptych 6
1978

PL 59
Acting Out
1976

All works by Steve Kahn. Unless otherwise indicated, all works are single gelatin silver prints.

Pls. 1–4: 8¼ x 6¼ in. Pls. 5–10: 6¼ x 8¼ in. Pls. 11–16, 18, 21–30, 33–46: 9⅝ x 12⅝ in. Pls. 17, 19, 20, 31, 32, 47–52: 12⅝ x 9⅝ in. Pls. 53, 55: Three gelatin silver prints. Each image: 12⅝ x 9⅝ in.; each sheet: 14 x 11 in. Pls. 54, 56: Three gelatin silver prints. Each image: 9⅝ x 12⅝ in.; each sheet: 11 x 14 in. Pl. 57: Four gelatin silver prints. Overall: 72¼ x 96¼ in. Pl. 58: Two gelatin silver prints. Each image: 9⅝ x 12⅝ in.; each sheet: 11 x 14 in. Pl. 59: Twelve Polaroids, with scratching. Each image: 2⅞ x 3¾ in.; overall: 18¾ x 20 in.

Collection of the Fine Arts Museums of San Francisco: Gift of Nancy Ganz and Mitchell Steir: Pls. 3, 5, 9, 10, 33–36, 38; Gift of Dr. Nancy Ascher and Dr. John Roberts: Pls. 4, 16–18, 20–22, 27, 30, 32, 37, 46–49

Mary and Dan Solomon Collection, Los Angeles: Pls. 1, 2, 6–8, 12–15, 23–26, 28, 29, 31, 39–45, 50–52, 55–57

Collection of the Stephen H. Kahn Trust: Pls. 11, 53, 54, 58

Private collection, courtesy of Howard Greenberg Gallery: Pl. 59

APPENDIX

NOTE

This appendix includes Steve Kahn's original first-generation Polaroids of *The Hollywood Suites*, which he later re-photographed to produce editions of gelatin silver prints (a selection of which appear in the plate section of this catalogue). Each Polaroid print is 3¼ by 4¼ inches and was taken on 3000 speed Type 107 format film packs. The appendix is organized by the date of manufacture of Kahn's film packs, which is contained in the production code on the verso of each print.

Note that apps. 1–4 are mounted on self-adhesive mounting cards that conceal the production codes. Two other Polaroids are unable to be located (apps. 61 and 81) and are reproduced here from Kahn's original 35 mm negatives. They have been placed in the sequence based on the production codes appearing on variants of those same subjects.

BD=Bound Door   * Surface of Polaroid retouched
D=Door   ** Not printed as a gelatin silver print in the 1970s
M=Mirror   *** Polaroid missing
N=Nude   **** No code visible
P=Portrait
R=Room
W=Window

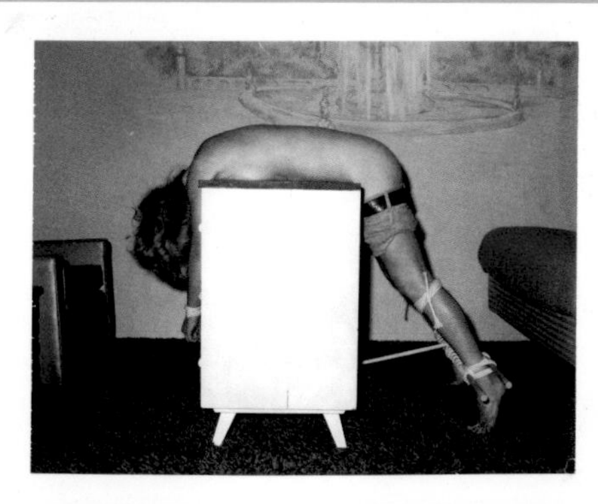

1
N1****
2017.84.2.24

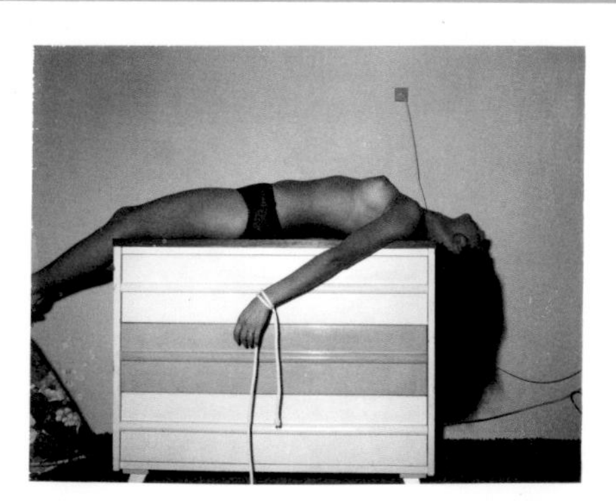

2
N2****
2017.85.2.15

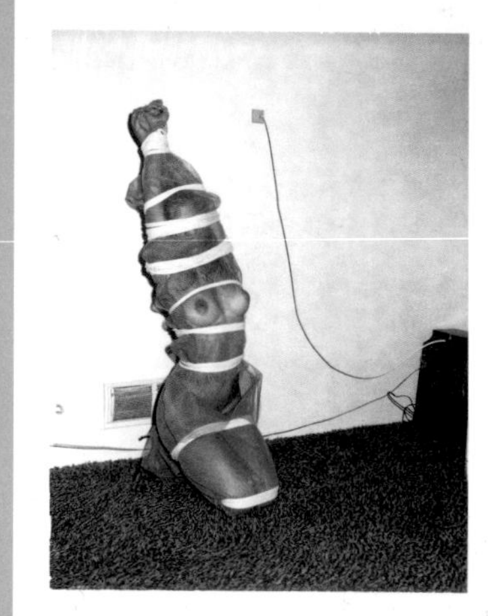

3
N3****
2017.85.2.19

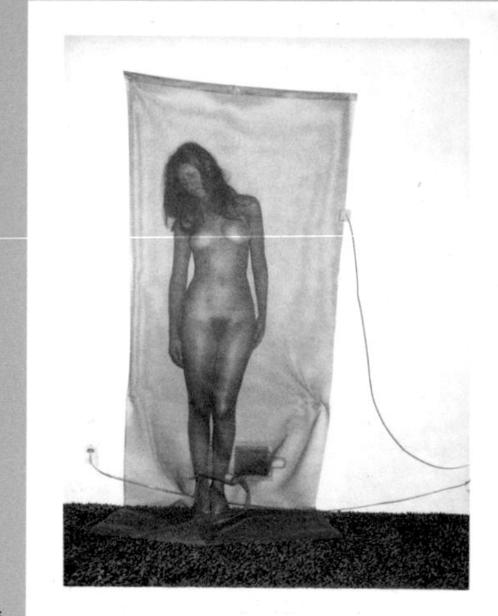

4
N4****
2017.84.2.28

C401821PC
MARCH 28, 1974

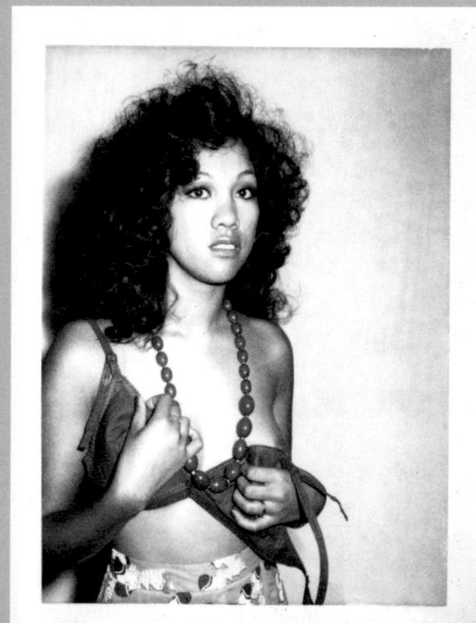

5
P1
2017.85.2.10

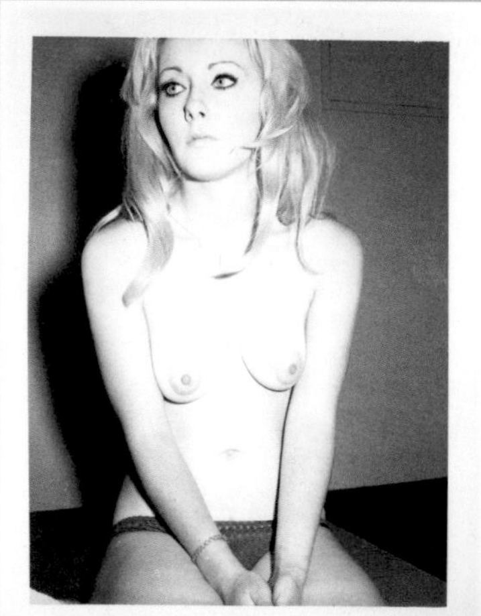

6
P2
2018.27.22

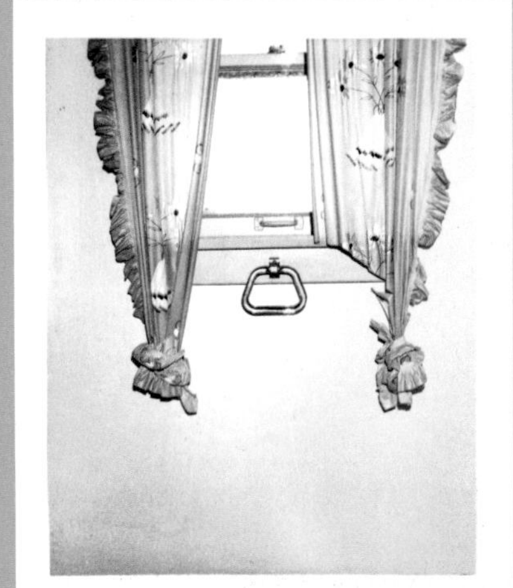

7
W1*
2018.27.24

E403031BC
MAY 1, 1974

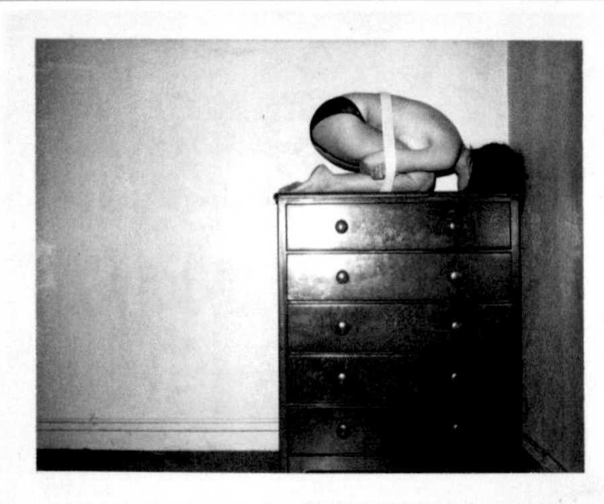

8
N6
2018.27.12

9
N7
2018.27.13

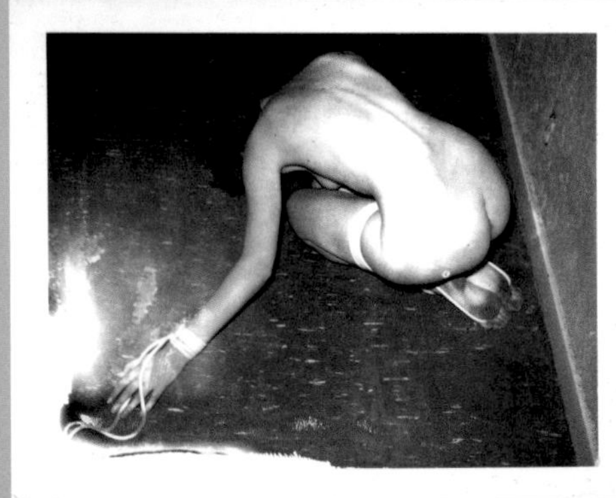

10
N8
2017.84.2.29

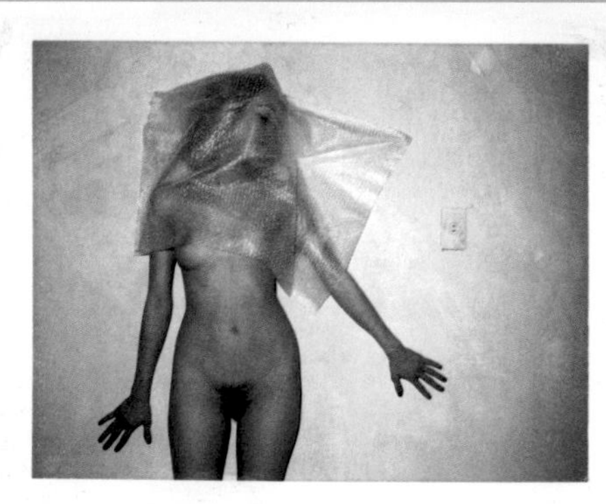

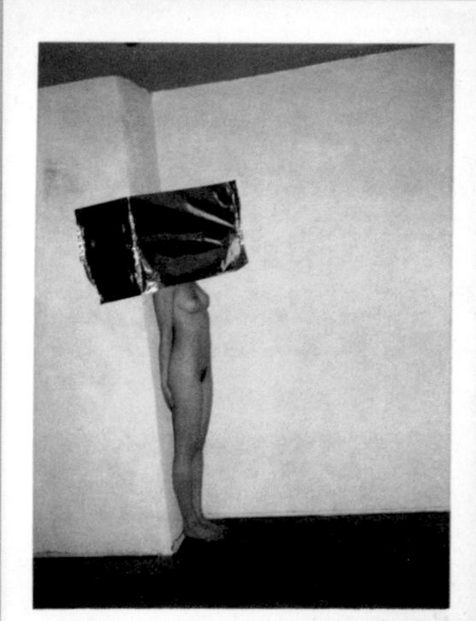

11
N30
2017.85.2.20

12
N9
2018.27.14

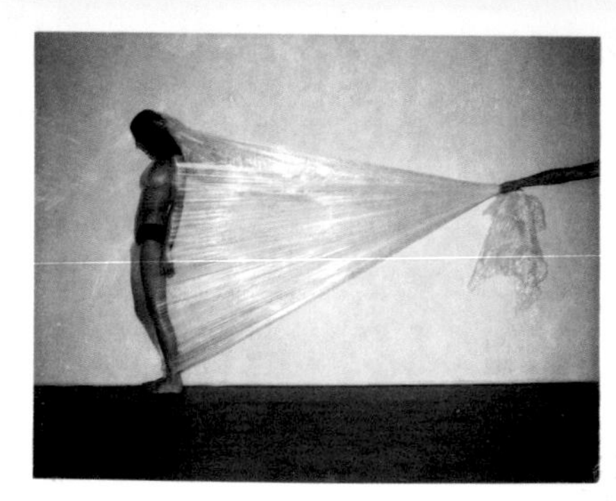

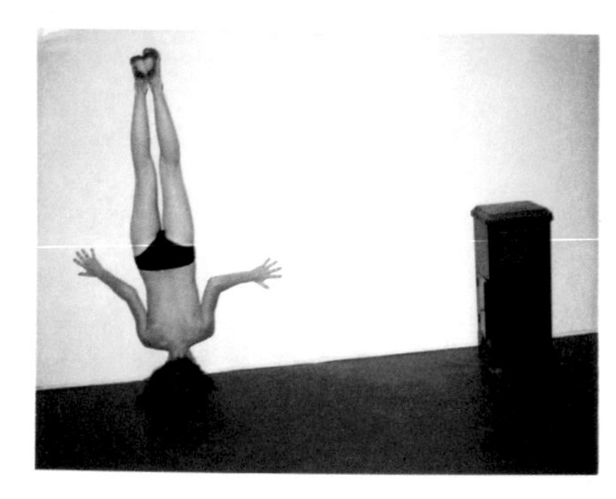

13
N10
2018.27.15

14
N11
2018.27.16

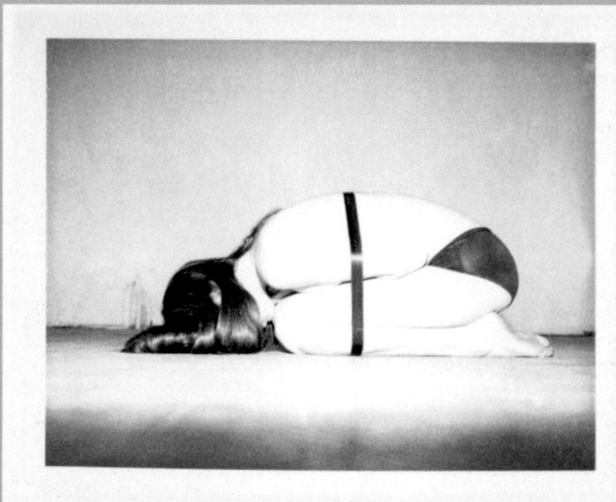

15
N32
2018.27.37

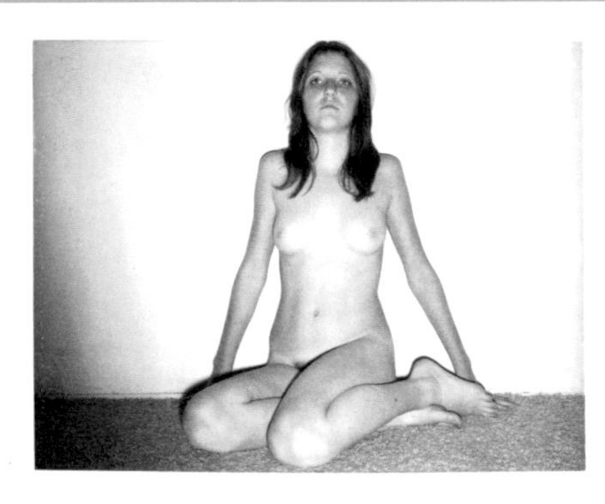

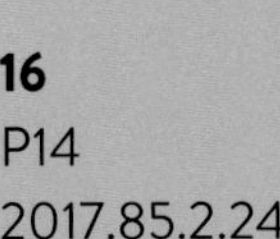

16
P14
2017.85.2.24

17
N15
2017.84.2.25

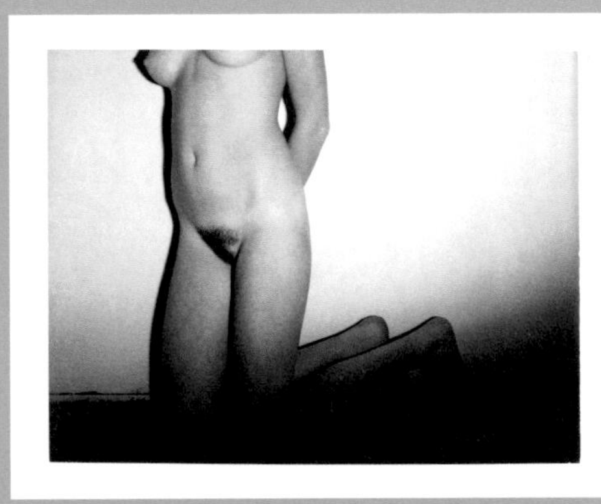

18
N16
2017.85.2.13

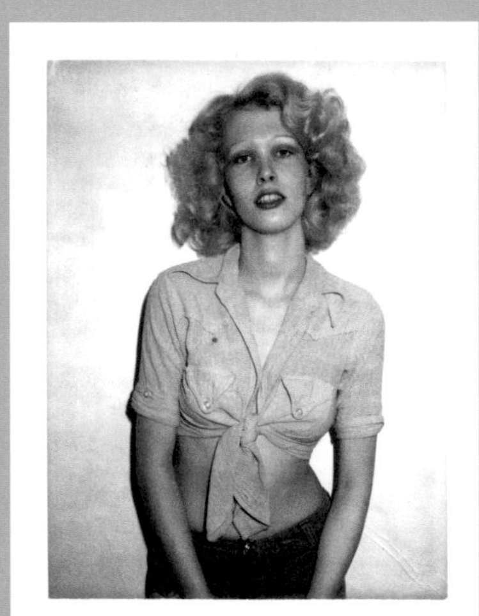

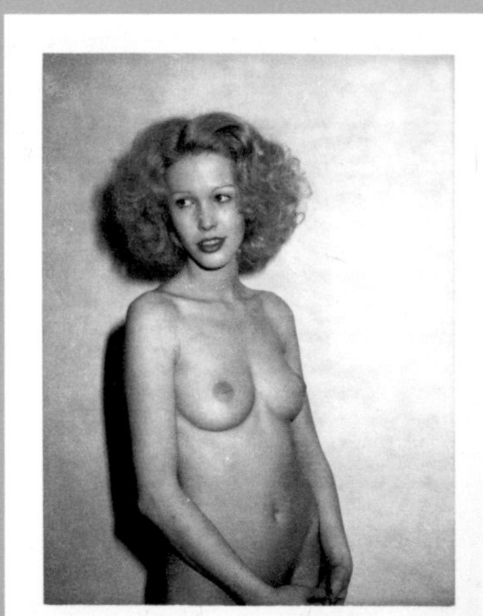

19
P7
2018.27.23

20
P13
2017.85.2.23

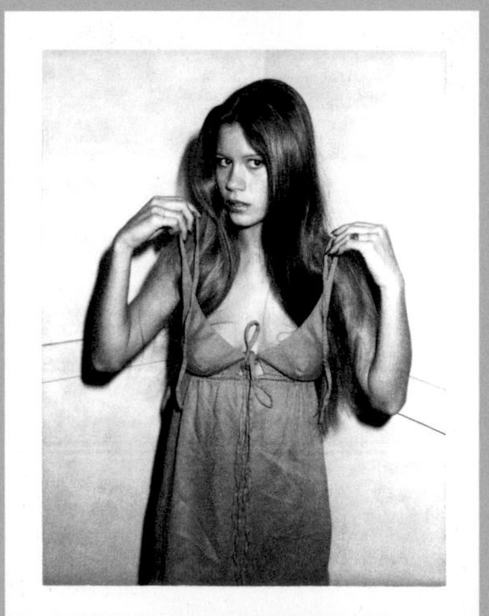

21
P6
2017.84.2.23

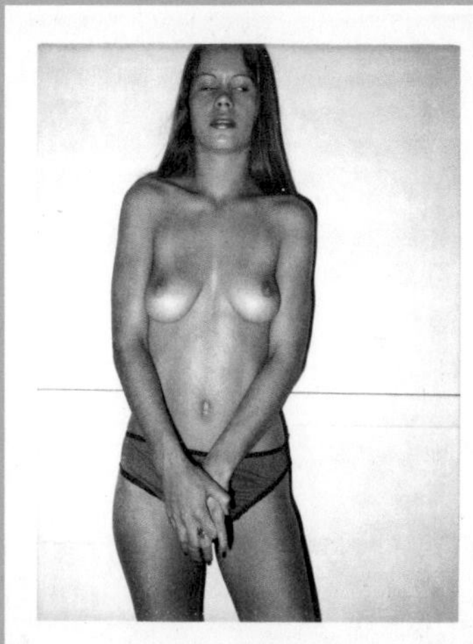

22
P4
2017.85.2.27

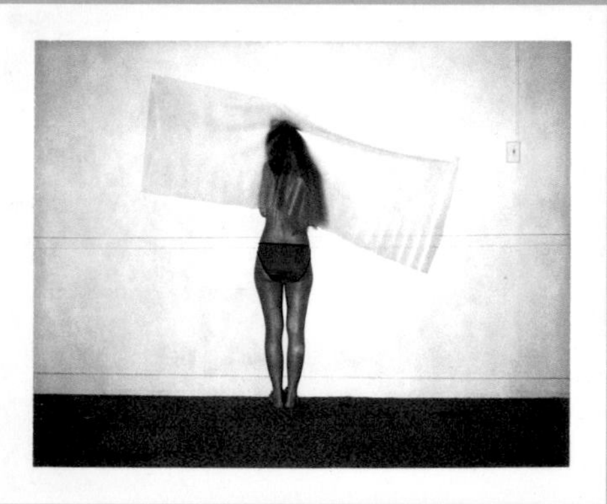

23
N12
2017.85.2.6

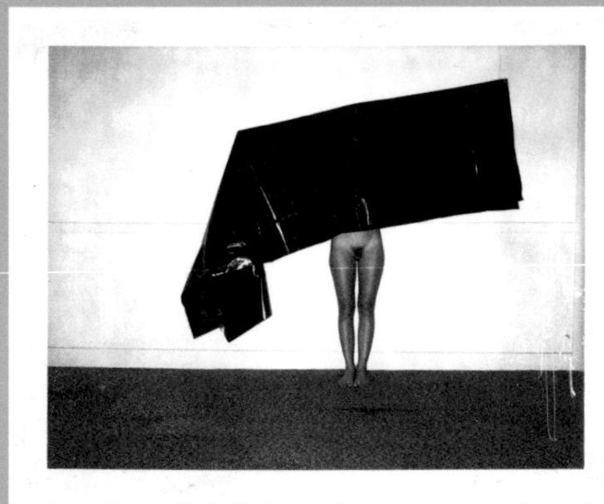

24
N35**
2018.27.39

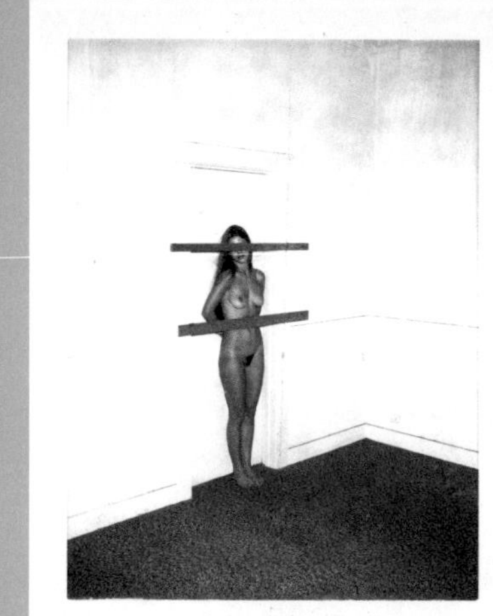

25
N5
2018.27.11

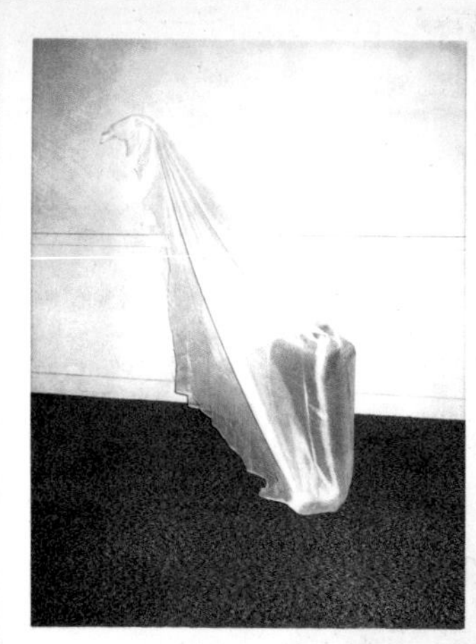

26
N14
2017.85.2.7

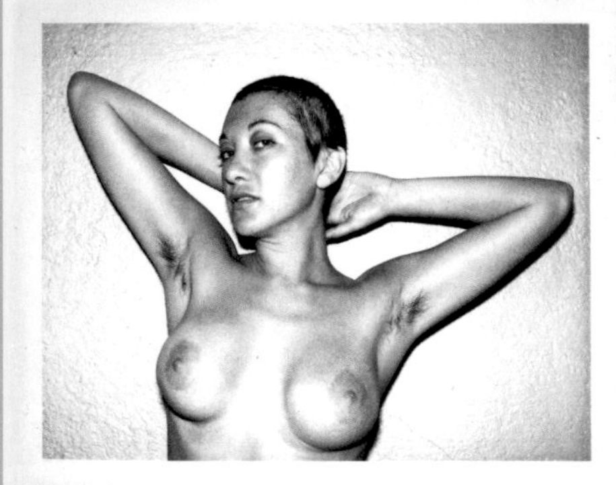

27
P8
2017.85.2.28

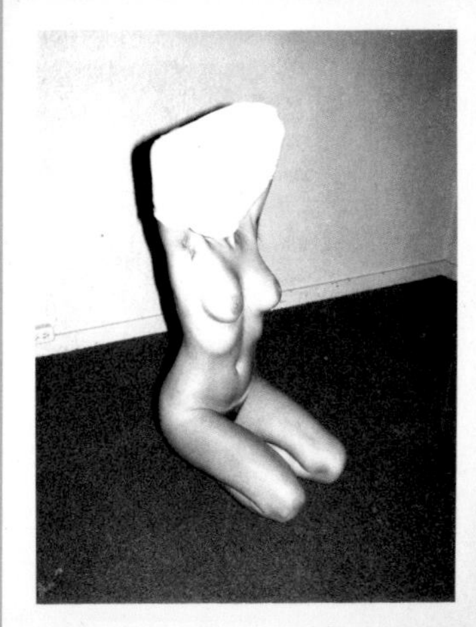

28
N13
2017.85.2.12

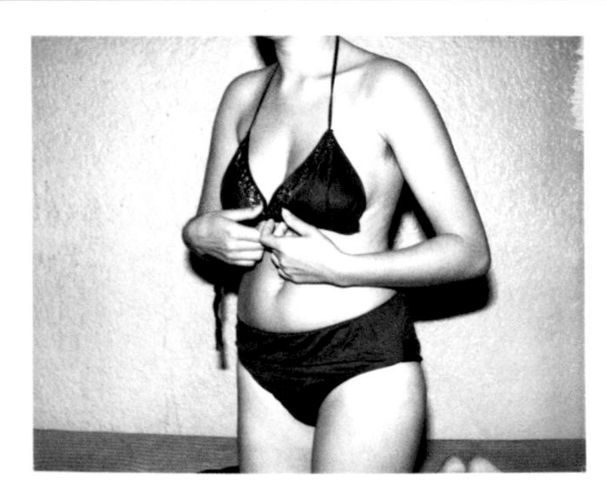

29
N17
2017.85.2.8

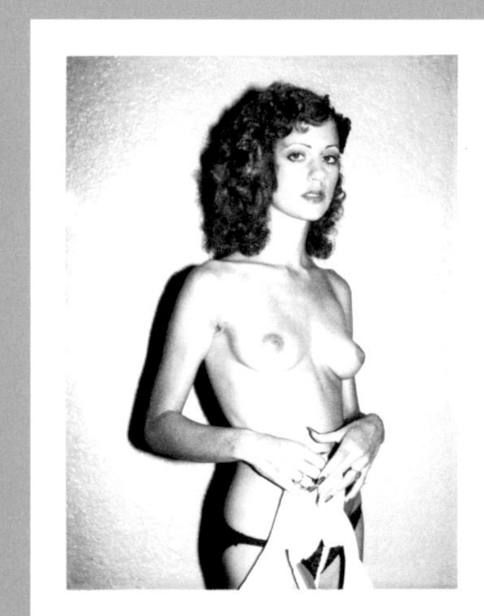

30
P16
2017.85.2.26

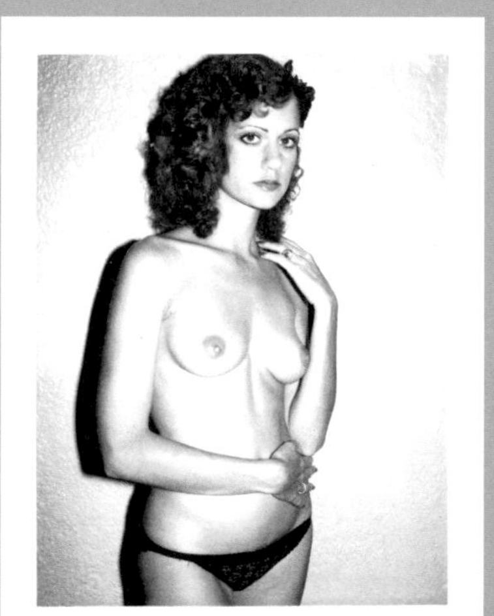

31
P9
2017.85.2.29

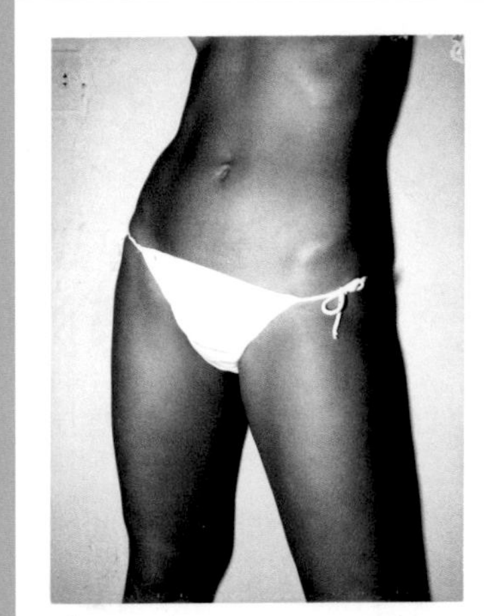

32
N20
2017.84.2.20

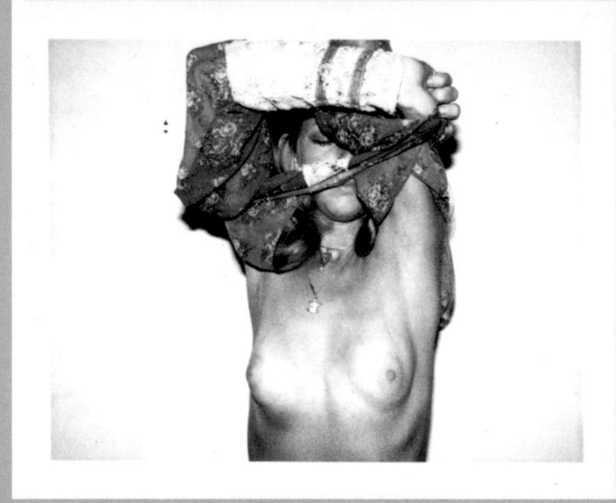

33
N27
2017.84.2.27

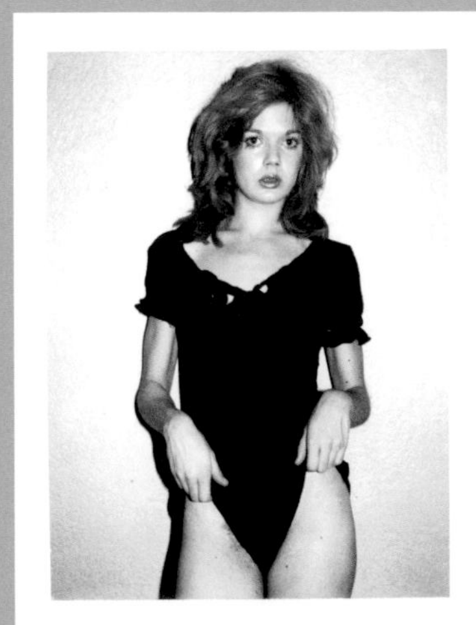

34
P11
2017.84.2.22

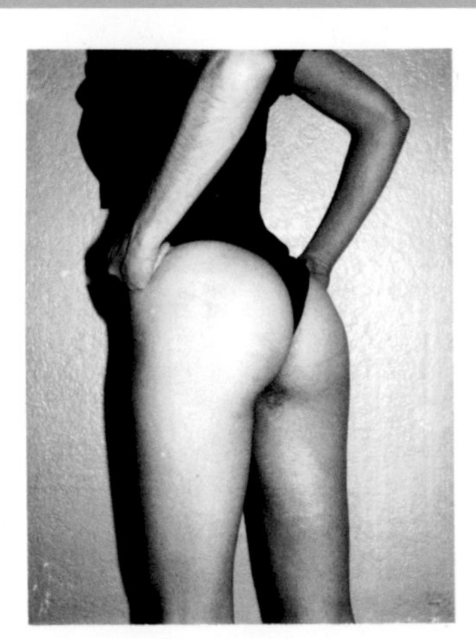

35
N21
2017.84.2.21

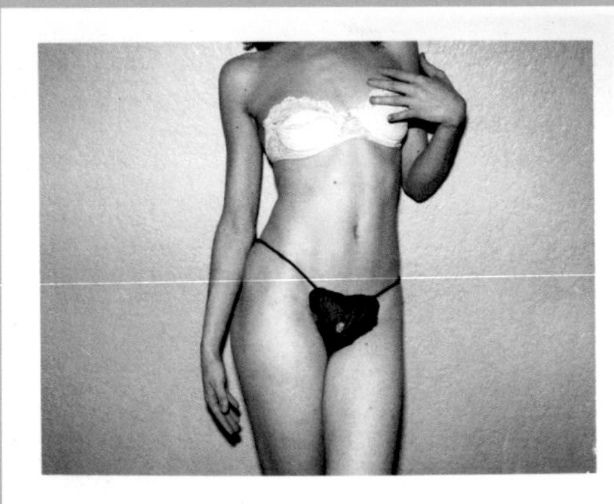

36
N18
2017.85.2.9

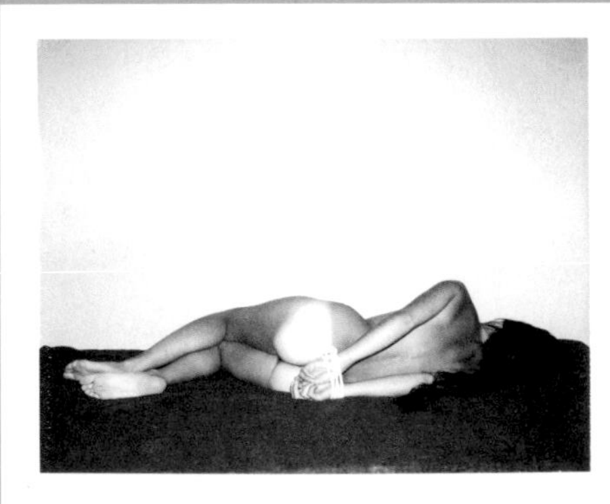

37
N33
2018.27.21

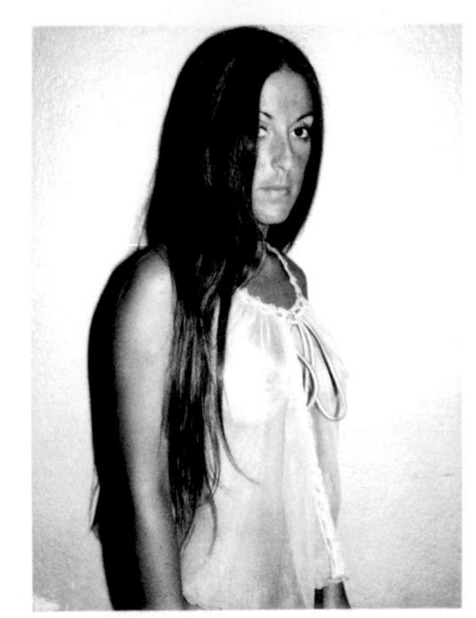

38
P3
2017.85.2.11

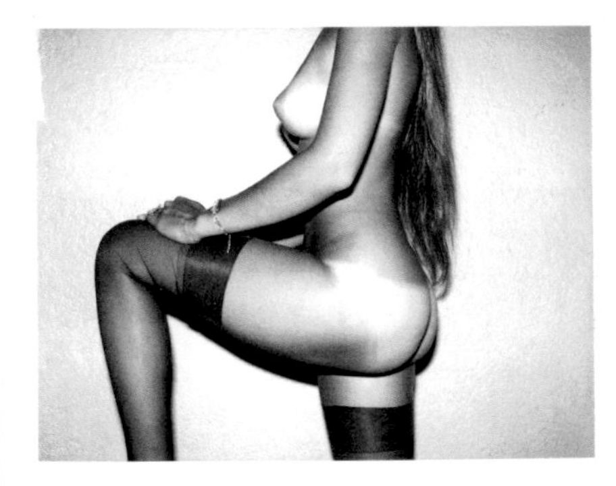

39
N19
2017.85.2.14

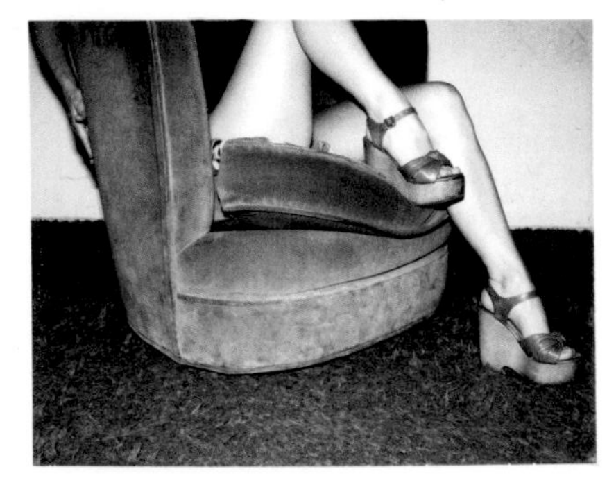

40
N23
2018.27.17

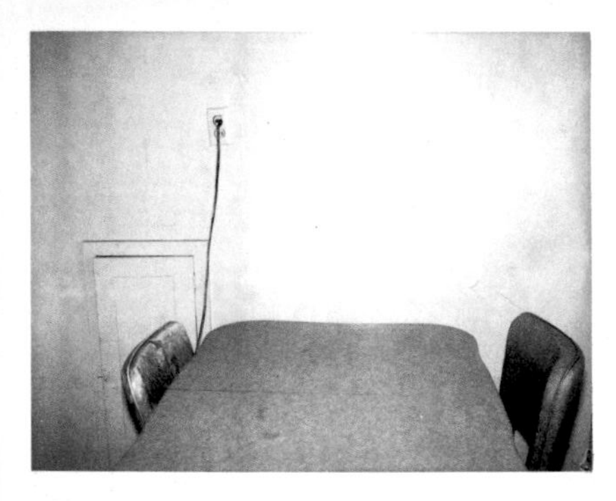

41
R1
2018.27.41

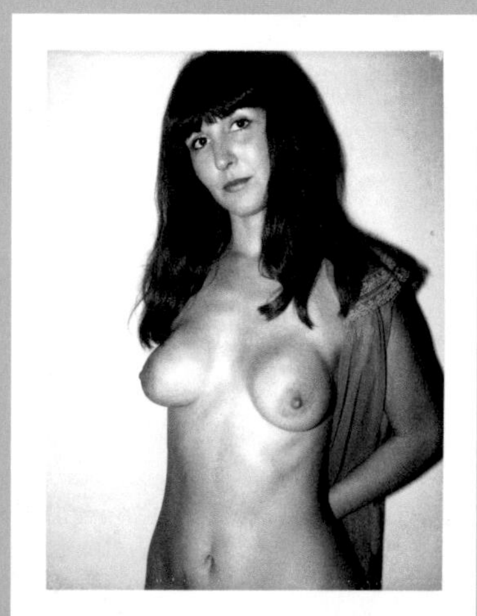

42
P12
2017.85.2.22

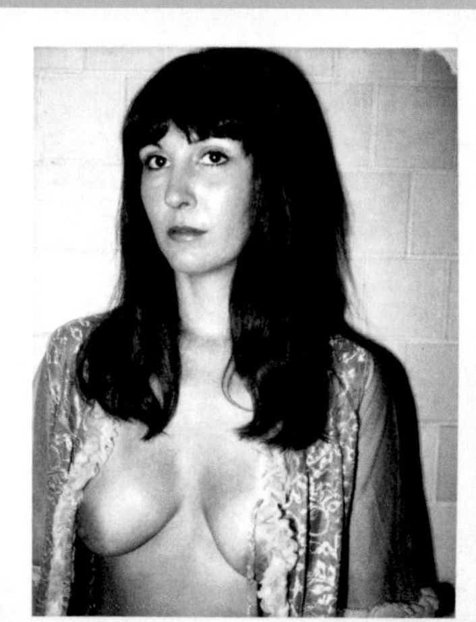

43
P17
2018.27.40

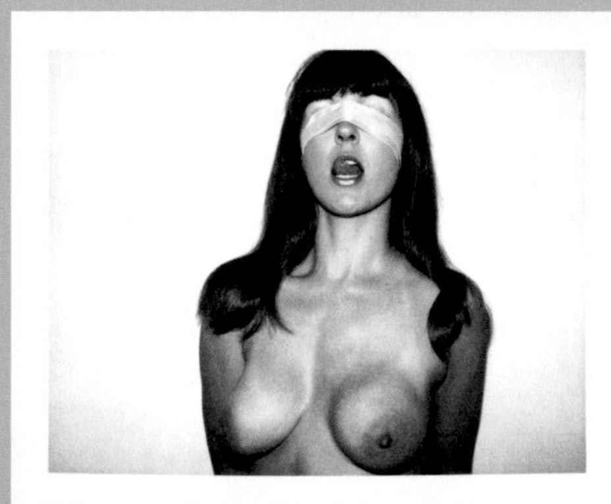

44
N22
2017.84.2.26

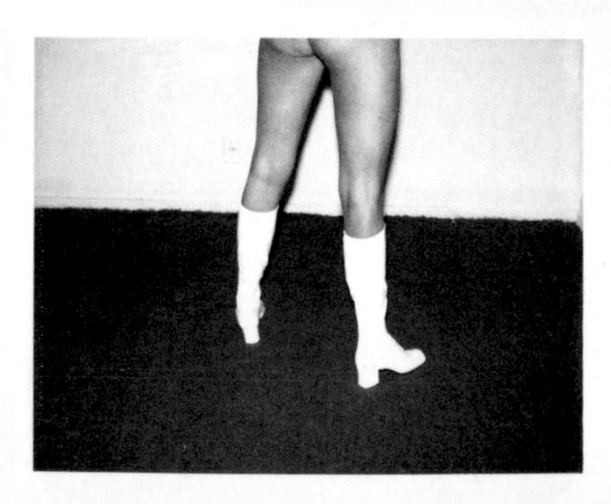

45
N28
2018.27.18

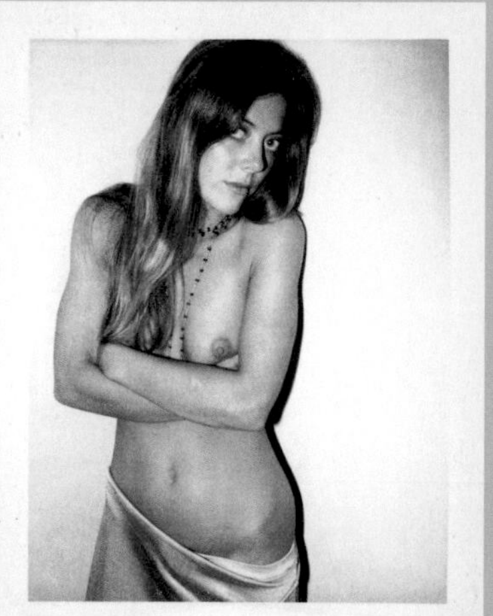

46
P5
2017.84.2.30

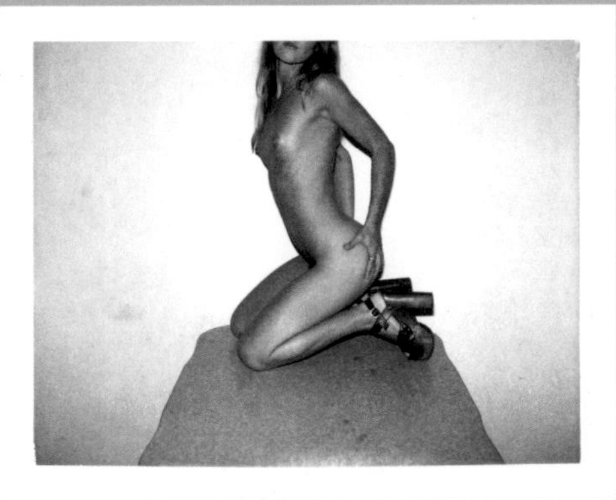

47
N26
2017.85.2.18

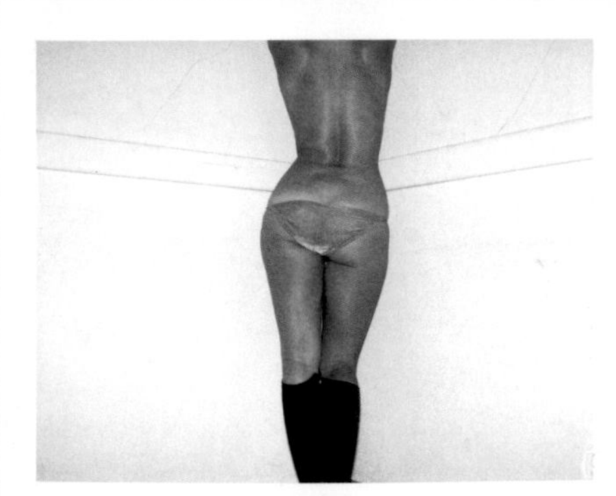

48
N34
2018.27.38

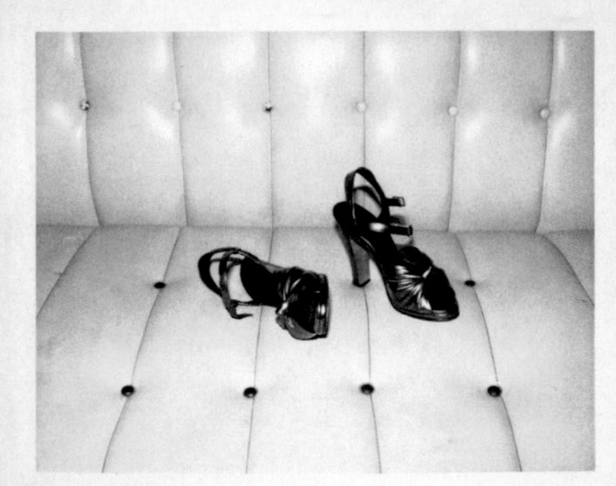

49
N31
2018.27.20

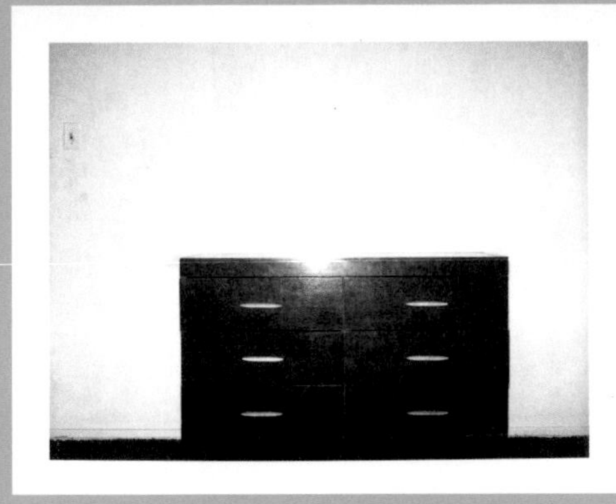

50
R5
2018.27.45

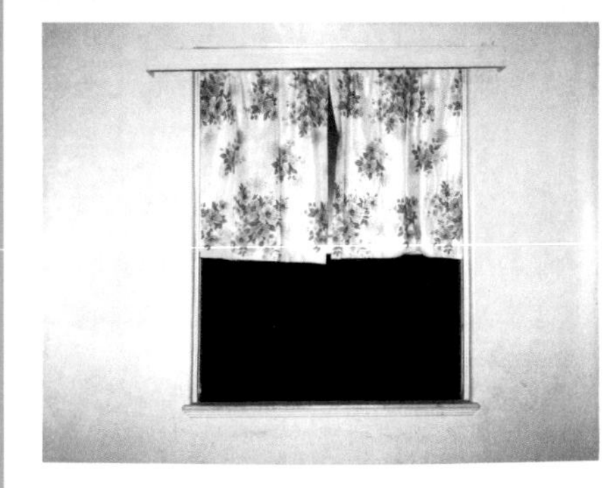

51
W4
2017.84.2.15

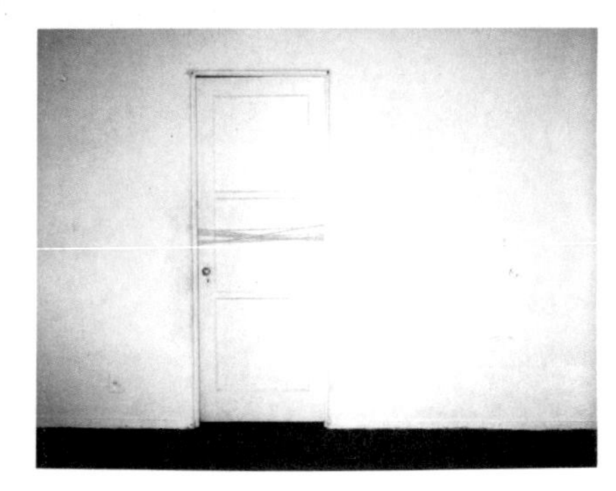

52
BD1
2018.27.1

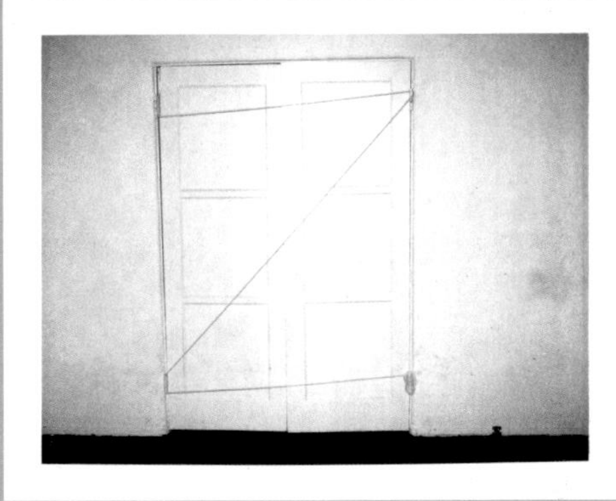

53
BD2
2018.27.2

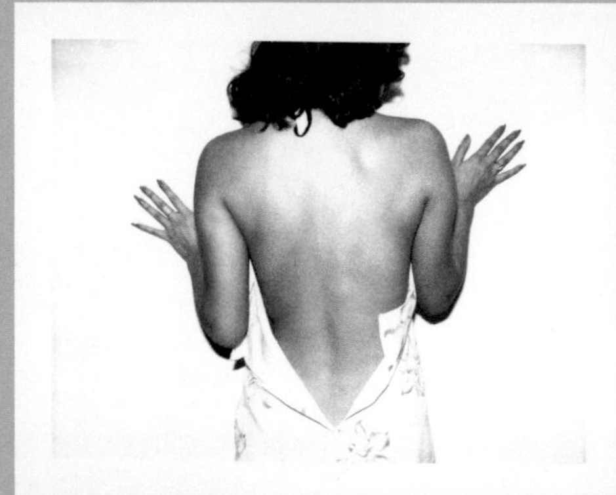

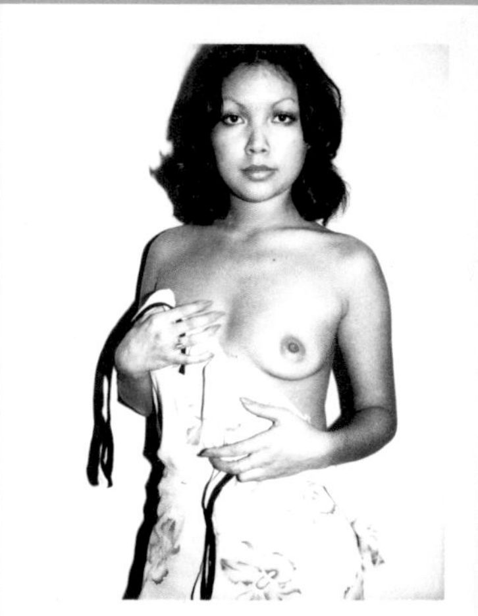

54
N29
2018.27.19

55
P15
2017.85.2.25

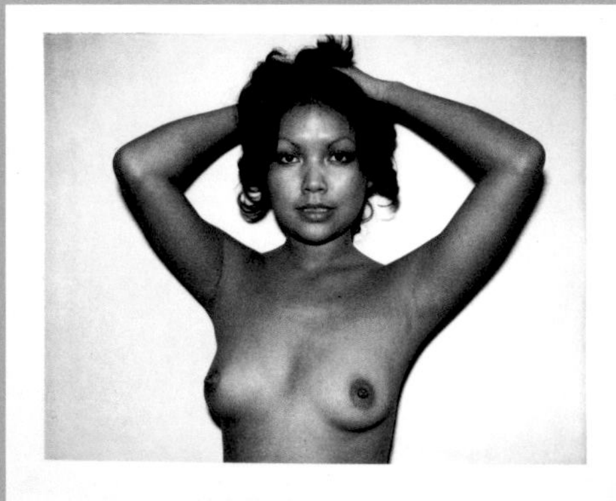

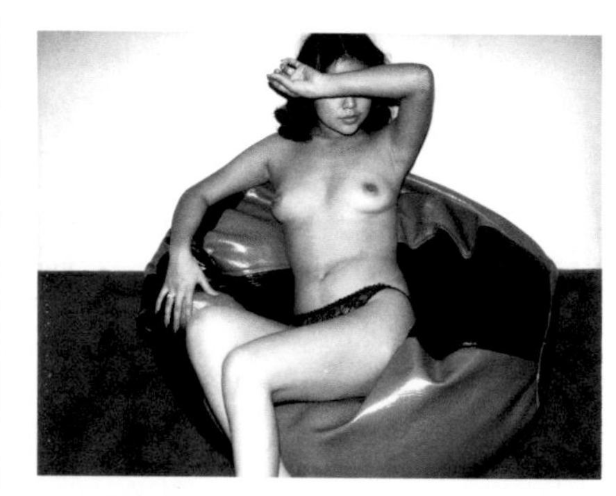

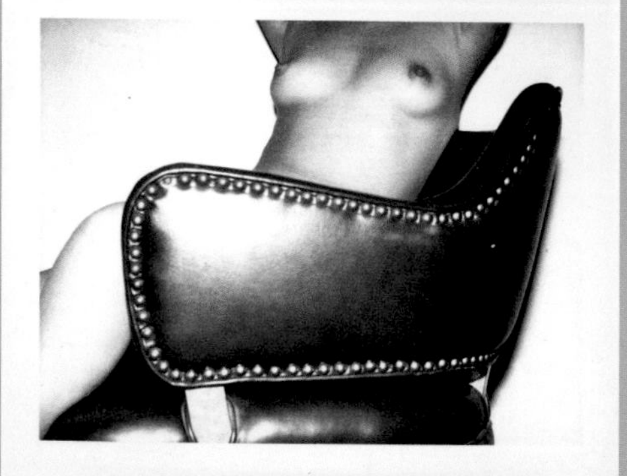

56
P10
2017.85.2.21

57
N25
2017.85.2.17

58
N24
2017.85.2.16

59
R2
2018.27.42

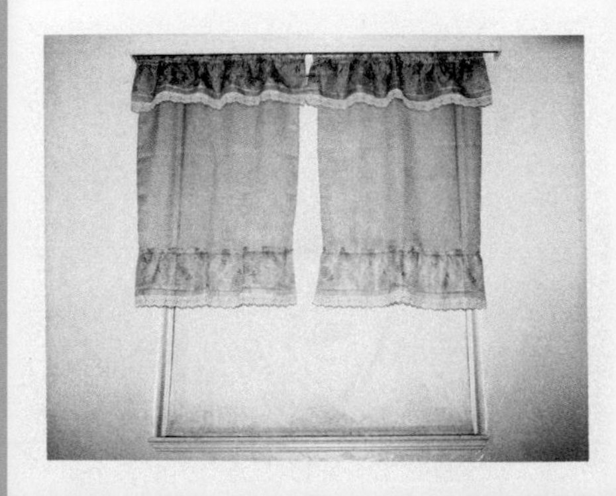

60
W3
2018.27.25

61
W2***

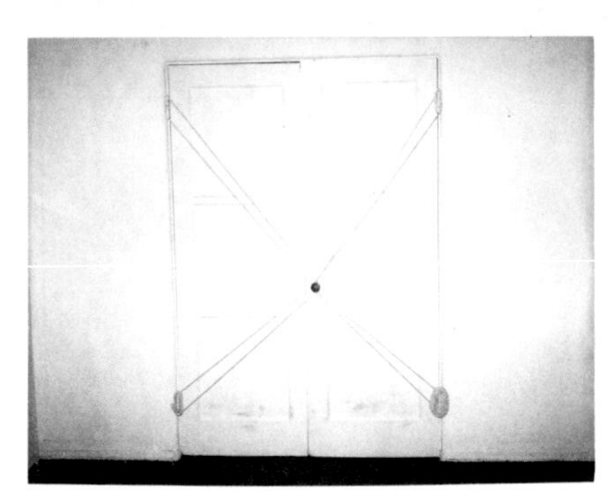

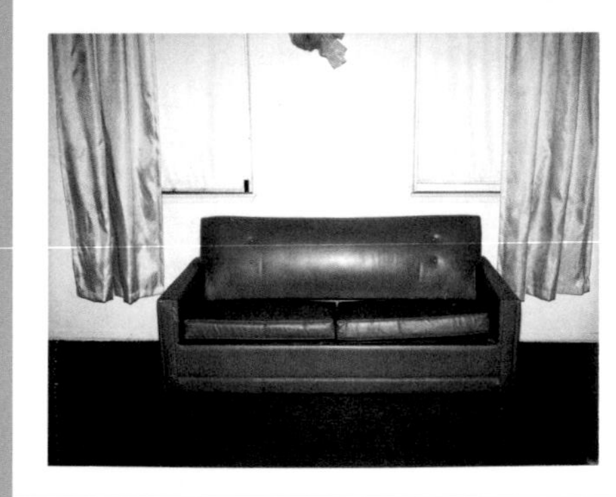

62
BD3
2018.27.3

63
R3
2018.27.43

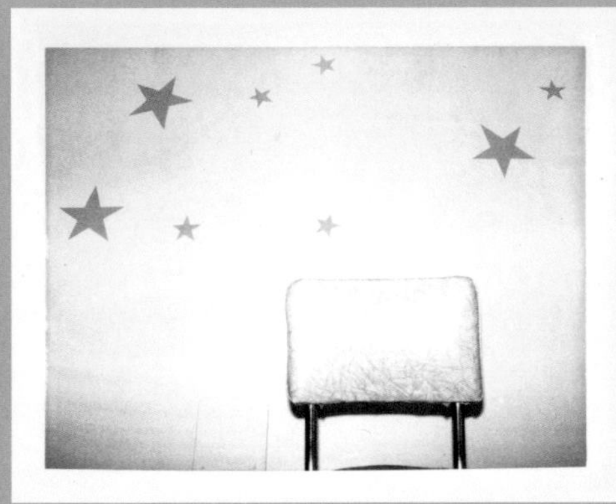

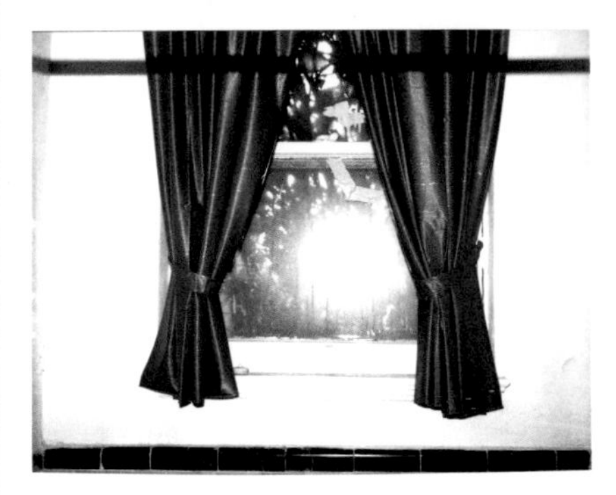

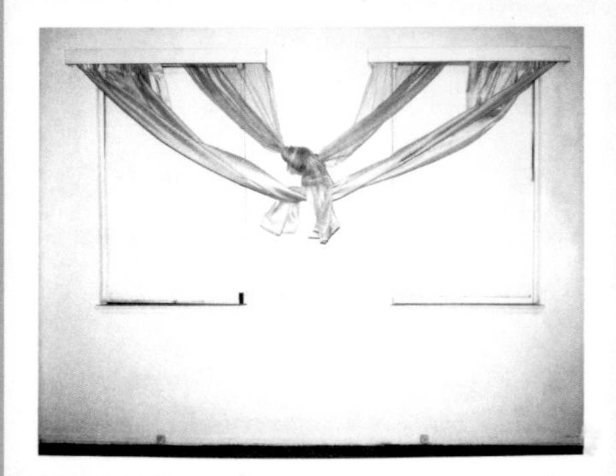

64
R8**
2018.27.48

65
W5
2017.84.2.16

66
W17
2018.27.28

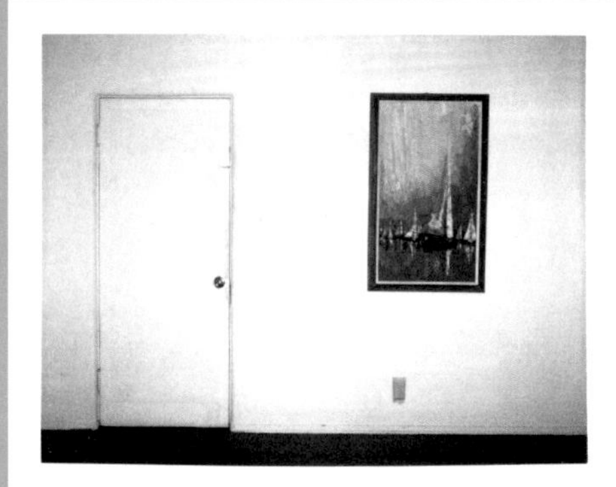

67
D2
2017.85.2.2

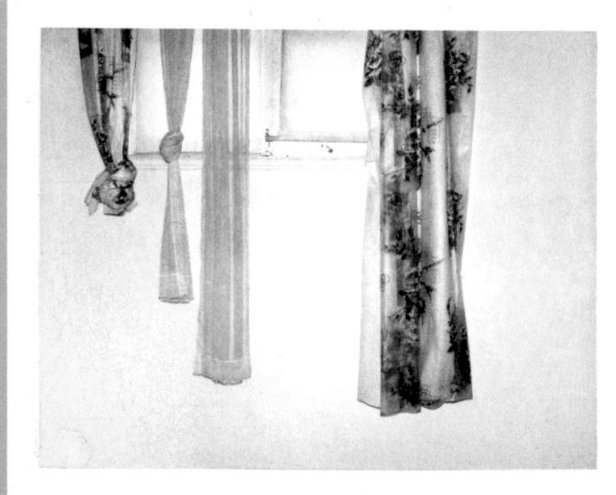

68
W20*
2018.27.29

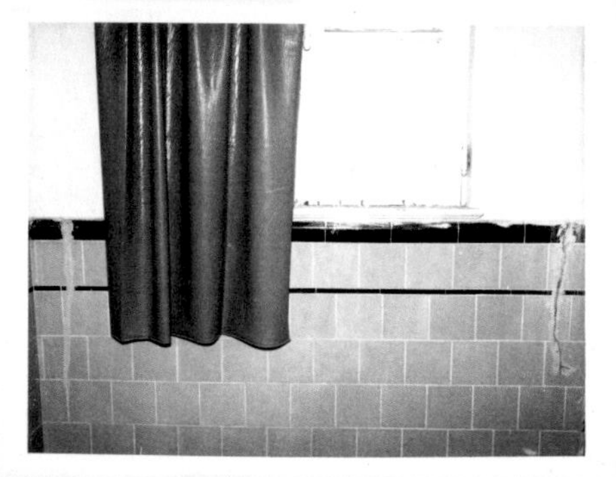

69
W18**
2018.27.52

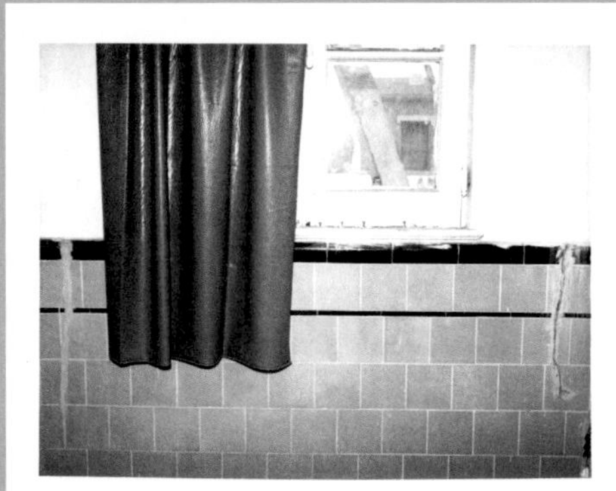

70
W18A
2017.84.2.13

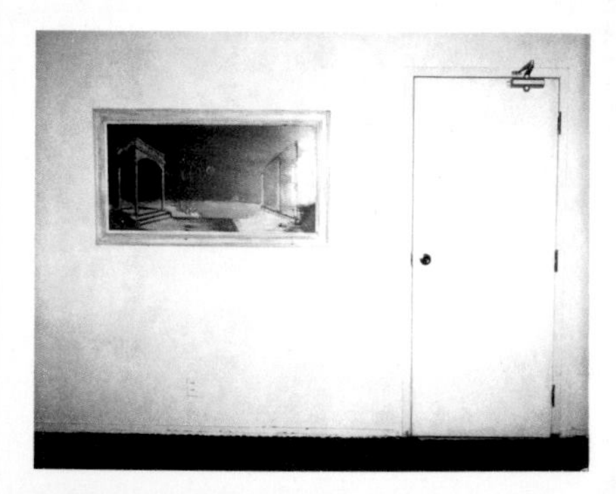

71
D1
2017.85.2.1

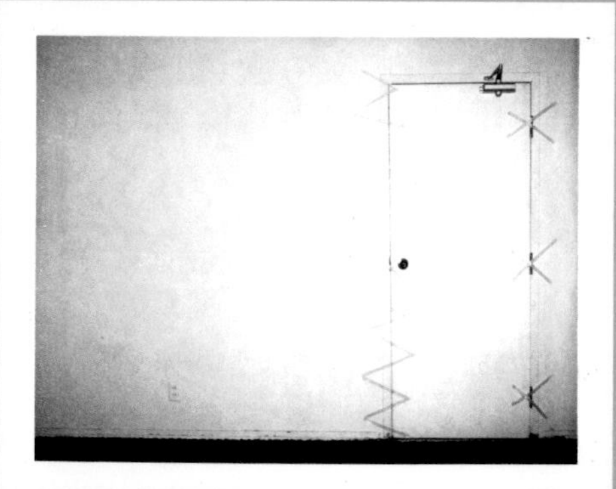

72
BD5
2018.27.5

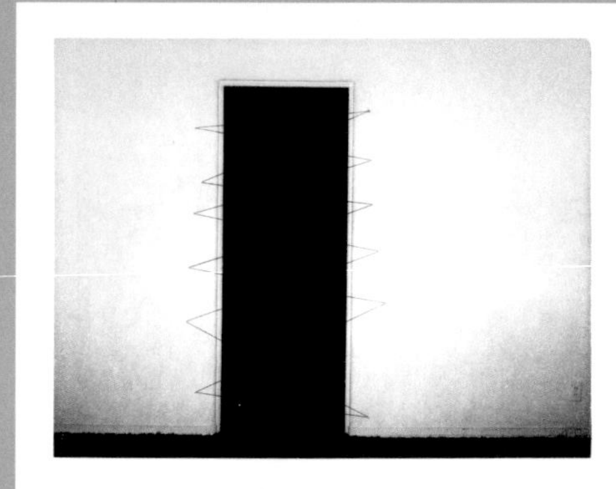

73
BD6
2018.27.6

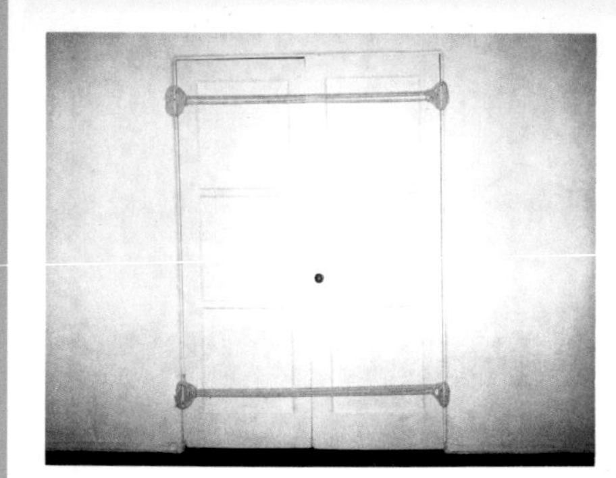

74
BD4
2018.27.4

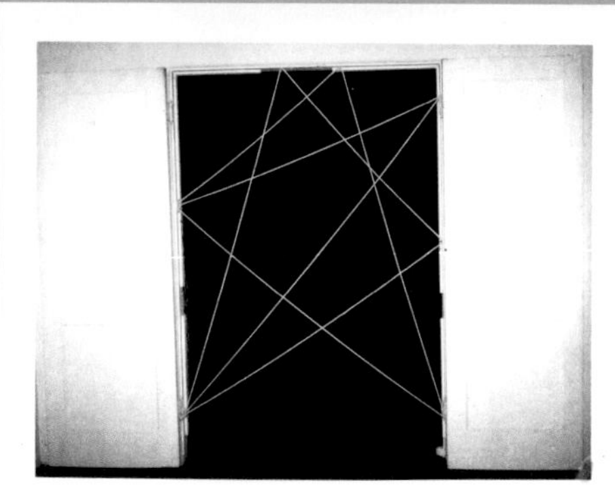

75
BD7
2018.27.7

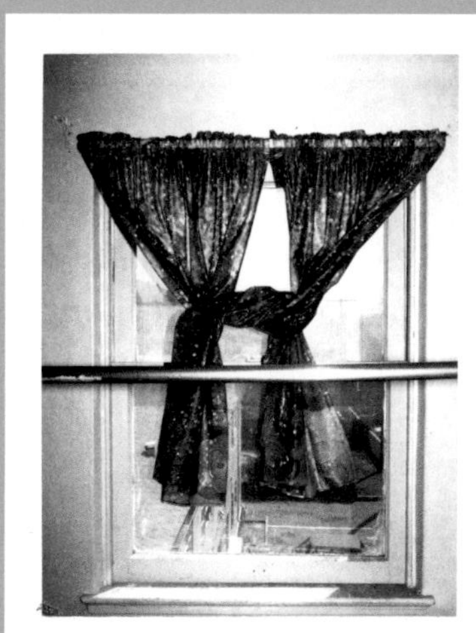

76
W6
2017.84.2.17

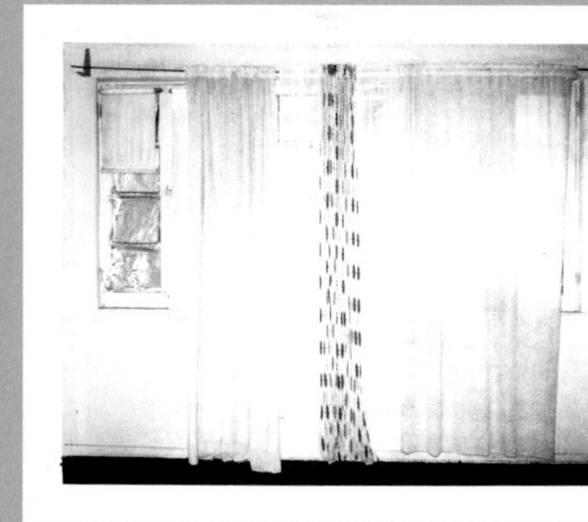

77
W23*
2018.27.32

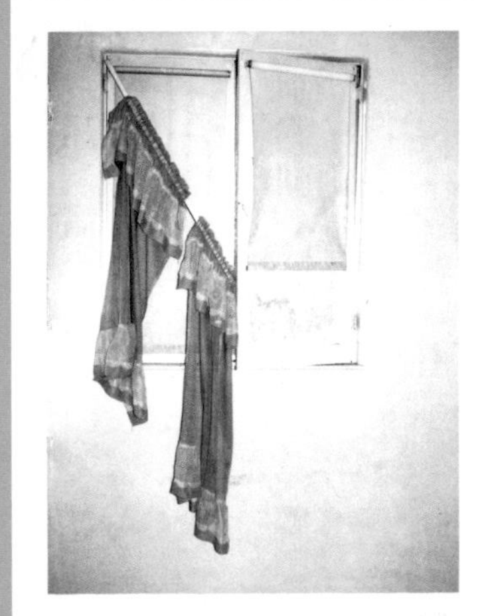

78
W7
2017.84.2.18

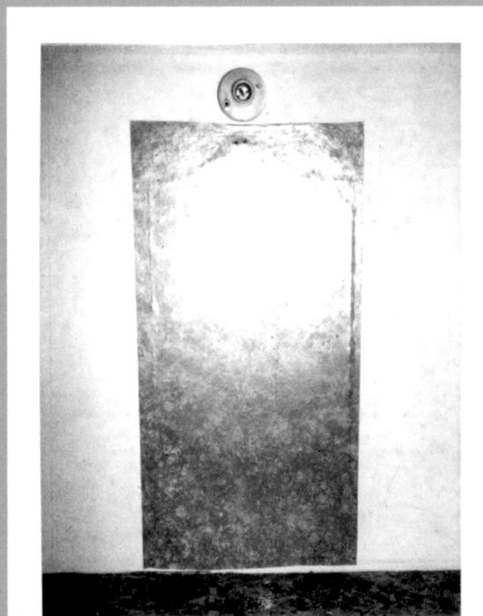

79
M2
2017.84.2.4

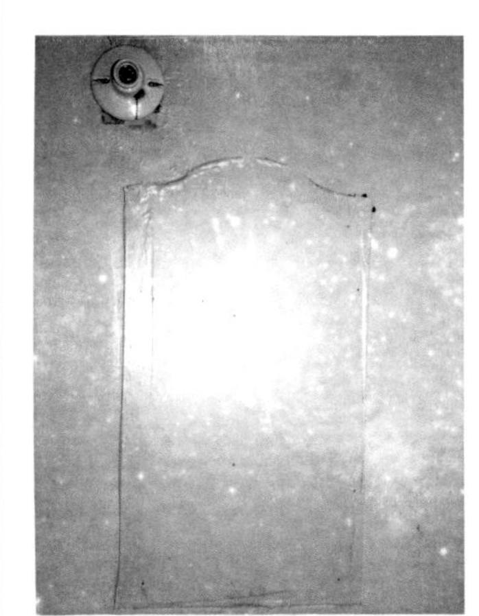

80
M3
2017.84.2.5

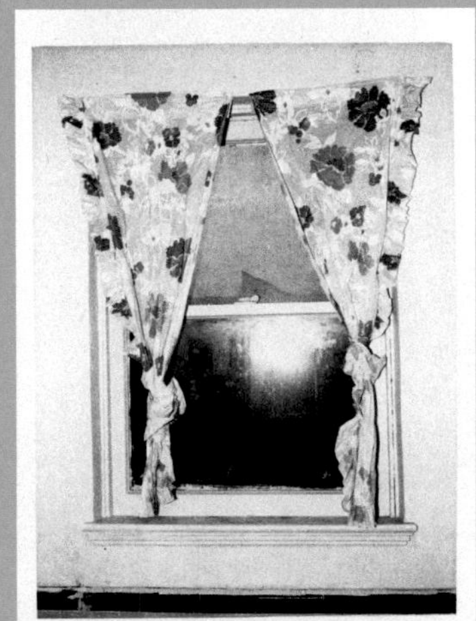

81
W9***

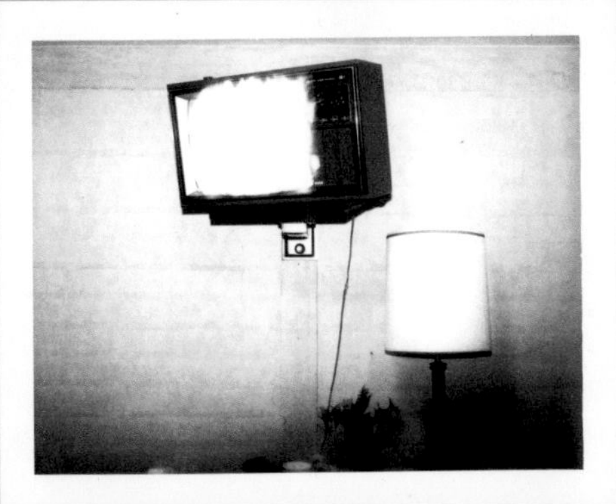

82
R4
2018.27.44

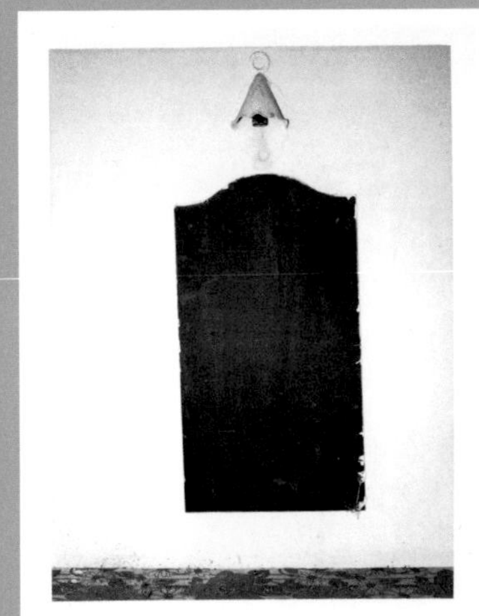

83
M6
2018.27.9

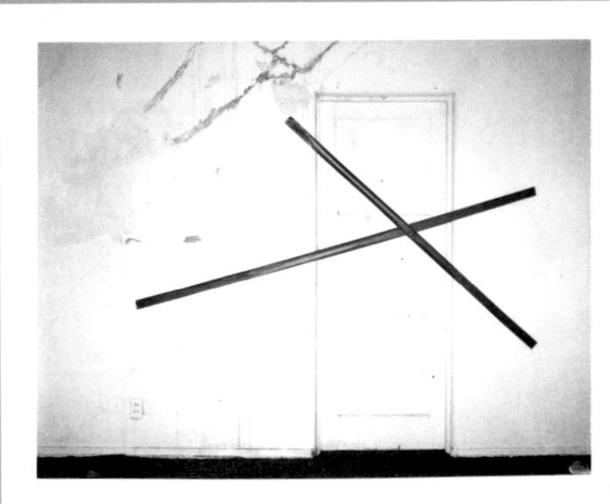

84
BD9**
2018.27.33

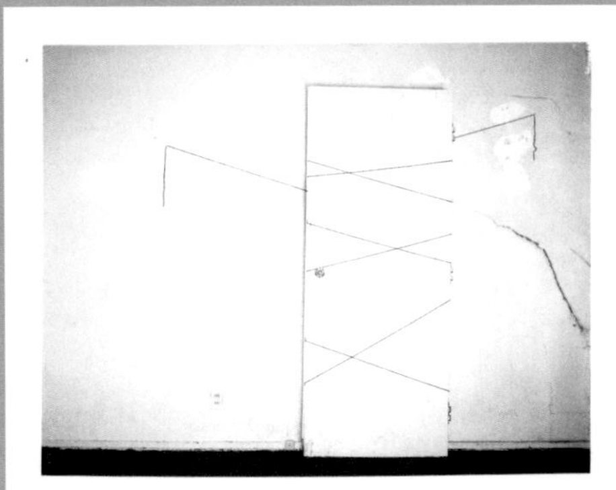

85
BD10
2018.27.34

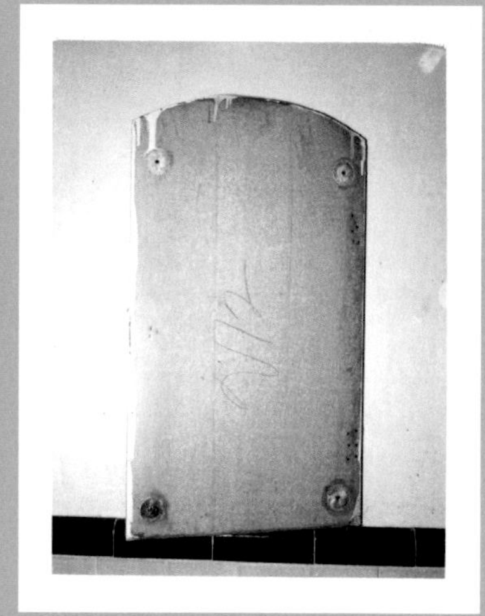

86
M1
2017.84.2.3

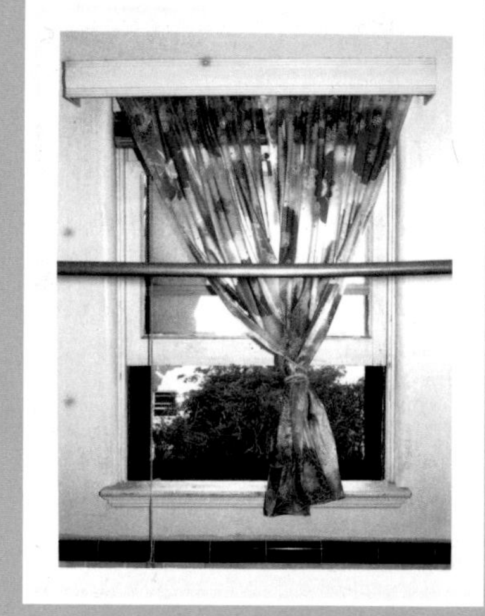

87
W10
2017.84.2.7

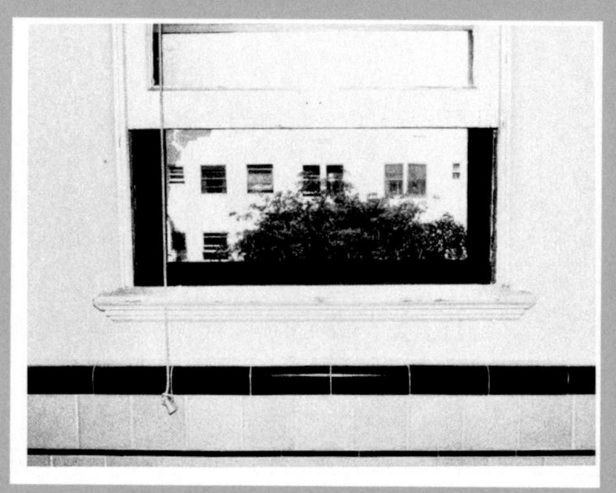

88
W12
2017.84.2.9

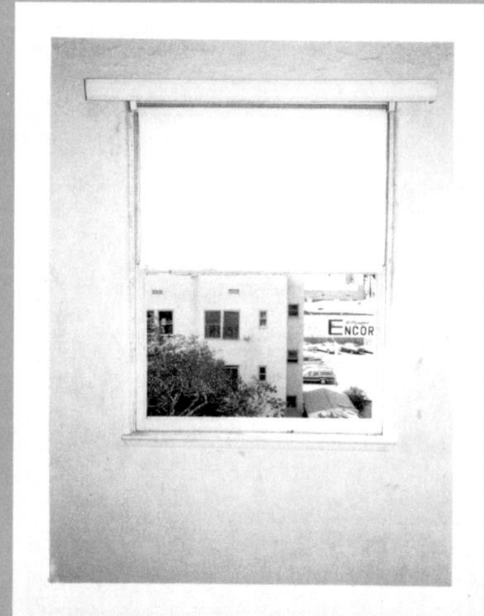

89
W21
2018.27.30

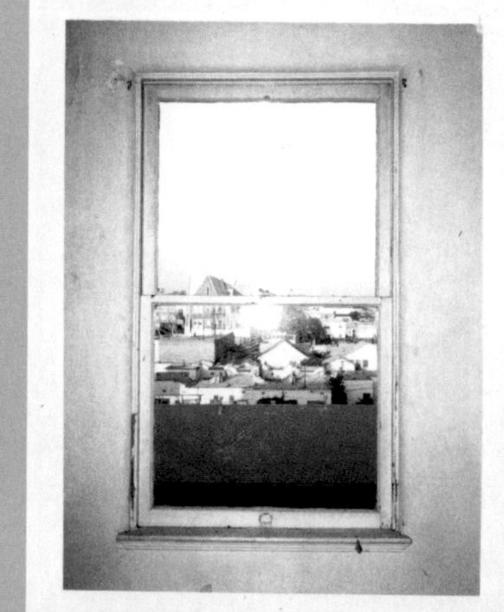

90
W24**
2018.27.49

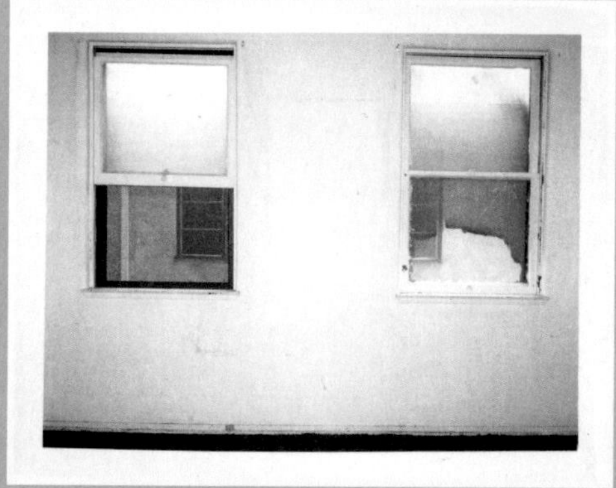

91
W15
2017.84.2.11

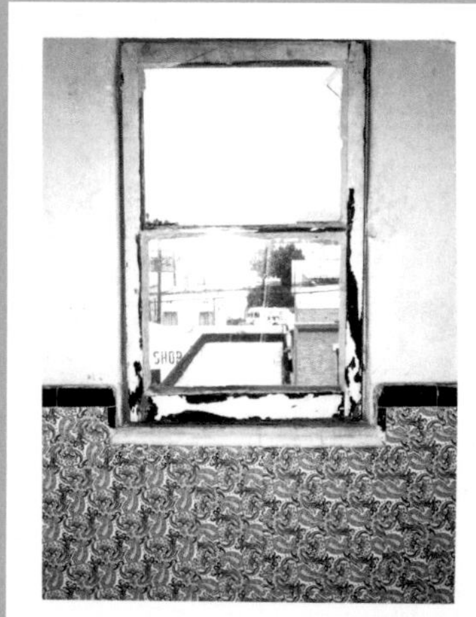

92
W11
2017.84.2.8

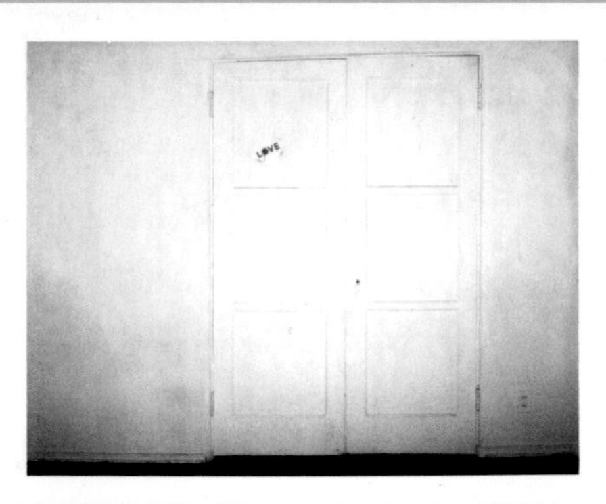

93
D7
2017.84.2.1

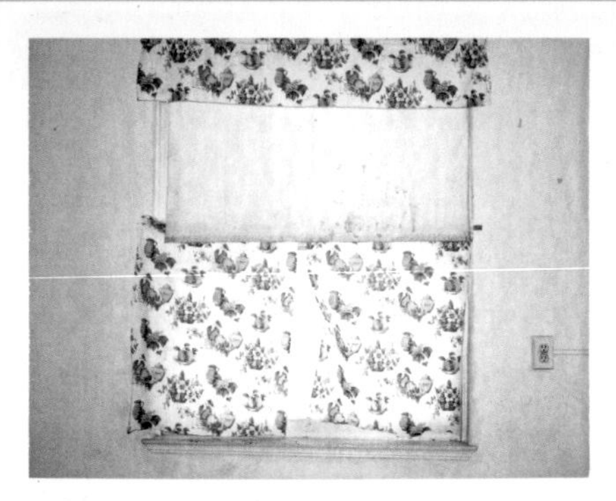

94
W19
2017.84.2.14

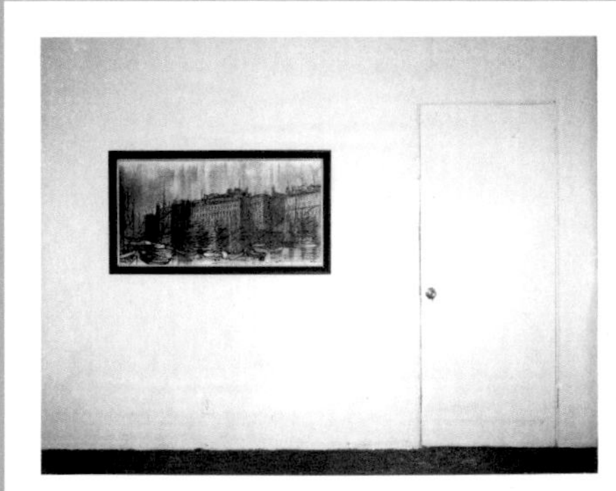

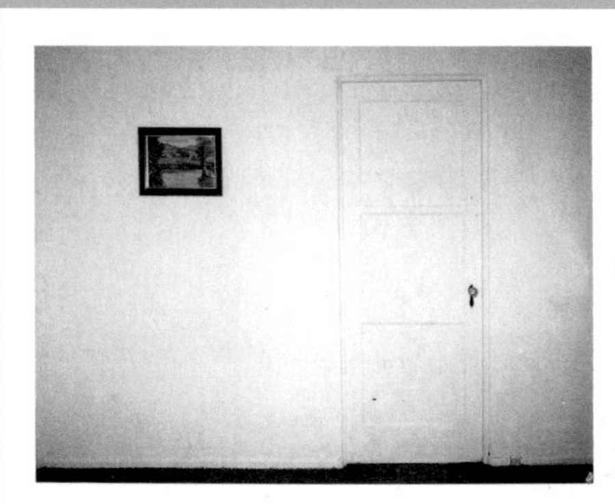

95
D3
2018.27.51

96
D4
2017.85.2.3

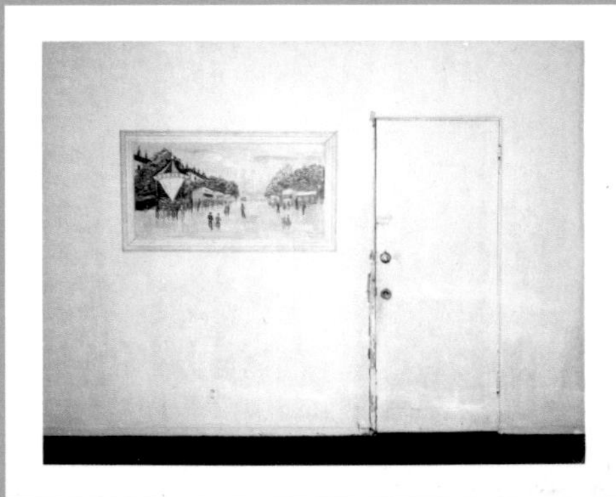

97
D5
2017.85.2.4

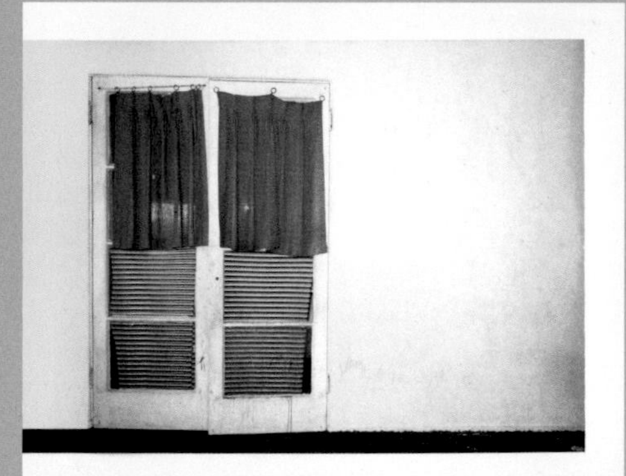

98
D6
2017.85.2.5

99
D9*/**
2018.27.35

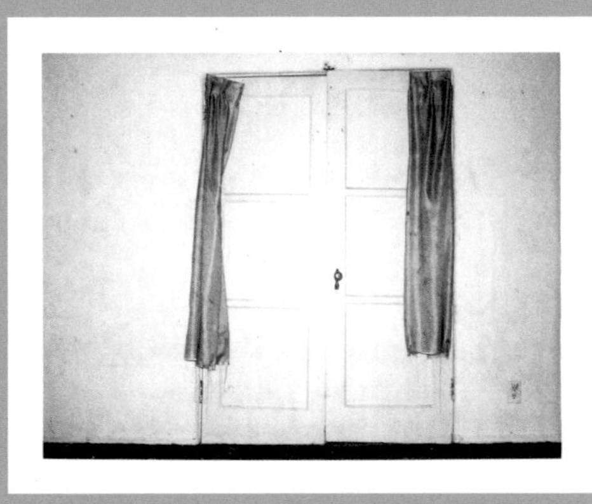

100
D8
2017.84.2.2

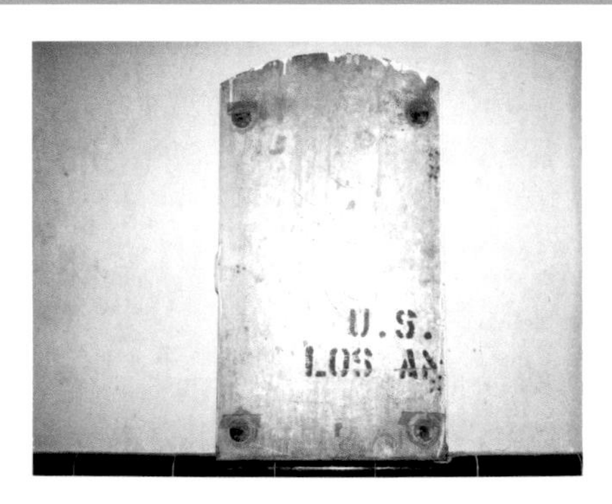

101
M5
2017.84.2.6

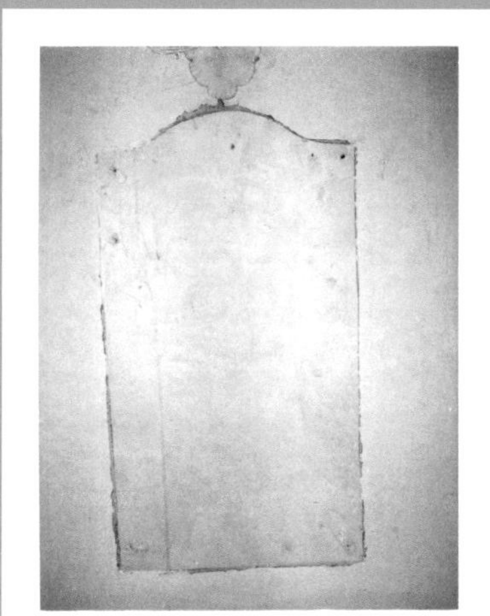

102
M4
2018.27.8

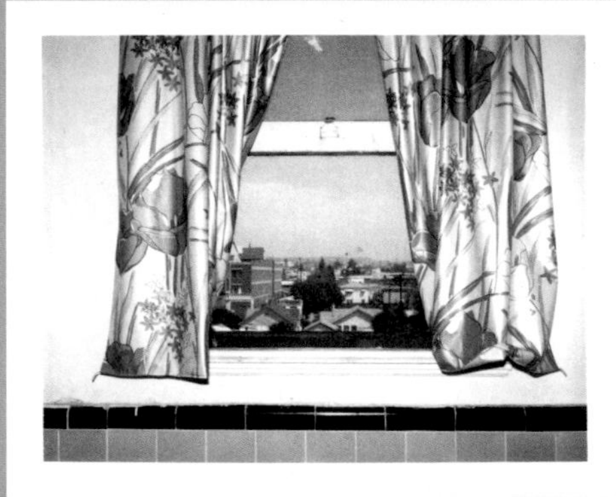

103
W13
2017.84.2.10

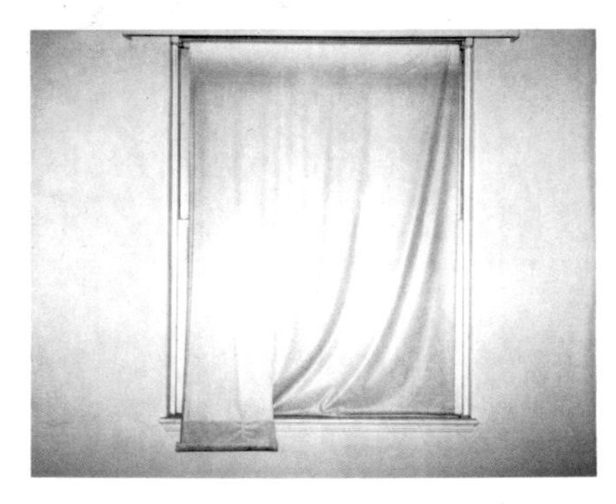

104
W22
2018.27.31

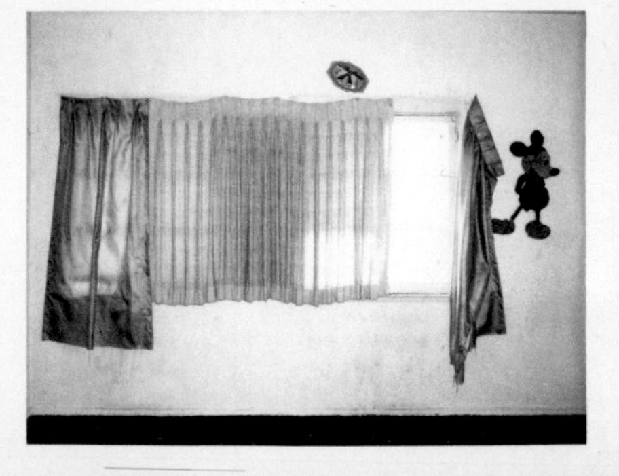

105
W25**
2018.27.50

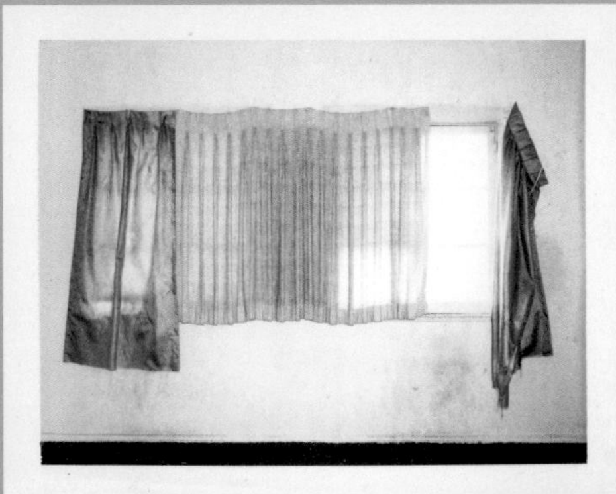

106
W14*
2018.27.27

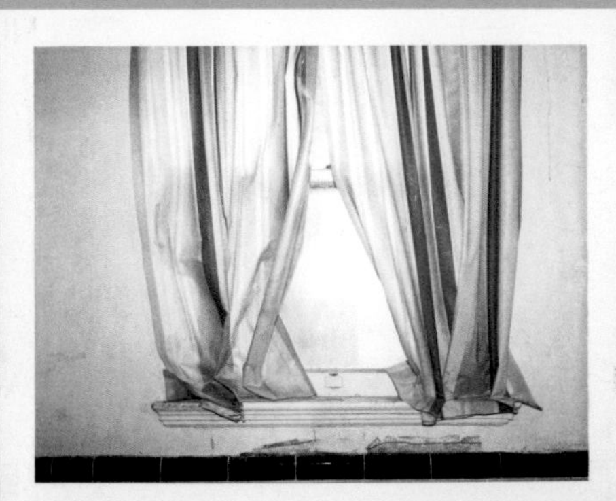

107
W8
2018.27.26

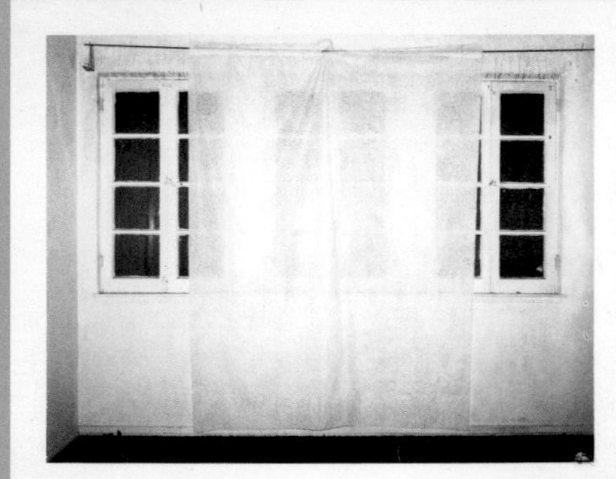

108
W16
2017.84.2.12

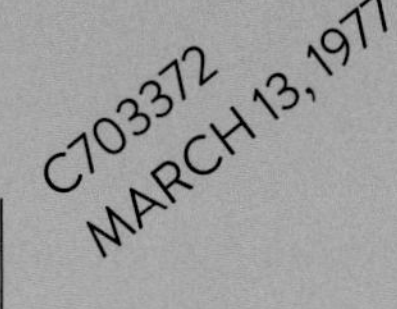

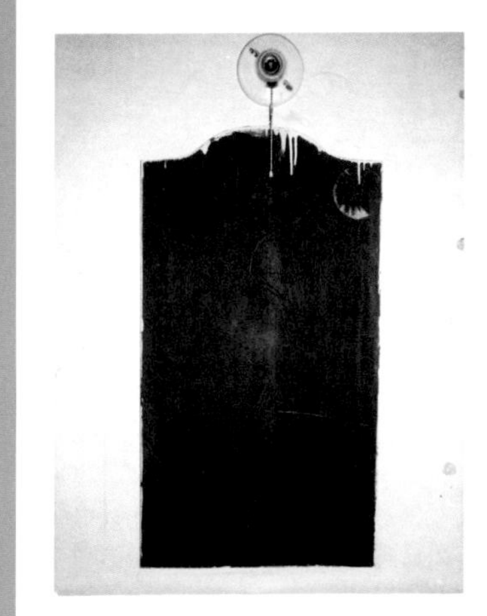

109
M7
2018.27.10

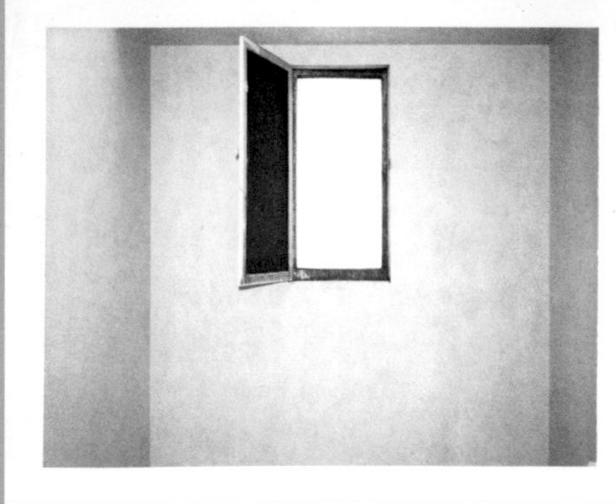

110
W26**
2018.27.53

Credits:

Collection of the Fine Arts Museums of San Francisco: Gift of
Dr. Nancy Ascher and Dr. John Roberts: Apps. 1, 4, 10, 17, 21,
32–35, 44, 46, 51, 65, 70, 76, 78–80, 86–88, 91–94, 100,
101, 103, 108; Gift of Nancy Ganz and Mitchell Steir: Apps. 2,
3, 5, 11, 16, 18, 20, 22, 23, 26–31, 36, 38, 39, 42, 47, 55–58,
67, 71, 96, 98; Gift of Mary and Dan Solomon: Apps. 6–9,
12–15, 19, 24, 25, 37, 40, 41, 43, 45, 48–50, 52–54, 59, 60,
62–64, 66, 68, 69, 72–75, 77, 82–85, 89, 90, 95, 97, 99,
102, 104–107, 109, 110

Collection of the Stephen H. Kahn Trust: Apps. 61, 81

ACKNOWLEDGMENTS

THE FINE ARTS MUSEUMS of San Francisco's exhibition *Steve Kahn: The Hollywood Suites* and its accompanying scholarly catalogue would not have been possible without the support of the Stephen H. Kahn Trust. At the Trust, we acknowledge specifically Jo Ann Montoya. The presentation has been enhanced by the kindness of the many lenders who have shared Steve Kahn's works with us. We extend our gratitude to Mary and Dan Solomon and the Howard Greenberg Gallery. We would also like to thank Nancy Ganz and Mitchell Steir, and Dr. Nancy Ascher and Dr. John Roberts, for their donations of Kahn's work to the Museums' collection. Additional gratitude is extended to Zoe Kahn, Farrol Mertes, Alex Lavayen, Jay Ruby, Karen Marks, Howard Greenberg, Stefan Kirkeby, Julie Casemore, and Larry Banka.

This project was initially conceived by Julian Cox, former chief curator and founding curator of photography, now chief curator and deputy director of the Art Gallery of Ontario in Toronto, and it has been led by James A. Ganz, former curator of the Achenbach Foundation for the Graphic Arts at the Fine Arts Museums of San Francisco, now senior curator of photographs at the J. Paul Getty Museum in Los Angeles. It is presented at the de Young by Janna Keegan, curatorial assistant. We are grateful to the outside scholars who contributed their insightful essays to this publication: Constance M. Lewallen, Matthew Simms, and Jodi Throckmorton.

This exhibition has been guided by Victoria Binder, conservator; Debra Evans, head conservator; Don Larsen, senior museum technician; Egle Mendoza, assistant registrar; and Douglas DeFors, associate registrar. We acknowledge the exhibitions team, who bring all of our shows to fruition, led by Krista Brugnara, director of exhibitions, and including Shannon Stecher Anandasakaran, exhibitions manager; and Genevieve Hulley, senior exhibitions coordinator; Ryan Butterfield, chief preparator, and his staff of technicians; and Chris Busch, exhibition designer.

Further staff members at the Museums have worked together to assist with the myriad of details related to this project and all of our programs. We thank our development team, led by Amanda Riley, director of development, alongside Kathleen Brennan, director of foundation and government giving; Emily Christian, director of individual giving; Karen Huang, director of major giving; Christa Sundell, director of corporate giving; and Larissa Trociuk, assistant director of major giving. We are appreciative of Linda Butler, director of marketing and communications, and her staff, including Joyce Alcantara, public relations assistant; Miriam Newcomer, director of public relations; Helena Nordstrom, international public relations manager; Wynter Martinez, associate director of marketing; and Francisco Rosas, creative and content assistant manager. In Education, we thank Sheila Pressley, director of education, alongside her staff, including Fay Dearborn, interim manager of public programs and adult learning; Emily Jennings, associate director of education, school and family programs; and Andrea Martin, museum educator.

Our Board of Trustees, led by Diane B. Wilsey, bring all of our valuable projects to life. Furthermore, we acknowledge many individuals and their teams who work dedicatedly behind the scenes to realize our many programs, including Ed Prohaska, chief financial officer, and Jason Seifer, director of finance; Megan Bourne, chief of staff; Melissa E. Buron, director of the art division; Patty Lacson, director of facilities; Tricia Robson, director of web and digital production; Skot Jonz, manager of board relations; Anna Zepp, manager of international business and special projects; and Jenny Moore, executive assistant to the director and CEO. We also extend our gratitude to Stuart Hata, director of retail operations; Rose Burke, merchandise manager; and Tim Niedert, book and media manager.

This catalogue was produced by the Publications department at the Fine Arts Museums, and was gracefully overseen by Leslie Dutcher, director of publications, and beautifully edited and project managed by Victoria Gannon. Danica Michels Hodge, managing editor; Trina Enriquez, associate editor; and José Jovel, publications assistant, also provided valuable assistance throughout the process of creating the book. Sue Grinols, head of photo services; Robert Carswell, digital assets and rights manager; and Randy Dodson, head photographer, helped to prepare the many visual materials required for reproduction. We thank Martin Venezky of Appetite Engineers for his innovative work as the designer of this volume. Conti Tipocolor is responsible for the impeccable printing, thanks to the stewardship of Roberto Conti, Marta Conti, and Laura Cuccoli. We are grateful of our partnership with DelMonico Books • Prestel for the distribution of this book in the trade; there, we acknowledge especially Mary DelMonico, who is always a passionate advocate for all of our projects together. This catalogue is published with the support of the Andrew W. Mellon Foundation Endowment for Publications.

MAX HOLLEIN
Director and CEO
Fine Arts Museums of San Francisco

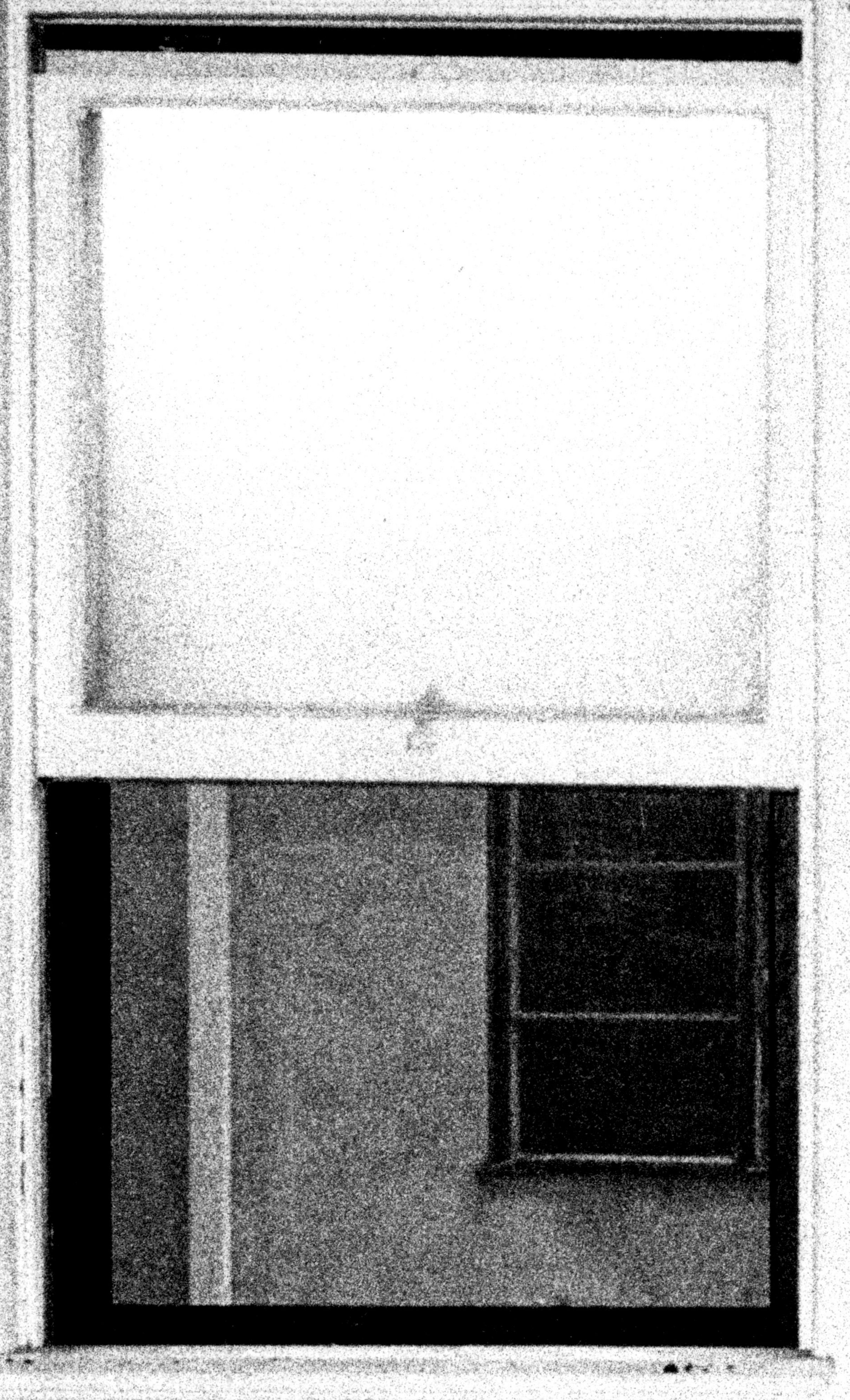

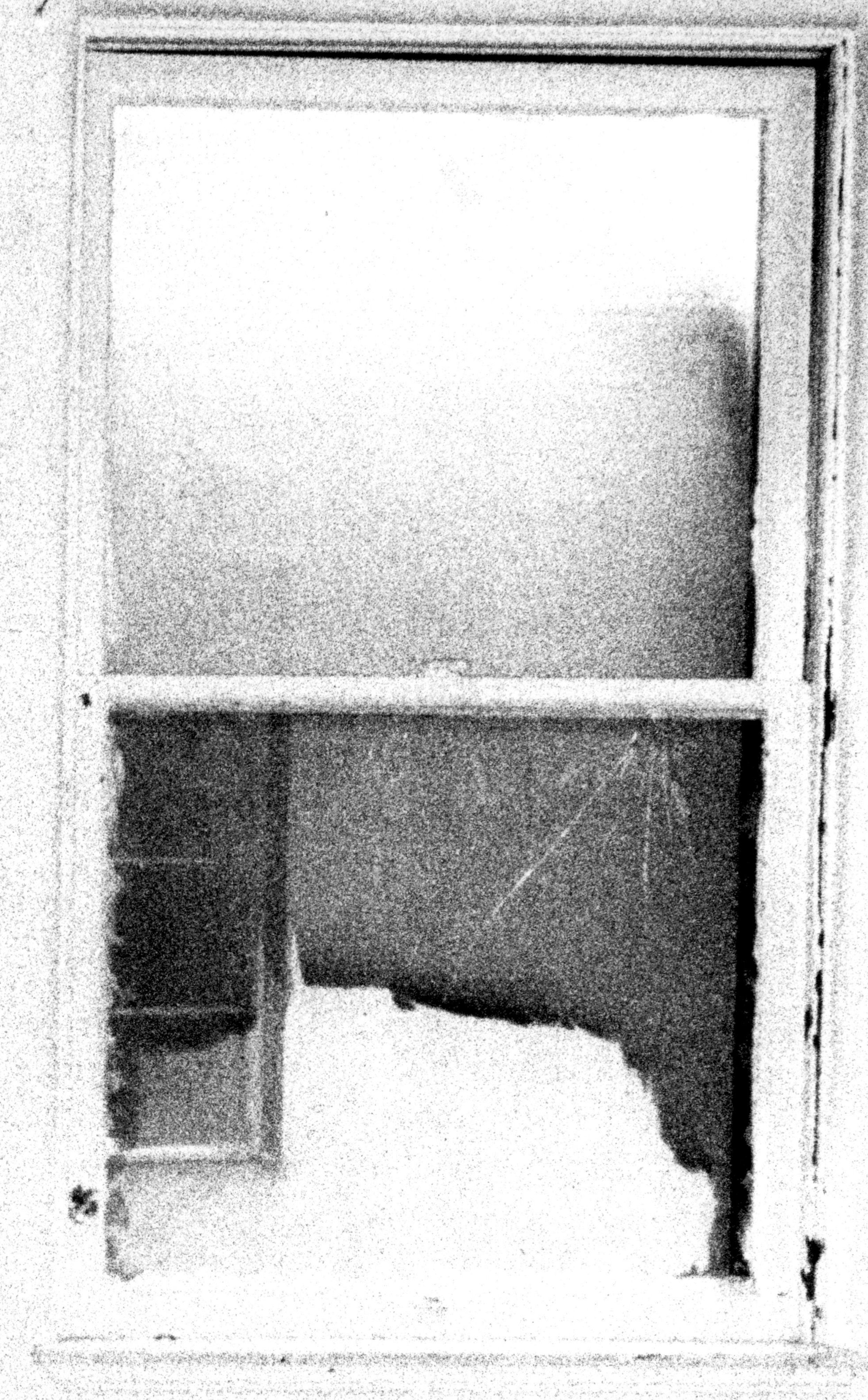

Published in 2018 by the Fine Arts Museums of San Francisco and DelMonico Books • Prestel on the occasion of the exhibition *Steve Kahn: The Hollywood Suites* at the de Young museum, San Francisco, from September 9, 2018, to March 31, 2019.

This exhibition is organized by the Fine Arts Museums of San Francisco.

This catalogue is published with the support of the Andrew W. Mellon Foundation Endowment for Publications.

Library of Congress Cataloging-in-Publication Data

Names: Ganz, James A., writer of supplementary textual content. | Lewallen, Constance M., writer of supplementary textual content. | Simms, Matthew, writer of supplementary textual content. | Throckmorton, Jodi, writer of supplementary textual content. | Kahn, Steve, 1943–2018 Photographs. Selections. | M.H. de Young Memorial Museum, editor.
Title: Steve Kahn: The Hollywood Suites / by James A. Ganz, Constance M. Lewallen, Matthew Simms, and Jodi Throckmorton.
Description: San Francisco: Fine Arts Museums of San Francisco/de Young; New York: DelMonico Books/Prestel, [2018]
Identifiers: LCCN 2018020981 | ISBN 9783791357997 (hardcover)
Subjects: LCSH: Photography of interiors—California—Hollywood. | Photography of the nude. | Bondage (Sexual behavior)—Pictorial works.
Classification: LCC TR620.S74 2018 | DDC 779/.21—dc23
LC record available at https://lccn.loc.gov/2018020981

A CIP catalogue record for this book is available from the British Library.

ISBN (hardback): 978-3-7913-5799-7

Fine Arts Museums of San Francisco
Golden Gate Park
50 Hagiwara Tea Garden Drive
San Francisco, CA 94118–4502
famsf.org

Leslie Dutcher, *Director of Publications*
Danica Michels Hodge, *Managing Editor*
Victoria Gannon, *Editor*
Trina Enriquez, *Associate Editor*
Adrienn Mendonça-Jones, *Editorial Assistant*
José Jovel, *Publications Assistant*

Edited and project managed by Victoria Gannon
Designed and typeset by Martin Venezky, Appetite Engineers
Proofread by Carrie Wicks
Separations, printing, and binding by Conti Tipocolor, Italy

DelMonico Books, an imprint of Prestel, a member of Verlagsgruppe Random House GmbH

Prestel Verlag
Neumarkter Strasse 28
81673 Munich

Prestel Publishing Ltd.
14–17 Wells Street
London W1T 3PD

Prestel Publishing
900 Broadway, Suite 603
New York, NY 10003

www.prestel.com